THE
BOOKSHOPS
OF
LONDON

THE
BOOKSHOPS
OF
LONDON

THE
BOOKSHOPS
OF
LONDON

CHARLES FREWIN
DEREK LUBNER

**TWO HEADS
PUBLISHING**

Copyright   TWO HEADS PUBLISHING
                   1993   All rights reserved

Published by   TWO HEADS PUBLISHING
                   12-50 Kingsgate Road
                   Kingston upon Thames
                   Surrey
                   KT2 5AA
                   081 974 8802

                   First edition

ISBN   1-897850-00-X

Cover Design   Kalligraphic Design
                   Horley
                   Surrey

Printed by   Caldra House Limited
                   Hove
                   Sussex

ACKNOWLEDGEMENT

COVER ILLUSTRATION

HENRY LEMOINE - *The Eccentric Bookseller and Author*
by
RALPH STEADMAN

The publishers are most grateful to Ralph Steadman for his kind
permission to use his superb drawing on the cover of this book.

The drawing and outlandish story of bookseller Henry Lemoine
appeared in *Tales Of The Weirrd* by Ralph Steadman, published by
Jonathan Cape in 1990.

USING THIS GUIDE

Welcome to the first edition of *The* Bookshops of London, a comprehensive guide to the wealth of bookshops in and around the capital. Its focus is the wealth of specialist booksellers but it also covers those who are best at being generalists, whether as part of a national chain or as local community bookshops.

Only bookshops open to the public are included in this guide. Books must be their main product, or they must carry a specialist range of books alongside other associated products. Book dealers trading from home have not been included as their business is mainly conducted by catalogue and mail order and if stock can be viewed it is by appointment only.

The shops are presented by main subject specialisation and the listings are intended to be descriptive rather than judgmental, conveying a feel for the character of a bookshop as well as providing essential facts. Where a section heading covers a wide scope of subjects, such as Academic, the individual subjects covered are listed at the start of the section. Within each section the bookshops are featured geographically or by a specific subject specialisation if appropriate. Categorising bookshops into one of twenty three subject sections is not always a straightforward task and inevitably there is an occasional element of overlap where a shop could fall into two categories. For example, a shop specialising in second-hand books on art & design will be found in Art & Design. Conversely, a shop selling antiquarian books on a wide range of subjects will be in the Antiquarian section.

There is a separate section on the chains which specialise in general bookselling. Where an individual branch has a true specialisation an entry will be found in the appropriate subject section.

The comprehensive indices allow users to quickly locate shops by name, to identify all bookshops in a chosen area and, by using the Subject Index, to find shops with particular specialisations more specific than those afforded by the main subject sections.

Whether you are involved in the book trade, a reader, collector, book buyer or book loving visitor to London, the publishers welcome feedback and suggestions for future editions from users of this unique guide .

CONTENTS

1   Academic
11   Antiquarian
20   Art & Design
29   Business
34   Chains
50   Children's
54   Comics & Science Fiction
59   Countries
69   Crafts & Pastimes
74   Environment & Nature
77   General
95   Languages
98   Literature
102   Mind, Body, Spirit
106   Museums & Galleries
113   Performing Arts
120   Politics & Social Sciences
127   Religion & Theology
137   Second-hand
149   Sport
152   Transport & Military
158   Travel
162   Women

164   Shop Index
172   Area Index
191   Subject Index

ACADEMIC

ARCHAEOLOGY CAMPUS SHOPS COURSE TEXTS
EDUCATION HISTORY HUMANISM MEDICAL
PSYCHOLOGY SCIENCE TECHNOLOGY

GOLDEN COCKEREL
25 Sicilian Avenue
WC1A 2QH
071 405 7979
M-F 10-5

The Golden Cockerel bookshop is a showroom and office for American academic publishers and Associated University Presses. The range of stock is therefore small but selective.

THE WELLSPRING BOOKSHOP
40A Museum Street
WC1A 1LT
071 831 1997
M-F 10.30-6, Sat-Sun 12-6

This bookshop moved to this location, which it shares with Vanbrugh Rare Books, two years ago. It is also known as Rudolph Steiner Books as the subject specialisation is based on Steiner culture and belief. You can find books on esoteric christianity, education, bio-dynamic agriculture, cosmology, spiritual science and inner development. There is also a selection of children's books with some toys and educational materials.

BRITISH MUSEUM
Great Russell Street
WC1B 3DG
071 323 8587
M-Sat 10-4.50, Sun 2.30-5.50

On entering this august institution turn right for the British Library Bookshop and left for the British Museum Bookshop. The emphasis is firmly in line with the major collections of the museum. Archaeology, classical history, ancient Egypt, Greece, medieval studies and ancient civilisations are the major areas. There is a small but selective range of educational children's books. A range of gifts, souvenirs and cards, caters for the hordes of tourists attracted to the museum.

THE MUSEUM BOOKSHOP
36 Great Russell Street
WC1B 3PP
071 580 4086
M-F 10-5.30, Sat 10.30-5.30

One of many bookshops in this area. After starting life as a generalist in 1978 it later developed into a specialist appropriate to its proximity to the British Museum. There are new and second-hand books in the specialist fields of Egyptology, archaeology, prehistoric and Roman Britain, classical history, museum studies and conservation. The works of T E Lawrence are well represented amongst the selection of books on the Middle East.

BRITISH MEDICAL JOURNAL BOOKSHOP
Burton Street
WC1H 9JR
071 383 6244
M-F 9.30-5

The BMJ Bookshop has recently moved to larger premises at the rear of the British Medical Association headquarters just a short walk from Euston Station. This move has provided an opportunity to greatly expand the range and depth of stock to encompass all areas of medicine and related fields. For students, professionals and members elsewhere in the country a postage-free mail order service is in operation.

WEATHER WISE
285 High Holborn
WC1V 7HX
071 430 5314
M-F 10-4

Given the penchant of the English to feed their national obsession, you would expect to see wall to wall people in this showroom of the London Weather Centre. What you can see is books both popular and technical, cloud charts for pilots and gifts for every weather buff. The 'Weather Trackers Kit' is a handbook with a complete monitoring station contained in a box the size of a hardback novel.

ROBERT CONNELLY THE BOOKSHOP
31-35 Great Ormond Street
WC1N 3HZ
071 430 1394
M-F 1-6

Opposite the Great Ormond Street Hospital, more than 3000 new, second-hand and antiquarian books exclusively devoted to the history of medicine and science. This shop is for enthusiasts only, but the curious are well served. Old prints and engravings related to medicine and science are stocked and a valuation, book-binding and search service is provided. The expertise is second to none. Robert Connelly publishes in this field under his own imprint.

PENGUIN BOOKSHOP
The City Lit
16 Stukeley Street
WC2B 5LJ
071 405 3110
M-F 12-7.30

The main purpose of the City Lit college is to provide a broad range of quality specialist courses on adult learning and development. The bookshop, within the college, mainly stocks course texts in the humanities, and language books from Arabic to Welsh.

MUSEUM OF MANKIND BOOKSHOP
6 Burlington Gardens
W1X 2EX
071 323 8045
M-Sat 10.30-4.30

The study of ethnography, the scientific description of human races and cultures, is featured in this bookshop which is part of a fascinating and educational museum. There are titles covering non-western civilisations and books relating to the variety of exhibitions at this museum for all ages.

MODERN BOOK COMPANY
15-21 Praed Street
W2 1NP
071 402 9176
M-F 9-5.30, Sat 9-1

With expertise built up over 55 years, the Modern Book Company is reputed to be one of the UK's largest medical, technical and scientific bookstores. There are experts in each department to meet the needs of students and professionals alike. The institutional and library supply department serves public bodies and industry worldwide. St Mary's Hospital is nearby and therefore medical books are a major specialisation with catalogues regularly issued. On the technical side, electronics and computing feature strongly with a complementary range of business books. In this welcoming bookshop popular general books are also available and there is a large paperback area.

DILLONS THE BOOKSTORE
Ealing College of Higher Education
St Mary's Road
W5 5RF
081 579 5730
M-F 9-5 term time

A small campus shop offering a wide range of academic texts to students and faculty. Technical and non-technical subjects are covered and there is access to the more substantial academic expertise at the Dillons flagship shop in Gower Street and other college branches in London.

DILLONS MEDICAL BOOKSHOP
The Reynolds Building
Charing Cross and Westminster Medical School
St. Dunstans Road
W6 8RP
081 741 0881
M-F 11-2.30

All required undergraduate textbooks for Medical school are found in this bookshop which is located within the library. In addition to general medical topics there is a specialist range of advanced texts in surgery, obstetrics and gynaecology. They specialise in supplying hospitals and medical institutes.

DILLONS MEDICAL BOOKSHOP
Royal Postgraduate
Medical School
Hammersmith Hospital
Du Cane Road
W12 0NN
081 742 9600
M-F 11-3

Another Dillons scalp, this shop carries a wide range of advanced medical texts for post-graduate study and standard medical texts for students of medicine. Specialisations include radiology and nuclear medicine, cardiology, molecular biology and orthopaedics. They also supply hospitals and research institutes and organise bookstalls for conferences.

CITY UNIVERSITY BOOKSHOP
Northampton Square
EC1V
071 608 0706
M-F 9-6 term time 9-5 non term

Owned by Dillons, the University bookshop is next to the main entrance. Text books and background reading for the variety of courses covered at the university, from computing to speech therapy, are represented in the large stock of books. There is a selection of popular stationery and some greetings cards.

MENCAP BOOKSHOP
123 Golden Lane
EC1Y 0RT
071 454 0454
M-F 9.30-5

Located off the entrance foyer to the MENCAP National Centre, this bookshop was set up 20 years ago as an extension to the reference library. All profits are devoted to the work of the Royal Society For Mentally Handicapped Children and Adults. There are around 1200 books on the needs and aspirations of people with learning difficulties and the services available for them. Every professional involved in caring for the mentally handicapped should know about the excellent range of services available here. The main subject categories covered are carers, disabilities, education, health, integration, legal, recreation and therapy. The bookshop's catalogue lists and describes all publications under the main subject areas and sets an example to any specialist bookshop in terms of clarity and comprehensiveness. The books are not just for professionals. There are learning packs for children and a book called 'Places That Care': a guide to places of interest suitable for elderly and disabled people which should be in the Travel and Guides section of every general bookshop. Videos are sold and can also be hired. Bookstall facilities are available by arrangement.

CITY POLY BOOKSHOP
84 Moorgate
EC2M
071 638 2793
M-F 10-6, October 'till 7

Formerly an Economist Bookshop before being swallowed by Dillons Bookstores. Located on the ground floor of the School of Business Studies to serve students in the areas of law, business and economics.

QUEEN MARY & WESTFIELD COLLEGE BOOKSHOP
Mile End Road
E1 4NS
081 980 2554
M-F 9-5.30, W 9-4.30

Located on the ground floor of the main campus building, this large shop stocks a range of academic books and student stationery. Biology, chemistry, computers, engineering and maths are prominent.

THE COLLEGE BOOKSHOP
Newham Community College
East Ham Centre
High Street South
E6 4ER
081 472 9946
M-Th 9-3, 6-8, F 9-3

The split in opening hours reflects the life of the student for whom this shop caters. College course texts and other academic subjects are stocked.

DILLONS MEDICAL BOOKSHOP
St. Thomas' Hospital Library
Lambeth Palace Road
SE1 7EH
071 928 7926
M-F 11-2.30

Another Dillons shop within a hospital library. There are undergraduate medical and dental text books plus various postgraduate specialist subjects. They will order any medical book not in stock.

THE PASSAGE BOOKSHOP
5 Canning Cross
Grove Lane
SE5 8BH
071 274 7606
M-F 10-6, Sat 10-5

A local general bookshop serving people from hospitals nearby. There is a genuine specialisation in nursing, dentistry and medicine.

IMPERIAL COLLEGE UNION BOOKSTORE
223 Sherfield Building
Imperial College
SW7 2AZ
071 225 6121
M-F 9-6 term time,
M-F 9-5 non term

Inside the college, on the Sherfield Walkway, 2000 square feet of books and college supplies can be found. The specialisation is science and technology: computing, maths, physics, geology and mining. Less cerebral popular titles are also on sale.

WATERSTONE'S
Goldsmith's College
New Cross
SE14 6NW
081 469 0262
M-F 9-7 term time
M-F 9-5.30 non-term

Waterstone's only college-based academic bookshop in London. University texts and reading in the arts, humanities and social sciences are the main focus with literature featuring strongly.

DILLONS THE BOOKSTORE
The Science Museum
Exhibition Road
SW7 2DD
071 938 8127
M-Sat 10-6, Sun 11-6

Hordes of visitors and tourists pass through this bookshop within the museum. The focus is on all aspects of science and technology, both popular and specialist. General subjects are well represented and the children's section is biased towards practical activities and basic science topics. The bookshop is closer to a general Dillons than a specialist shop but still offers an interesting range of books reflecting the collections within the museum. Unfortunately, the museum's own shop, adjacent to the bookshop, is disappointing.

INSTITUTE BOOKSHOP
DIGBY STUART COLLEGE
Roehampton Lane
SW15 5PH
081 392 3030
M-F 8.45-5.30

Teachers use this bookshop for reference works, teacher training material and a range of other subjects from psychology to reading. You can even buy your favourite chocolate bar.

ST GEORGES HOSPITAL
MEDICAL SCHOOL
BOOKSHOP
University of London
Cranmer Terrace
SW17 0RE
081 672 9944
M-F 10-2.15

The limited opening hours probably reflect the fact that nurses and doctors have little time to browse. Specialist books and texts for students and those practising medicine are available here.

MERCURY BOOKSHOP
University of Greenwich
12/14 Wellington Street
SE18 6PF
081 317 0646
M-F 8.45-5.30, W 8.45-5

Adjacent to the University of Greenwich, the bookshop covers all academic subjects studied at the university. Business, computing, social sciences, engineering, chemistry, biology and mathematics. Light relief is provided by the selection of paperback fiction.

DULWICH COLLEGE BOOKSHOP
Dulwich Common
SE21 7LD
081 693 4565
M-F 8.30-4.45

Bookshop for the students with school and college textbooks dominant.

TLON BOOKS
The Pavillions
Merton Abbey Mill
Watermill Way
SW19 2RD
081 540 4371
W-Sun 11-5

History is the main subject specialisation, but books on politics and other academic topics also feature. The wide selection provides a welcome second-hand alternative to new texts and academic title. The nearest tube station is South Wimbledon.

MERTON COLLEGE BOOKSHOP
London Road
Morden
SM4
081 685 0157
M-F 10-1.30, 5.45-7.15

You have to be a student to shop at this college bookshop. Books on education dominate.

HEATH EDUCATIONAL BOOKS
Sutton Business Centre
Restmor Way
SM6 7AH
081 773 8344
M-F 9-5.30

Formerly Fielders Educational, this is a large showroom for teachers and librarians who can choose from the wide range of educational books up to 6th form level.

COLLEGE BOOKSHOP
St Marys College
Waldegrave Road
TW1
081 891 4255
M-F 9-5

All they are prepared to say is 'academic titles only for colleg (*sic*) courses.' With a number of other excellent outlets in the area the choice is yours!

OPEN BOOKS
West London Institute of Higher Education
Gordon House
300 St. Margarets Road
TW1 1PT
081 898 5520

Lancaster House
Borough Road
Isleworth
M-F 11-4.30 term time

Two campus bookstores serving students on site. Subjects covered at Lancaster include occupational therapy, nursing, business, computing, geography and geology. At Gordon House, literature, the media, sociology and American studies are the majors along with music and religion.

OPEN BOOKS
Richmond-upon-Thames College
Egerton Road
Twickenham
TW2 7SJ
081 898 5520
M-F 10-2 term time

Linked to the above shops, this college store concentrates on A Level, GCSE, BTEC textbooks and revision aids with a wide variety of general stationery. It is open to students and the general public alike.

DILLONS THE BOOKSTORE
Royal Holloway and Bedford
New College
Egham Hill
Egham
TW20 0EX
0784 71272
M-F 9-6

This college bookshop provides an invaluable service to students and lecturers who would otherwise have to travel to London for their academic textbooks and associated reading. It is worth visiting this location purely to see the magnificent main college building.

HARROW SCHOOL BOOKSHOP
7 High Street
Harrow
HA1 3HU
081 869 1212
M-Sat 9-5

Providing the students with textbooks, educational titles and gifts branded with the school crest. Open to all, unlike the school.

BRUNEL UNIVERSITY BOOKSHOP
Cleveland Road
Uxbridge
UB8 3PH
0895 257991
M-F 9-5

Previously owned by the Economists group and now possessed by Dillons Bookstores. A wide range of texts and books to serve the needs of students at the university covering business, management, computing, engineering, law, social sciences and politics.

MARYLEBONE BOOKS
University of Westminster
35 Marylebone Rd
NW1 5LS
071 911 5049
M-F 9.30-5

Originally the Town and Country Planning bookshop, it now stocks 3000 titles on a wide range of subjects. The shop can be found on the ground floor and specialises in planning, building,

architecture, housing and
business topics.

NURSING BOOK SERVICE
52 Phoenix Road
NW1 1ES
071 387 9378
M-F 7.30-4.30

Primarily a mail order specialist
with books on nursing and
medicine.

KARNAC BOOKS
118 Finchley Road
NW3 5HJ
071 431 1075

58 Gloucester Road
SW7 4QY
071 584 3303
Both shops M-Sat 9-6

It may help to have a lie down on
the nearest couch before you
venture inside here. A mind
blowing array of books on
psychoanalysis, analytical
psychology, child care and the
family, psychotherapy,
philosophy and gender studies.
Allied topics are equally well
covered with special sections on
books related to childhood
problems, sexual abuse and eating
disorders. The choice of location
was not coincidental as Karnac is
close to the Tavistock Clinic,
Anna Freud Centre and other
similar institutions. Karnac Books,
as an independent, is unique in
operating a publishing
programme which has in recent
years expanded into original texts
and translations. This followed an

earlier reputation for keeping
alive classics of psychoanalytical
writing. Within these
specialisations Karnac claims to
be the world leader, and the size
of the international mailing list of
over 20000, to whom an annual
catalogue is sent, supports this
proud boast. General books are
also available as is one of the most
competitive ranges of art
postcards and cards in London.
The substantial mail order
business is handled by the
Gloucester Road branch.

THE LIBRARY BOOKSHOP
Westfield College
Kidderpore Avenue
NW3 7ST
071 794 7911
M-F 9.30-5.30

A small academic bookshop for
the courses taught at the College.
Open University course books are
sold in the summer.

FACULTY BOOKS
98 Ballards Lane
N3 2DN
081 346 7761
M-Sat 9.30-5.30

Education, law and business are
featured as is a range of general
books.

FACULTY BOOKSHOP
Middlesex University
Burroughs
Hendon
NW4
081 202 3593

M-F 10-4, M,W 10-6.30

The bookshop is adjacent to the University's car park. Business is the speciality and there is a particularly large law section. They sell computers at very competitive prices, taking advantage of the student discounts offered by most manufacturers.

HISTORY BOOKSHOP
2 The Broadway
Friern Barnet Road
N11 3DU
081 368 8568
By appointment only

No surprise to find that books on history are in abundance, with a military leaning. Why make an appointment to see books that can be found elsewhere on demand ?

TRENT BOOKSHOP
Middlesex University
Bramley Road
Oakwood
N14 4XS
081 440 9653
M,T,W 10-4.30, Th,F 10-3.30

College bookshop serving the students well with a comprehensive range of texts and associated reading from art and design to women's studies. A second-hand section provides a cheaper option.

NATIONAL SECULAR SOCIETY & G.W. FOOTE
702 Holloway Road
N19 3NL
071 272 1266
M-F 9.15-5

Run for members of the society and as a service to readers of their monthly magazine, '*The Freethinker*,' and not for browsers. This bookshop has all you want to know about freethought, anti religion and anti superstition, in fact all humanist beliefs. They will also offer guidance on non-religious funerals.

ALL SAINTS BOOKSHOP
MIDDLESEX UNIVERSITY
Queensway
Enfield
EN3
081 443 4684
M,Th, F 10-3.30, Tu-W 10-6

Course books and materials for students of this north London college. The general range is wider than many with children's and fiction amongst the drama, geology and philosophy.

SCEPTRE BOOKS
2 Chingford Road
E17
081 503 2600
M-Sat 10-5.30

College and university texts from business to social sciences with a small selection of stationery.

ANTIQUARIAN

VANBRUGH RARE BOOKS
Ruskin House
40A Museum Street
WC1A 1LT
071 404 0733
M-F 10.30-6, S-S 12-6

Bookcases filled with attractive leather bound volumes line the walls of Vanbrugh. Ruskin House is a listed building once occupied by George Allen, the engraver and publisher, who named the premises in honour of his mentor John Ruskin. Manuscripts and fine books of the 17th century is the main area of expertise with a selection that is one of the best in London.

THE AVENUE BOOKSHOP
11 Sicilian Arcade
Southampton Row
WC1A 2QH
071 831 7486
M-Sat 11-6

A small general stock of 'interesting and unusual books.' Art reference, monographs and Italian books from 1500-1800 are the speciality.

LOUIS BONDY
C/O The Avenue Bookshop
Hours and 'phone as above

In business for in excess of forty years and a leading authority on miniature books. Samples of the intruiging stock are on display in the window. Mr Bondy is the author of a standard reference book on miniatures and in addition carries books on caricature, fine illustrated volumes and examples of early printing.

JARNDYCE ANTIQUARIAN BOOKSELLERS
46 Great Russell Street
WC1B 3PA
071 631 4220
M-F 9.30-5

Look for the brass plate on the wall of the house occupied by Randolph Caldecott, artist and book illustrator, from 1846-1886. Ring the bell to obtain access to the first floor showroom but visit preferably by appointment to inspect the special pre 1900 range of fine, rare and interesting books. Victorian triple deckers, Yellowbacks and Dickens first editions can be found here alongside English literature, social, economic and political history.

FREW MACKENZIE
106 Great Russell Street
WC1B 3NA
071 580 2311
M-F 10-6, Sat 10-2

Pleasantly situated adjacent to the British Museum and dealing in good quality antiquarian books, especially English literature, illustrated, travel and sets.

ANTIQUARIAN DEPT DILLONS BOOKSTORE
82 Gower Street
WC1E 6EQ
071 636 1577
M, W, Th, F 9-7, Tu 9.30-7, Sat 9.30-6

A separate department inside the Dillons megastore with a large selection of mainly second-hand books in academic fields. Genuine antiquarian stock is in the minority. It loses out to stand-alone competitors in terms of quality books and perceived levels of expertise, probably due to its position as a department within the largest bookstore in Europe.

COLLINGE & CLARK
13 Leigh Street
WC1H 9EW
071 387 7105
M-F 11-6.30, Sat 11-3.30

Humanities and the arts with particularly fine illustrated books, history (books, pamphlets and ephemera) and private press books.

TOOLEY, ADAMS & CO
13 Cecil Court
WC2N 4EZ
071 240 4406
M-F 9-5

R V Tooley, one of the original founders, was author of many authoritative works on the subject of antique maps and atlases. The current business claims to hold one of the largest stocks of antiquarian maps and atlases in the world. The book stock is therefore a small but highly specialist selection of antiquarian atlases and cartobibliographies.

P J HILTON
12-14 Cecil Court
WC2N
071 379 9825
M-F 9.30-8, S 10.30-7.30

Two years ago P J Hilton doubled in size by acquiring the shop next door to cater for more books and more customers. There is an appealing range of secondhand and antiquarian books, especially English Literature, both first editions and reading copies. The section devoted to recent acquisitions is worthy of regular inspection.

FOOD FOR THOUGHT
27 Cecil Court
WC2N 2EZ
071 379 1993
M-Sat 10.30-8

Following in the tradition of HM Fletcher who traded at this Cecil Court address since the 1930s. The sign on the pavement says 'fine and antiquarian books bought and sold' and the stock is best described as selective with a bias towards literary. The shop itself resembles a library with dark wooden shelving and an array of books. There is a 'quality secondhand' room in the basement: this is a new term largely based on a value judgement with a subsequent effect on price.

HAROLD T STOREY
3 Cecil Court
WC2N 2EZ
071 836 3777
M-Sat 10-6

Specialising primarily in prints, maps and engravings in military and naval subjects with a small selection of rare books and fine bindings.

BERNARD QUARITCH LTD
5-8 Lower John Street
Golden Square
W1R 4AU
071 734 2983
M-F 9.30-1, 2-5.30

A formidable business with an intimidating atmosphere and strictly not for the casual visitor who fancies a nice old leather-bound book. The stock is divided into separate sections and covers all the classic antiquarian topics. It is a scholarly and earnest place of international repute.

MAGGS BROTHERS
50 Berkeley Square
W1X 6EL
071 493 7160
M-F 9.30-5

A rare treat indeed. Maggs Brothers was founded in 1853, and John Maggs carries on the family tradition of overseeing a London landmark known to serious collectors all over the world. Maggs moved to this present location, a magnificent Georgian residence, reputed to be the most haunted house in London, in 1939. Staffed by 20 experts each with a section of the shop in their charge and supported by reference facilities and records of historical note. The rarest first editions, manuscripts, fine bindings and an unparalleled collection of autographs fill the four floors in the most gracious manner. The travel room is quite superb. Stop on the landing to look at the signed letters from Einstein and Churchill. Unlike many other antiquarian specialists it is not all ivory towers and although the atmosphere is earnest and learned, it is far from elitist and all visitors are treated with courtesy and given expert advice.

RUSSELL RARE BOOKS
18 Queen Street
W1X 8JN
071 629 0532
M-F 9.30-5.30

A short walk from Green Park will lead you to a general range of antiquarian books with an emphasis on nicely bound sets and illustrated books.

E. JOSEPH BOOKSELLERS
1 Vere Street
W1M 9HQ
071 493 8353
M-F 9.30-5.30

From their own well presented literature, 'more akin to the library of a country house than a conventional bookshop,' E Joseph caters for the collector of fine books. Modern major first editions like James Joyce's *Ulysses* share the cabinet shelf space with early editions of Shakespeare. Illustrated volumes, Churchilliana and library sets line the walls. The quality is self evident and the prices serious. The mail order department caters for the visiting collector and despatches books world wide.

HENRY SOTHERAN LTD
2, 4 & 5 Sackville Street
W1X 2DP
M-F 9.30-6, Sat 10-4
071 439 6151

For over 200 years, this historic bookshop has been offering rare opportunities to collectors and enthusiasts. The pedigree, both historic and contemporary, is hard to match. It was established in London in 1815 by Thomas Sotheran, but was originally founded in York over 50 years previously. Landmarks in Sotheran's history include the purchase of the library of Lawrence Sterne in 1768, the complete stock and copyright of John Gould in 1881 and the acquisition of Dickens' library. It is no wonder that you feel you are

visiting a national treasure. The departments include: English literature, architecture, natural history, naval & military, travel and autograph letters. The free book search service will attempt to satisfy any special need that cannot be met from stock. The legacy of Gould means that the ornithology department is superb and includes new books as well as the earliest works. The print department specialises in the magnificent work of John Gould. A complete portfolio of services is also on offer, from book repair and binding to regular catalogues.

Their second shop is at
80 Pimlico Rd, SW1
071 730 8756.

A huge range of architectural and topographical prints can be found here.

SAM FOGG RARE BOOKS
14 Old Bond Street
W1X 3DB
071 495 2333
M-F 10-6

All antiquarian booksellers claim to sell 'rare' books but here is rarity indeed. Medieval and illuminated manuscripts only.

JONATHAN POTTER
125 New Bond Street
W1Y 9AF
071 491 3520
M-F 10-6

A first floor retail gallery with a magnificent collection of original antique maps of all types on every part of the world. Antique atlases and reference books on the history of cartography comprise the book element.

MARLBOROUGH RARE BOOKS
144-146 New Bond Street
W1Y 9FD
071 493 6993
M-F 9.30-5.30

Opposite Sotheby's, in fourth floor offices, this is a haven for collectors. Appointments are advised in order to inspect the fine stock of architectural titles, illustrated books and literature.

ASH RARE BOOKS
25 Royal Exchange
EC3V 3LP
071 626 2665
M-F 10-5.30

Two hundred years ago The Royal Exchange was one of the great centres of the book trade and is now a most appropriate location for the City's leading specialist in antiquarian and rare books. The stock is small but highly selective and their customers include museums, libraries and collectors all over the world. Literature to 1900, fine bindings and first editions are the main specialisations with a select range of antique maps and prints.

SANGORSKI & SUTCLIFFE ZAEHNSDORF LTD
175 Bermondsey Street
SE1 3UW
071 407 1244
M-Thu 8-4.30, F 8-1

Not a bookshop but known to fine book specialists all over the world. For 150 years this firm has produced the most exquisite bindings of modern literature, children's illustrated, special editions and commissions. Expertise in repair and conservation is supplemented by the sale of high quality stationery and general bookbinding supplies.

D MELLOR & A L BAXTER
121 Kensington Church Street
W8 7LP
071 221 8822
M-F 10-6.30, Sat 10-4

Literature of the 16th and 17th centuries is a speciality along with history, fine bindings and sets of standard authors.

DEMETZY BOOKS
113 Portobello Road
W11
0993 702209
Sat only 7-3pm

A Saturday-only stall in this popular market. The stock is small and covers a broad area with a leaning towards leather bound sets, cookery, natural history, miniatures and Dickens first editions.

BRIAN L BAILEY
113 Portobello Road
W11
071 229 1692
Sat only 8.30-4

A long established market trader
in rare, antiquarian and out of
print books only. Travel,
topography, books with
engravings and maps and natural
history are in the majority with
some antique maps.

S K BILTCLIFFE BOOKS
Antique Arcade
289 Westbourne Grove
W11
081 740 5326
Sat only 8.30-3.30

Different and ultimately more
interesting than the fellow
bookstalls in Portobello Market.
The genuine specialisation is all
aspects of the British Industrial
Revolution. This includes life and
leisure, architecture, science and
technology, social and economic
life in London. Book searches and
valuations are undertaken in this
field.

PICKERING & CHATTO
17 Pall Mall
SW1Y 5NB
071 930 2515
M-F 9.30-5.30

Founded in 1820 by William
Pickering, a leading publisher of
the early 19th century, it is one of
the oldest antiquarian booksellers
in the capital. They specialise in
economics and philosophy,

medicine and science as well as
the core business of English
literature. They have rare medical
books, as well as continental
books dating from the 16th and
17th centuries. Indicative of the
rarity of the English literature
stock is the only copy in private
hands of Bunyan's *Pilgrim's
Progress*.

SIMS, REED LTD
58 Jermyn Street
SW1Y 6LX
071 493 5660

Hidden away and accessible by
ringing a bell, this shop stocks
rare, out of print and new
reference books on fine and
applied art. It is not all historical
as contemporary design is
handsomely covered. Catalogues
are produced frequently and the
mail order business is active. Not
a place for the uninitiated.

CHRISTOPHER EDWARDS
63 Jermyn Street
SW1Y 6LX
071 495 4263
M-F by appointment or chance

Above a restaurant on the fourth
floor at the St James's Street end.
This is where most of the interest
ends. Strictly antiquarian, and a
very small range of English
literature and history to 1900 and
early continental books.

BARBARA STONE
Antiquarius
135 King's Rd
SW3 4PW
071 351 0963
M-Sat 10.30-5.30

In a busy and varied antique market, Barbara Stone stocks only rare books. Subjects include children's, 19th and 20th century illustrated books and private press books. The policy of dealing only in rare items means that quality and selectivity shine through.

IL LIBRO
Chenil Gallery
181-183 Kings Rd
SW3
071 352 9041
M-Sat 10-6

Dealers in illustrated, natural history and leather bound literature. Some decorative prints and maps.

HARRINGTON BROS
The Chelsea Antique Market
253 Kings Road
SW3 5EL
071 352 5689
M-Sat 10-6

Located within the antique market and carrying a very large range of antiquarian books. There is much of interest here from library sets to rare inscribed items and modern first editions. The illustrated books are most appealing with a sub-specialisation in fore-edge paintings. Despite the erudite characteristics of the antiquarian stock, it is a browsers delight and is definitely a shop selling affordable and accessible books.

CHELSEA RARE BOOKS
313 Kings Road
SW3 5EP
071 351 0950
M-Sat 10-6

A good mixture of second-hand and antiquarian books in a nicely furnished shop with space and chairs to sit and inspect the stock. English literature of the last two hundred years, art, architecture and illustrated books are the attraction. In addition to the normal range of prints, the book furniture of stands and book ends catches the eye.

VANDELEUR ANTIQUARIAN BOOKS
69 Sheen Lane
SW14 8AD
081 878 6837
Usually M-F pm telephone first

Irregular hours to match the stock but no less attractive because of it. There are around 10000 titles from cheap second-hand books to expensive and rare antiquarian volumes. All subjects are covered but special mention must be made of the main areas which are: travel and exploration, big game and mountaineering, with particular emphasis on Africa. A unique feature is probably the largest stock in the world of 19th century rowing publications, prints and books. Local topography prints are sold, catalogues issued, subject lists prepared on request and all enquiries welcome. Although the range of stock is vast the service is expert and knowledgeable enough to cope.

IAN SHERIDAN'S BOOKSHOP
34 Thames Street
Hampton
TW12 2DX
081 979 1704
M-Sun 10.30-7

A large and largely uninspiring stock of second-hand and antiquarian books in the centre of Hampton on Thames.

DERRICK NIGHTINGALE
32 Coombe Road
Kingston upon Thames
KT2 7AG
081 549 5144
M-Sat 9-1, 2-5, W 9-1

Antiquarian and second-hand books, including review copies, covering the popular range of general subjects in a small bookshop.

ELIZABETH GANT
52 High Road
Thames Ditton
KT7 0SA
081 398 0962
M-Sat 11-5, closed W

A pleasing bookshop in an attractive village with good books for collectors in all subjects.

Children's and illustrated books are the main specialisations.

MICHAEL FINNEY
BOOKS & PRINTS
11 Camden Passage
N1 8EA
071 226 9280
Tue-Sat 10-5

Located in the Camden Passage antique market, which opens on Wednesday and Saturday with a small book market on Thursday. The stock is no bigger than 200 titles and concentrates exclusively on antiquarian plate books in the areas of natural history, travel and architecture. The prints of Spain and the Mediterranean are the main attraction along with general antiquarian prints and some watercolours.

FISHER AND SPERR
46 Highgate High Street
N6 5JB
081 340 7244
M-Sat 10-5

This bookshop is housed in a majestic building, dating back to the 1670's. It is home to over 50000 volumes of second-hand and antiquarian books housed on four floors and in a garden annexe. The wide sweep of subjects defies accurate description. There are some superb volumes, and Mr. Sperr knows his stock personally as a life-long collector. Help could not be more forthcoming and you get the feeling that he has read every book in his bookshop. Definitely worth a visit and

clearly one of the best bookshops
of its type in London.

ROGERS TURNER BOOKS
22 Nelson Road
Greenwich
SE10 9JB
081 853 5271
Tu-Sun 10-6

A very specialised stock, hence
the mail order orientation, awaits
the visitor and collector.
Horology, especially books on sun
dials, history of science and
scientific instruments, linguistics
and Germanic studies. Six
catalogues are issued every year.

ART & DESIGN

APPLIED ARTS ARCHITECTURE BUILDING DESIGN FINE ART GRAPHICS PHOTOGRAPHY SURREALISM

BALLANTYNE & DATE
38 Museum Street
WC1A 1LP
071 242 4249
M-Sat 10.30-6, Sun 12-6

Antiquarian and second-hand books in art and design, photography, architecture and industrial history. Illustrated books is the main theme throughout the stock with the 1930s featuring prominently. Prints and ceramics are also stocked.

ROE & MOORE
29 Museum Street
WC1A 1LH
071 636 4787
M-Sat 10.30-6

Once in Chenil Galleries on King's Road but now in the book enclave near the British Museum. A large collection of out of print and some antiquarian books on all aspects of fine art. Art of the 19th and 20th centuries predominates: on artists, exhibition catalogues, modern illustrations and reference. Modern French first editions, children's and fine bindings complete a well rounded and appealing stock. They also stock books for Bookworks and Carol Manheim.

TRIANGLE BOOKSHOP
36 Bedford Square
WC1B 3EG
071 631 1381
M-F 10-6

Located in the Architectural Association's basement, 4000 titles covering architecture, landscaping and design. Some superb international magazines and many overseas publications.

THE BUILDING BOOKSHOP
26 Store Street
WC1E
071 637 3151
M-F 9.30-5.15, Sat 10-1

Located within the Building Centre, the bookshop complements a well thought out complex. See the materials on display then obtain the know how in the bookshop. They cover all building techniques and other topics from architecture to town planning. DIY enthusiasts are catered for as well as students and professionals of the various trades.

DILLONS ARTS BOOKSHOP
8 Long Acre
Covent Garden
WC2E 9LH
071 836 1359
M-Sat 9.30-10, Tu 10-10,
Sun 12-7

Once the Arts Council Shop and acquired by Dillons in the mid eighties, it has been impressively refurbished to give the welcoming appeal of a gallery with the modern design of a Dillons Bookstore. There are books on applied and fine art, at all levels and for all tastes. In addition other general subjects are covered from bargain books to fiction. The selection of specialist magazines is particularly impressive and there is a modest range of art posters.

A ZWEMMER
24 Litchfield Street
WC2H 9NJ
071 836 4710
M-W, F 9.30-6, Th-Sat 10-6

A specialist of international repute as a leader in both new and out of print books on art. The two floors are packed with books on all aspects of the visual arts. On entering the shop the walls to the right and left are decked with books on artists A-Z. Comprehensive sections on art history, medieval art, national schools, art reference, oriental art and 20th century art occupy the rest of this floor. The basement is devoted to architecture and decorative arts. There is everything you could ever wish for on architectural monographs,

journals, furniture, ceramics, metalwork, fashion and textiles. General and specific subject catalogues are frequently issued and mailed world-wide to appreciative connoisseurs. To the uninitiated, service can be as superior as some of the stock.

A ZWEMMER OUP BOOKSHOP
72 Charing Cross Road
WC2H 0BE
071 379 7886
M-F 9.30-6, Sat 10-6

All books in print, and some that are not, published by Oxford University Press. Why?

A ZWEMMER
80 Charing Cross
WC2H 0BE
071 240 1559
M-F 9.30-6, Sat 10-6

A sister shop to the arts emporium around the corner. Graphics, film and photography in abundance. An applied arts specialist on the Charing Cross Road book browser belt. It feels compelled to display a rather worn notice saying ' no note taking or title making without prior permission.' The service is good enough for enthusiasts but casual browsers beware.

SHIPLEY SPECIALIST ART BOOKSELLERS
70 Charing Cross Road
WC2H 0BB
071 836 4872
M-Sat 10-6

This specialist bookseller concentrates exclusively on the visual arts and stocks new, out of print and some antiquarian books. The range is slightly more expansive than elsewhere and covers the following areas: art and architecture, typography and graphics, photography and fashion, interior design and furniture, Japan and the Orient, aesthetics, writings on art and exhibition catalogues.

ANN CREED BOOKS LTD
22 Cecil Court
WC2N 4HE
071 836 7757
M-Sat 10.30-6.30

A charming shop specialising in out of print and antiquarian books only. Over 5000 books on art, design, typography and fine bindings of artistic merit. There is some interesting original material including artists' books, ephemera and documentation related to the 20th century Avant Garde. There is also a fine set of 19th and 20th century photographs. Magazines and periodicals feature too, as demonstrated by the folio size editions of 'The Manipulator' in the window.

ALAN BRETT
24 Cecil Court
WC2N 4HE
071 836 8222
M-Sat 9-5.30, Sun 10-4

Known also as the 'J R Hartley' shop since the launch of the spoof fly fishing book. The shop is mainly a gallery with a small selection of second-hand and antiquarian books. There are plate books and volumes illustrated by the likes of Arthur Rackham and Dulac. The main specialisation is Vanity Fair prints and albums and there are always many Illustrated London News volumes to peruse. A notice in the window boasts that all the Vanity Fair prints are genuine and no reproductions are sold. So invest in a 1879 Verdi for £200 or a Sarah Bernhardt for £100 in complete confidence.

PHOTOGRAPHERS GALLERY BOOKSHOP
5 & 8 Great Newport Street
WC2H 7HY
071 831 1772
Tu-Sat 11-7

The Photographers Gallery was founded over twenty years ago and following a refit and redesign in late 1992, offers the largest space devoted to photography in London. There are twenty four exhibitions a year in four galleries, an education programme, a print sales room, library(members only), cafe and a bookshop. It has London's leading specialist photography bookshop with publications on every aspect of the art. The mail order service keeps you in touch whilst away on assignment and the broad selection of posters, cards and magazines is one of the best in any arts venue. The shop layout is both innovative and clear, thanks to the design skills of Nick England. You will experience no difficulty in finding and enjoying books by British, American and European photographers, photo journalism, new work, landscape, architecture, history, theory and technique.

NATIONAL PORTRAIT GALLERY BOOKSHOP
St Martin's Place
WC2H 0HE
071 306 0055
M-F 10-4.45, Sat 10-5.45,
Sun 2-5.45

Situated within the Gallery to the left of the foyer at the main entrance, or enter direct through the side entrance. The extensive range of books and merchandise reflects the magnificent art collections of the gallery. National Portrait Gallery publications, British art and portraits, art history and biography are the major areas of expertise. There is a selection of literature and children's educational books, including tapes and videos. Posters, postcards, cards and stationery feature the famous images within the Gallery. The range of crafts is of interest to the art lover and tourist alike, with bags, jigsaws, bookends, mugs and other gift items.

RIBA BOOKSHOP
66 Portland Place
W1 4AD
071 251 0791
M-F 9.30-5.30, Sat 10-1.30

Exclusively architecture inside the premises of the Royal Institute of British Architects. The books cover the theory and practice of architecture and allied topics such as management and law. The comprehensive selection of magazines include the glossy design periodicals from Italy. In addition to providing a comprehensive and up to date range of publications to both students and those in practice, mail order, catalogues and book lists are available.

HOLSTEIN CAMPBELL ART BOOKS
46 Maddox Street
W1R
071 495 4412
M-F 10-6
Modern art reference and illustrated books and prints.

BOOK DEPARTMENT LIBERTY
210 Regent Street
W1R 6AH
071 734 1234
M-W, F-Sat 9.30-6, Th 9.30-7.30

In this world famous department store full of character is a bookshop to match. From Fine Art to children's, a medium sized range of books attractively laid out in a comfortable setting. Good cookery, gardening, textiles and Liberty titles available.

ROYAL ACADEMY OF ART BOOKSHOP
Piccadilly
W1V ODS
071 439 7438
M-Sun 10-5.30

Small range of current art books, featuring exhibition catalogues, art history and artists. There is a complementary range of cards, calendars and gift items.

BOUTLE AND KING
23 Arlington Way
EC1R
071 278 4497
M-Sat 10.30-7

The owners started with a stall in Exmouth Market and opened here in 1990. The shop is in a conservation area of early Victorian terraces, a minute's walk from Angel tube and even closer to Sadler's Wells Theatre. The second-hand stock is as interesting as the location. Surrealism is the main specialisation with a fine selection on expressionism, experimental writing and Atlas Press. Art, history and poetry are represented with a small selection of modern first editions. General subjects are carried selectively with an emphasis on the performing arts and literature. Arguably better than a local pub to while away pre-performance time.

ZWEMMER AT THE WHITECHAPEL GALLERY
80 Whitechapel High Street
E1 7QX
071 247 6924
Tu, Th, Sun 11-5, W 11-8

The Zwemmer empire continues at this well known art venue. The concentration is firmly 20th century art - Bloomsbury to Pop art, architecture and design. Special displays always back up current exhibitions providing background titles, tie-ins and catalogues. There is a good selection of magazines, posters and cards.

DESIGN COUNCIL BOOKSHOP
28 Haymarket
SW1Y 4SU
071 839 8000
M-Sat 10-6, Sun 1-6

The Design Council showroom is a fine example of taking a national talent and presenting it to visitors for interest and to generate new ideas. There is a host of superb designers in this country and one reward is for their work to be shown here. The bookshop complements the displays by presenting a complete range of associated books and publications in an innovative setting. Design management, technical design, packaging products, landscape, history, furniture, architecture and education are all covered. Cards, stationery and gifts are also available.

ICA BOOKSHOP
Nash House
12 Carlton House Terrace
SW1
071 930-493
M-Sun 12-10

Art, media, design, women's studies, culture and fiction. Wide range of design and art magazines. Become a member or pay for the day and enjoy the bookshop, gallery, movie theatre, vegetarian restaurant and bar.

THE PLANNING BOOKSHOP
17 Carlton House Terrace
SW1Y 5AS
071 930-8903
M-F 9.30-5.30

Conveniently located at the Town and Country Planning Association in the architectural splendour of Carlton House Terrace. All planning subjects, in sympathy with the aim of revitalising rural and urban Britain, are covered. There are books on land use, planning law, energy usage, housing, transportation and environmental studies and reports. Subject catalogues are issued and a mail order service is provided.

ST. GEORGES GALLERY BOOKS
8 Duke Street
SW1Y 6BN
071 930 0935
M-F 10-5.30

New titles only here on the fine and decorative arts. St. Georges'

unusual specialisation is the range of international exhibition catalogues. Books cover the wide spectrum of Western art, from pre-historic to the present.

THOMAS HENEAGE ART BOOKS
42 Duke Street
St. James's
SW1Y 6DJ
071 930 9223
M-F 10-6

Publishing an impressive catalogue, Thomas Heneage carries one of the largest range of specialist art books in the world. From interiors to oriental art, reference to Islamic, there's little chance they won't have what you are looking for. Multi-lingual staff in a friendly atmosphere.

CHRIS BEETLES
10 Ryder Street
St. James's
SW1Y 6QB
071 839 7551
M-Sat 10-5.30

This is an art gallery, but there is a range of art books.

TATE GALLERY SHOP
Millbank
SW1 4RY
071 834 5651
M-F 10.30-5.45, Sat 10-5.45, Sun 2-5.45

The Tate boasts three selling areas. The Gallery shop is to the right of the gallery, off the rotunda; the Clore sales desk which is on the ground floor of the Clore gallery and the Exhibition sales desk which is only open to coincide with special exhibitions. The range of books reflects the collections at the Tate and includes all aspects of art throughout the ages. British painting from 1570 to the present and foreign 20th century painting and sculpture are the main specialities. There are always displays of catalogues, books and other items relating to special exhibitions and events in the Gallery. Prints, posters, slides, cards and gifts are included in the repertoire.

HAYWARD GALLERY SHOP
Hayward Gallery
South Bank Centre
Belvedere Road
SE1 8SX
071 928 3144
M-Sun 10-6, W,Th 10-8

A specialist stock on art: artists from A-Z, photography, art reference, sculpture and contemporary art. There is always a comprehensive selection of publications related to current exhibitions arranged to cover the culture, art and literature of the main topic. The other products include a wide selection of cards, posters and calendars connected to the exhibitions and the selection of associated diaries is a real feature.

DESIGN MUSEUM BOOKSHOP
Butlers Wharf
Shad Thames
SE1 2YD
071 403 6933
Tue-Sun 11.30-5.30

A small shop inside the entrance to the Design Museum. There is a wide selection of Design Museum publications, exhibition catalogues, posters and postcards all with a designer theme. A mail order service is available, as is a stock list, on request.

DON KELLY BOOKS
Antiquarius M13
135 King's Road
SW3 4PW
071 352 4690
M-Sat 10-6

The popular antique market at the heart of King's Road is home to Don Kelly's bookstall specialising in reference books on the fine and applied arts, including a selection of foreign language titles. On Saturday mornings, visit his stall at 65 Portobello Road. It was originally founded to supply art and antique dealers with reference material, both new and second-hand.

VICTORIA & ALBERT MUSEUM SHOP
Cromwell Road
SW7 2RL
071 938 8434
M 12-5.30, Tu-Sat 10-5.30,
Sun 2.30-5.30

After a walk around this stupendous museum, spend some time in this equally excellent shop just on the left as you enter the museum, inside the woodwork gallery. The books cover the study, conservation and preservation of the major collections in the V & A: textiles, ceramics, furniture, metalwork, sculpture and the arts and crafts of the Far East, Indian and Islamic cultures. The books form only part of what is a gift givers delight, as the range of products inspired by the sumptuous collections will attract the most jaded culture vulture. If you can't decide what to buy take a V & A gift voucher.

BATTERSEA ARTS CENTRE BOOKSHOP
Old Town Hall
Lavender Hill
SW11 5TF
071 223 2223
Tu-Sat 12-8, Sun 12-6

This bookshop has an appropriate location inside the Arts Centre, a premiere spot for visual theatre. This is essentially a local community bookshop and has a range of popular general subjects: fiction, health, psychology, poetry, literature, women's and children's with an arts bias. There is a good selection of magazines, cards, wrapping paper and cheap CD's.

THE CAMBERWELL BOOKSHOP
28 Camberwell Road
SE5 8RE
071 701 1839
M-Sat 10-7

Situated in a quiet street of Georgian houses a short walk from the High Street. Camberwell Art college is nearby. The building has been a bookshop for the last twelve years and is soon to be expanded to accommodate an upstairs gallery reached by a spiral staircase. The stock is second-hand with a small proportion of antiquarian books. Applied and fine arts, illustrated books and periodicals of the 20th century are the main specialisations. The sections on modern architecture, cartoon and caricature and design offer a wide choice of well selected books. There is normally a good range of titles on Camberwell and its environs. Literary and arty periodical sets can be found here: The Humorist, Night and Day, The Bystander, The Sketch, Lilliput, The Strand and many others. Many of the more attractive and unusual books are displayed face up on the low units in the centre of the shop and a large section of mainly hardback fiction dominates one wall. This is a fine arts bookshop with a strong customer following but the overall quality of stock is reflected in higher than average prices.

BOOKS AND THINGS
Arbras Gallery
292 Westbourne Grove
W11 2PS
071 370 5593
Sat 7-4

Formerly on Portobello Road,
now as a part of this market's
antique gallery. The books
specialise in decorative art, some
modern first editions and fine art.
Ask to see the original posters and
book illustrations.

STEPHEN FOSTER
95 Bell Street
NW1 6TL
071 724 0876
M-Sat 10-6

The Lisson Gallery of modern art
is also in Bell Street, a home of
bookshops for a generation. The
Arts- architecture, decorative arts,
photography and literature is the
main specialisation and there is a
stock of Gould facsimile prints. A
large stock of second-hand books
offers a selection at all price
levels. See the bookshop, stroll
through the Gallery and feast at
the world renowned fish and chip
shop around the corner.

BUSINESS

ACCOUNTING COMPUTING FINANCE
INSURANCE LAW MARKETING

P C BOOKSHOP
21 Sicilian Avenue
WC1A 2QH
071 831 0022
M-F 9.30-6, S 10-12.30

A truly specialist bookshop and
the only one of its kind in
London. Over 3000 books, some
videos, software and computing
magazines. Applications for
business, personal computing
(from Macs to Wizards) and
Virtual Reality are all
comprehensively covered.
Beginners are as welcome as
advanced users and friendly,
helpful advice is dispensed on
demand. Book catalogues and
subject lists are available to enable
customers to take advantage of
the mail and telephone order
service.

PARKS BOOKSHOP
244 High Holborn
WC1V 7DZ
071 831 9501
M-F 8.30-6.30

The first Parks outlet which
opened in 1982. Located 50 yards
from Holborn Underground,
Parks reputation as a leading
specialist is reinforced by the
depth of stock, extending to some
9000 titles. Accounting, Banking,
Finance and Investment,
Management, Marketing, Law,

Taxation, Training, Computing
and general business are treated
as true specialisations and in
many areas the extensive range is
second to none. It is not all big
corporations, the small business
section is worthy of note. The
burgeoning range of business
audio cassettes on sales and
marketing techniques, especially
U S inspired, is well presented. A
van delivery service will cater to
account customers in central
London.

PARKS BOOKSHOP
At the South Bank University
202 Wandsworth Road
SW8 2JZ
071 815 8302
M-F 9-5.30 term time only

Serves the specialised
requirements of the students at
the South Bank. You will find
books on building, construction,
architecture, building law and
economics.

PARKS BOOKSHOP
18 London Road
SE1 6JX
071 928 5378
M-F 9-6

A short walk north of the
Elephant and Castle tube station,
this Parks shop stocks over 4000

titles and is the parent store to the shop at the South Bank University. Computing and computer science, engineering, law, finance, accounting and general business subjects are covered. The delivery service to central London is available from this and all other Parks bookshops.

PARKS BOOKSHOP
11 Copthall Avenue
EC2R 7DJ
071 638 1991
M-F 9-5.30

The ICAEW (Institute of Chartered Accountants in England and Wales) plays host to this shop which primarily serves its members. A superb business reference section including directories and yearbooks sits alongside the full range of Institute publications. All topics close to an accountant's heart-taxation, auditing, finance, investment and commercial law-are here in all their glory. Mail-order and catalogues provided.

BUTTERWORTHS BOOKSHOP
9-12 Bell Yard
Temple Bar
WC2A 2LF
071 405 6900
M-F 9-5, Th 10-5

Next to the law courts is the appropriate location for a shop devoted to books on law and finance with a not unnatural emphasis on books published by Butterworths.

LAW SOCIETY SHOP
227 Strand
WC2
071 242 1222
M-F 9.30-5.30

A one-stop shop for legal eagles. Law Society publications, careers and recruitment services.

BOOKS *etc*
54 London Wall
EC2M 5TR
071 628 9708
M-F 8.30-6.30

Half of the 6000 sq ft of bookselling space is devoted exclusively to professional and business books: law, taxation, insurance, banking, accountancy, computing, business and management. If Books *etc* are as successful with business books as they have been with setting the standard for general bookselling in London, then stiff competition is in store for the more established specialists in the City.

HAMMICKS PROFESSIONAL BOOKSHOP
Corner of Chancery Lane
191/192 Fleet Street
EC4A 2AH
071 405 5711
M-F 9-6

The successor to the Sweet & Maxwell bookshop, founded in 1799, occupies a prominent corner site just inside the borders of the City of London. Middle Temple and Inner Temple are just across the road, The Public Records

Office is nearby and The Royal Courts of Justice are a short walk along Strand. It was previously known as a Law bookshop and although this sector is still pre-eminent, other ranges of business books have been developed. The result is a fine business bookshop offering many specialist services. An extensive mail order operation and Subscriptions Agency is controlled from the head office in Hounslow. The annual Law Book Catalogue has been established for the last 11 years and is considered by legal librarians to be the leader in this field. There is also a Business Books Catalogue.

THE CITY DEPARTMENT WATERSTONE'S
1/7 Whittington Street
EC3V 1LE
071 220 7882
M, W-F 8.30-5.30, Tu 9.30-5.30

Lunch-time in the city and hordes of workers gather to browse, buy and attend author events in one of the most convivial environments in the area. Before Waterstone's moved to this new site a famous old grey, Desert Orchid (horse not doyen author), provided the sort of attraction you associate with this leading chain by making a personal appearance. The City Department, located in the basement, meets the needs of the financial sector with a comprehensive range on investment, insurance, banking and all subjects of import to business. Delivery to Institutional Account Customers is free within the City and even business book

launches can be interesting. At the party to celebrate 'Bankrupt: the BCCI Fraud' the only thing missing was the book which was absent due to legal action!

BANKERS BOOKS
17 St Swithins Lane
EC4N 8AL
071 929 4306
M-F 9-6

You won't have to wait in a line to look at the books on banking. That's because the shop measures a miserly 88 square feet. But if it's banking books you're after, then the publications of the Chartered Institute of Bankers and its American counterpart as well as financial titles will keep you in the black.

WITHERBY & CO LTD
32-36 Aylesbury Street
EC1R 7BR
071 251 5341
M-F 9-4.30

They claim to stock more insurance books than any other bookshop in the world. The roots of this specialisation go back to 1740 when a printing business was founded. Bookselling and publishing developed from producing books for the world of insurance in the City. The range of books on insurance and shipping includes many imported titles. As you would expect from a business with such a long history, it exports to customers world-wide and issues subject catalogues.

BARBICAN BUSINESS BOOK CENTRE
9 Moorfields
EC2Y 9AE
071 628 7479
M-F 9-5.30

A variety of titles from finance to computers, management to strategy.

OYEZ STATIONERY
144 Fetter Lane
EC4 1BT
071 405 2847
M-F 9-5.15

Part of a nation-wide group supplying the needs of the legal profession. The main range is legal and commercial stationery. The book stock is small and on law only.

WILDY AND SONS
Lincoln's Inn Archway
Carey Street
WC2A 2JD
071 242 5778
M-F 8.45-5.15

A legal atmosphere hangs in the air like a premium Havana. Situated in the picturesque Archway, all books legal are in abundance. The shop boasts a stock control system containing details dating back hundreds of years. Books are arranged by the area of law to which they relate and a large adjacent room houses antiquarian and second-hand titles. Newspaper cuttings and other relics from famous criminal cases add to the atmosphere.

LAW NOTES BOOKSHOP & LENDING LIBRARY
25-26 Chancery Lane
WC2A 1NB
071 740 1294
M-F 9-5.30

A library and a bookshop exclusively for the legal profession.

INPUT SOFTWARE
32 Rathbone Place
W1P 1AB
071 636 2666
M-Sat 9.30-6

Primarily a computer software store, with a small range of computer books and manuals.

HOLBORN COLLEGE BOOKSHOP
200 Greyhound Road
W14 9RY
071 385 3377
M-F 9-5.30, Sat 9-12

Specialising in law, but business books are in stock.

THE ECONOMIST BOOKSHOP
25 St. James Street
SW1A 1HG
071 839-7000
M-F 9.30-6

Dedicated business bookshop, with the Economist publications occupying pride of place.

Specialist business reports by the Economist Intelligence Unit are obtainable here. Also available are Economist diaries, calendars and back copies of the magazine. The stock of general business books, from biographies to college texts will not fail to please readers of The Economist.

EXPORT MARKET INFO CENTRE BOOKSHOP
123 Victoria Street
SW1E 6RB
071 215 5444
M-F 9.30-5

Everything you need to know about export and trade whether it be selling machine tools with possible dual use to potentially hostile nations in the Middle East, or expanding into Europe. Part of the DTI, all Department of Trade and Industry publications are available. It was previously known as The Statistics and Market Intelligence Library and Production Data, so the range of information available to businesses on exporting goes beyond mere publications.

ROYAL INSTITUTE OF CHARTERED SURVEYORS
12 Great George Street
SW1P 3AD
071 222 7000
M-F 9.30-5.30

Books centred around property and related law. Contracts, land and construction, engineering and surveying all appear on the shelves.

THE BUSINESS BOOKSHOP
72 Park Road
NW1 4SH
071 723 3902
M,W,F 9-6, Tu 9.30-6

Serving the London Business School just beside Regent's Park, this shop offers a wide variety of business publications to reflect the demanding needs of MBA types. General management, strategy, marketing and personnel management is the strong point. Unusually, there is a wide range of directories, including Kellys and Compass, and BPP publications. Stationery products are sold and the extensive selection of London Business School logo branded products provides a unique selling point. The mail order department is very active serving alumni around the world. A comprehensive stock catalogue is available on request.

THE TRAINER'S BOOKSHOP
35 Harbour Exchange Square
off Marsh Wall
E14 9GE
071 987 8989
M-F 9-5

The new location for the British Association for Commercial and Industrial Education, consisting of a business bookshop, library and information service and training centre. The range of business books is small and concentrates exclusively on management, presentations, training and development.

CHAINS

This section is devoted to the branches of the book chains which specialise in general bookselling. There are a number of bookshops in this category with a genuine specialisation in a particular subject and where this is the case, full details are included in the appropriate section of the guide.

In almost every instance a Books *etc*, Dillons, Waterstone's and larger WH Smith bookshop will carry a superior selection of general books than the smaller independently owned general bookshop. The size of the modern general bookstore means that they now carry an enormous range within individual subjects, but in most cases the specialists listed in this guide will offer superior expertise and range of titles in their specific topics.

BOOKS *etc*

The company was formed in 1981 by father and son, Philip and Richard Joseph who bought four shop leases from the liquidator of the bankrupt Words and Music chain. Three of these original four shops still exist today - two are now twice as large and one is three and a half times bigger. This is indicative of the growth and impact on London bookselling that Books *etc* have had.

They now have 10 shops and are the only specialist general books chain devoted exclusively to London. This focus gives the shops a unique character and an enviable reputation in the capital. The shops exude a relaxed air and although there is a modern design common to each location, they all have something individual to offer. Books are to the fore in every shop, with service provided by booksellers who are also staff and managers.

Special promotions and author events are a Books *etc* feature. One innovative promotion centred around an offer to customers to return a hardback novel if it was found to be an unsatisfactory read. There's no shortage of readable fiction: the range of paperback and hardback novels is predominant in all branches of Books *etc* and the selection in the Charing Cross Road flagship is second to none. Postage on mail orders in London is free and Books *etc* gift vouchers are available.

163 Oxford Street
W1R 1TA
071 734 8287
M-Sat 9.30-8, Sun 12-6

263 High Holborn
WC1V 7EE
071 404 0261
M-F 8.30-6.30, Sat 10-4.30

26 James Street
Covent Garden
WC2E 8PA
071 379 6947
M-Sat 10-10, Sun 12-8

120 Charing Cross Road
WC2H 0JR
071 379 6838
M-W, F, Sat 9.30-8, Th 9.30-8.30,
Sun 12-6

19 Whiteleys of Bayswater
W2 4YQ
071 229 3865
M-Sat 10-10, Sun 12-8

54 London Wall
EC2M 5TR
071 628 9708
M-F 8.30-6.30
SEE BUSINESS SECTION

30 Broadgate Circle
EC2M 2QS
071 256 8590
M-F 8-8

60 Fenchurch Street
EC3M 4AQ
071 481 4425
M-F 8.30-6.30

176 Fleet Street
EC4A 2AB
071 353 5939
M-F 8.30-6.30

66 Victoria Street
SW1A 5LB
071 931 0677
M, Tu, F 8.30-6.30, W, Th 8.30-7
Sat 9-6

DILLONS THE BOOKSTORE

In terms of shop numbers, Dillons is second only to WH Smith, with over thirty bookstores in and around London. The design of their stores is innovative and striking and they were pioneers in revolutionising specialist general bookselling at a time of enormous growth in the book trade. The key to their expansion is the retailing expertise within the Pentos Retailing Group, the owners of Dillons. They have approached this business as retailers whose product is books.

Dillons have 11 general bookstores in London, including two of the world's most famous bookshops: Dillons in Gower Street and Hatchards of Piccadilly. Each has its own distinct character. Hatchards has the history, the pedigree, the Royal Warrants and the snobbery whilst Gower Street has sheer size, an unrivalled range of subjects and a strong academic record. Acquisitions in recent years have added an impressive array of specialist shops to the empire. At Dillons in Margaret Street is A R Mowbray, a leading light in religious bookselling reborn as a specialist department in a worthy general bookstore. At Long Acre in Covent Garden can be found Dillons Arts Bookshop and down the road from Gower Street is a specialist children's and educational bookshop.

There are ten shops at colleges and universities of which three are medical specialists and one is a dedicated business bookshop at the prestigious London Business School. The Economists Bookshop near the London School of Economics continues to provide books on politics and social sciences under Dillons ownership. The business community is further served by a bookshop at the Barbican and Dillons has a bookstore in the Science Museum. There are five bookstores around London: at Bromley, Croydon, Richmond and two in Kingston.

Dillons are at the forefront of a campaign to sell new books at less than the published prices and if this mould-breaking campaign doesn't make books cheap enough in the general bookstores, try the two shops devoted exclusively to bargain books.

DILLONS THE BOOKSTORE
82 Gower Street
WC1E 6EQ
071 636 1577
M, W-F 9-7, Tu 9.30-7, Sat 9.30-6

The flagship of the Dillons chain and undoubtedly the most impressive bookstore in Europe.
SEE GENERAL SECTION

DILLONS ARTS BOOKSHOP
8 Long Acre
Covent Garden
WC2E 9LH
071 836 1359
M-Sat 9.30-10, Tu 10-10
SEE ART & DESIGN SECTION

**THE ECONOMISTS
BOOKSHOP**
Clare Market
Portugal Street
WC2A 2AB
071 405 8643
M-F 9.30-6, W 10.30-6,
Sat 10.30-1.30
**SEE POLITICS & SOCIAL
SCIENCES SECTION**

HATCHARDS
390 Strand
WC2R 0LT
071 379 6264
M-Sat 9.30-6

On the corner of Southampton
Street.

DILLONS THE BOOKSTORE
37 Upper Berkeley Street
W1H 8AS
071 706 3040
M-F 9-7, Sat 9.30-5.30
SEE CHILDREN'S SECTION

**DILLONS THE BOOKSTORE
A R MOWBRAY**
28 Margaret Street
W1N 7LB
071 580 2812
M-Sat 9-6, Th 9-7
SEE RELIGION SECTION

DILLONS THE BOOKSTORE
19-23 Oxford Street
W1R 1RF
071 434 9759
M-Sat 9.30-8

An ex-Claude Gill bookshop.

DILLONS THE BOOKSTORE
10-12 James Street
W1R 2AQ
071 629 8206
M-F 9.30-8, Sat 9.30-6

An ex-Claude Gill bookshop.

119 Oxford Street
W1R 1TF
071 734 3383
M-Sat 9.30-8, Tu 10-8

Once an Athena Bookshop and
now renamed Claude Gill
Bargains. At street level there is a
'...full range of quality books at
bargain prices.' In the basement is
an Athena Gallery with the
expected selection of posters,
cards, gifts and stationery.

DILLONS THE BOOKSTORE
213 Piccadilly
W1V 9LD
071 434 9617
M-Sat 9-7, Sun 11-7

An ex-Claude Gill bookshop.

HATCHARDS
187 Piccadilly
W1V 9DA
071 439 9921
M-Sat 9-6

A most historic bookshop of
international repute.
SEE GENERAL SECTION

DILLONS THE BOOKSTORE
64 Ealing Broadway Centre
Ealing
W5 5JY
081 840 5905
M-Sat 9.30-6

An ex-Claude Gill bookshop.

Barkers Arcade
63 Kensington High Street
W8 5HW
071 937 0858
M-Sat 9.30-6

Formerly Hatchards, now a
bargain bookshop in deference to
the Dillons Bookstore below.

DILLONS THE BOOKSTORE
48-52 Kensington High Street
W8 4PE
071 938 2228
M-Sat 9.30-9, Tu 10-9, Sun 12-7

DILLONS THE BOOKSTORE
150 Kings Road
SW3 3NR
M, W-Sat 9.30-10, Tu 10-10,
Sun 12-10

Progressive opening hours and
one of the best places for new
books in London.

**DILLONS THE BOOKSTORE
THE SCIENCE MUSEUM**
Exhibition Road
SW7 2DD
071 938 8127
M-Sat 10-6, Sun 11-6
**SEE MUSEUMS & GALLERIES
SECTION**

**BARBICAN BUSINESS BOOK
CENTRE**
9 Moorfields
EC2Y 9AE
071 628 7479
M-F 9-5.30
SEE BUSINESS SECTION

THE BUSINESS BOOKSHOP
72 Park Road
NW1 4SH
071 723 3902
M, W, F 9-6, Tu 9.30-6
SEE BUSINESS SECTION

HATCHARDS
782 High Road
North Finchley
N12 8JY
071 439 9921
M-Sat 9-5.30

DILLONS THE BOOKSTORE
12 High Street
Croydon
CR9 1UT
081 688 3811
M-Sat 9-5.30, Tu 9.30-5.30

DILLONS THE BOOKSTORE
7-11 The Mall
Bromley
BR1 1TR
081 460 3232
M-Sat 9-5.30

DILLONS THE BOOKSTORE
Bentalls Shopping Centre
Kingston
KT1
081 974 6811
M-Sat 9-6, Th 9-9

Opened in late 1992 and fits effortlessly into the marble and chrome of the new shopping centre. A magnificent general bookshop, on one floor, that has been needed in Kingston for some time.

HATCHARDS
2 Brook Street
Kingston
KT1 2HA
081 546 7592
M-Sat 9-5.30

Dillons operates a number of specialist bookshops at Colleges and Universities in and around London. Full details of the following bookshops may be found in the **ACADEMIC SECTION.**

CITY UNIVERSITY BOOKSHOP
Northampton Square
EC1V

CITY POLY BOOKSHOP
84 Moorgate
EC2M

QUEEN MARY & WESTFIELD COLLEGE BOOKSHOP
Mile End Road
E1 4NS

MEDICAL BOOKSHOP
St Thomas' Hospital Library
Lambeth Palace Road
SE1 7EH

DILLONS BOOKSTORE
Ealing College of H E
St Mary's Road
W5 5RF

MEDICAL BOOKSHOP
Hammersmith Hospital
Du Cane Road
W12 0NN

MEDICAL BOOKSHOP
Westminster Medical School
St Dunstans Road
W6 8RP

BRUNEL UNIVERSITY
Cleveland Road
Uxbridge
UB8 3PH

DILLONS BOOKSTORE
Royal Holloway and Bedford
New College
Egham
TW20 0EY

HAMMICK'S

With the exception of the Professional Bookshop in Fleet Street, Hammick's is not a force in London bookselling, but they do have a number of branches in small towns around the country. In addition to the specialist business bookshop, there are six general bookshops around London: Barnet, Harrow, Hammersmith, Epsom, Sutton and Kingston. They were owned by John Menzies until a management buy-in in 1992 and so far the shops retain the flavour of a local general bookshop, with the backing of a larger organisation.

Professional Bookshop
192 Fleet Street
EC4A 2AH
SEE BUSINESS SECTION

0372 742533
M-Sat 9-5.30

2 Church Street
Kingston-upon-Thames
KT1 1RJ
081 541 5411
M-Sat 9-5.30, Th 9-8

9 King's Mall
Hammersmith
W6 0QW
081 954 7373
M-Sat 9-6

60-62 St Anns Road
Harrow
HA1 2PL
081 863 4578
M-Sat 9-5.30

13 Times Two
Sutton
SM1 1LF
081 642 6842
M-Sat 9-5.30

2 The Spires
111 High Street
Barnet
081 449 8229
M-Sat 9-5.30, Th 9-7

18 The Ashley Centre
Epsom
KT18 5DA

JOHN MENZIES

Menzies shops have a similar stock profile to W H Smith: newspapers, magazines, cards, stationery, videos and books. The books are restricted to bestsellers and basic stock in the popular subjects. However, there is a good selection of popular paperback fiction and bargains in the Strand branch, and Old Broad Street is a comprehensive and established general bookshop which is known for its signing sessions and events. The shop in Staines shares the local book market with W H Smith.

JOHN MENZIES
Villiers House
40 Strand
WC2N 5HZ
071 930 0033
M-F 8-7, Sat 9-6

50 Cheapside
EC2V 6AT
071 248 5315
M-F 7.30-5.30

56 Old Broad Street
EC2M 1RX
071 588 1632

M-F 8.30-5.30
36 Ashley Centre
Epsom
KT18 5DB
0372 728292
M-Sat 8.30-5.30

42 Elmsleigh Centre
Staines
TW18 4QB
0784 461107
M-Sat 8.30-5.30

VOLUME ONE

Volume One is a national chain with an aggressive expansion plan to give the business 100 outlets by the late nineties. It was founded by the family which started the Superdrug chain and has a link with a major retailer of discount books in the USA. The firm intention is to attract new buyers of books and this aim manifests itself in the design and stocking policy of each store. Elitism is out and the atmosphere is far from intimidating. What is evident is centralised efficiency and face-out displays arranged in accordance with photograph plans supplied from Head Office.

It is impossible to miss the displays of bestsellers, and the general range of popular subjects consists of a carefully chosen and arranged selection of titles. Getting customers into the shop is paramount here, and the wide range of videos and stationery in the larger shops helps achieve this. The fast customer order service counter-balances the lack of depth of stock. It may not be a chain for the purists but that's not the point. If they can sell books to the non-purists, that is the 75% of the population who are not dedicated book buyers, then all those who love books should be happy.

Unit L542
Centre Court
Wimbledon
SW19
081 944 8879
M-Sat 9.30-7

112 North End
Croydon
CR0 1UD
081 688 0231
M-W, F, Sat 9-6, Th 9-8

107 Clarence Street
Kingston-upon-Thames
KT1 1QT
081 541 5481
M-Sat 9-6

26 Treaty Centre
Hounslow
TW3 1ES
081 569 6686
M-W 9-5.30, Th 9-8, F, Sat 9-6

2A Mercer Walk
The Pavillions
Uxbridge
UB8 1LY
M-Sat 9-5.30

Unit 55-56
Exchange Shopping Centre
Ilford
IG1 1AS
081 553 5035
M, Tu, Th 9-5.30, W 9-8,
F, Sat 9-6

WATERSTONE'S

If Dillons revolutionised bookselling with prime sites and glitzy design, Waterstone's changed the face of book retailing with bookshops crammed with the best of art and literature and an exciting array of new books. Waterstone's shops were not designed to be finely tuned centres of retailing excellence or showrooms with every book in its place. They are splendid bookshops with a literary ambience and are absolutely packed with appealing books, on the shelves and often all over the floor. Late opening hours, previously anathema to booksellers, are a characteristic of Waterstone's bookshops and this has done much to make good books more accessible.

In recent years W H Smith purchased Waterstone's and a skilful marriage was effected with Sherratt & Hughes, the specialist book division of Smith's. There is now a nationwide blend of excellent bookshops, in city centres and on university campuses. In London, the emphasis is on general bookselling with only one of the thirteen inner London branches being located at a university. There is an arts-oriented shop at the Royal Festival Hall, South Bank, which is open eleven hours a day, every day except Christmas Day.

The Leadenhall Market shop is the largest in the City and has a specialist business section to rival any of the exclusive business book specialists. Out of town, there are shops competing head-to-head with Dillons in Bromley, Kingston, Richmond and Croydon. The Croydon shop is one the best general bookshops in the south, although it enjoyed this reputation long before becoming a Waterstone's.

Other chains strive to emulate the readings, book launches, signing sessions and literary events held at Waterstone's and although it is a close run thing it is one area where Waterstone's has a genuine edge. The other shops lack the literary cachet.

WATERSTONE'S
121-125 Charing Cross Road
WC2H 0EA
071 434 4291
M, W, F, Sat 9.30-8, Tu 10-8,
Th 9.30-9.30, Sun 12-7

9-13 Garrick Street
WC2 4LA
071 836 6757
M-F 10-8, Sat 10-7.30, Sun 12-7

193 Kensington High Street
W8 6SH
071 937 8432
M-F 9.30-9, Sat 9.30-7, Sun 11-6

39-41 Notting Hill Gate
W11 3JQ
071 229 9444
M-F 9.30-9, Sat 9.30-8,Sun 12-7

1 Whittington Avenue
Leadenhall Market
EC3V
SEE BUSINESS SECTION

Harrods
2nd Floor
87 Brompton Road
SW1X
071 225 5916
M-Sat 9-6, W 9.30-7

266 Earls Court
SW5 9AS
071 370 1616
M-F 10-9, Sat 10.30-9, Sun 12-8

99-101 Old Brompton Road
SW7 3LE
071 581 8522

12 Wimbledon Bridge
SW19 7NW
081 543 9899
M-F 8-8, Sat 9-6, Sun 12-6

The South Bank Centre
Royal Festival Hall
SE1 8XX
071 620 0403
M-Sun 11-10
**SEE PERFORMING ARTS
SECTION**

Goldsmith's College
University of London
New Cross
SE14 6NW
081 469 0262
SEE ACADEMIC SECTION

128 Camden High Street
NW1 0NB
071 284 4948
M-F 9.30-8, Sat 9.30-6, Sun 12-6

68-69 Hampstead High Street
NW3 1QP
071 794 1098
M-F 10-9, Sat 10-8, Sun 11-7

1063-7 Whitgift Centre
Croydon
CR0 1UX
081 686 7032
M, W, F,Sat 9-6, Tu 10-6, Th 9-9

23-25 Thames Street
Kingston-upon-Thames
KT1 1PH
081 547 1221
M-F 9.30-8, Sat 9-7, Sun 11-6

2-6 Hill Street
Richmond-upon-Thames
TW10 6UA
081 332 1600
M, W-F 9.30-8, Tu 10-8,
Sat 9.30-7, Sun 12-7

75 The Mall
Broadway Shopping Centre
Bexleyheath
DA6 7JJ
081 301 4411
M-Sat 9-5.30, Th 9-9

20-22 Market Square
Bromley
BR1 1NA
081 464 6562
M-F 9-5.30, Sat 9-6

W H SMITH

WH Smith has over sixty shops in and around London, and sells more books than anyone else in the country. Dyed-in-the-wool booksellers are snobbish about WH Smith and consider that they only deal in bestsellers, paperbacks and illustrated cookery books. This is a fallacy even in the smallest branch. The W H Smith shops listed below are grouped by size and depth of books carried and are split into eight groups, from the largest to the smallest.

All shops carry stationery, cards, newspapers and magazines. Around 75% also carry music, videos and computer software. You can expect to find the same subject areas in all shops, but the larger shops will carry a wider range within the subject. At Brent Cross, one of the largest stores, you will see over 30000 titles, whereas the smallest shops will carry only 10% of that. The largest branches, Brent Cross, Croydon and Wood Green compete closely with the average Dillons or Waterstone's. W H Smith is surprisingly good in the areas of popular paperback fiction, reference, maps and guides and illustrated non-fiction such as crafts, gardening and cookery. Children's books and basic titles for primary and secondary education are to be found in every shop. You will not find specialist books and tertiary level academic texts.

All shops are supplied from a central warehouse and they aim to supply special orders in 72 hours, providing it is for a book normally stocked by WH Smith. Supplying customer orders for books outside this range is not yet an area where WH Smith competes with other general bookshops.

Despite the central control, there is some latitude for individual shops to develop locally inspired selections of books, in addition to local history. Brent Cross has a sizeable range on Jewish topics, Wood Green and Lewisham carry sections on Black interest and Sloane Square concentrates on crafts, design and interiors.

In a number of areas of London WH Smith is the only general books outlet: Wood Green, Romford, Catford, with only one other competitor in Putney and Staines. They may not be the most inspiring bookshops but they facilitate the reading and buying of books and offer reassuring uniformity to the High Street shopper.

Brent Cross Shopping Centre
Brent Cross
NW4 3FB
081 202 4226

110 High Road
Wood Green
N22 6HE
081 889 0221

Whitgift Centre
Croydon
CR0 1US
081 688 5211

----

36 Sloane Square
SW1W 8AP
071 730 0351

50 The Exchange
Ilford
IG1 1DQ
081 553 5344

21-23 The Broadway
Ealing
W5 2NH
081 567 1471

----

124 Holborn Circus
EC1N 2TD
071 242 0535

King's Mall
King Street
Hammersmith
W6 0PZ
081 748 2218

59 Riverdale
Lewisham Centre
SE13 7EP
081 318 1316

68-72 Powis Street
Woolwich
SE18 6LQ
081 854 7108

132-138 High Street
Bromley
BR1 3EZ
081 464 5044

Bentalls Centre
Kingston-upon-Thames
KT1 1PQ
081 549 7631

49-51 High Street
Staines
TW18 4QR
0784 452700

8 The Liberty
Romford
RM1 3RL
0708 762317

7-11 Palace Gardens
Shopping Centre
Enfield
EN2 6SN
081 366 3633

125 High Street North
East Ham
E6 1HZ
081 552 4875

Hornton Court
132-136 Kensington High Street
W8 7RP
071 937 0236

148 High Street
Uxbridge
UB8 1JY
0895 56221

111-115 Putney High Street
Putney
SW15 1SS
081 788 2573

The Plaza
120 Oxford Street
W1N 9DP
071 436 6282

118 High Street
Sutton
SM1 1LU
081 643 4512

189-193 High Street
Orpington
BR6 0PF
0689 71516

180-182 High Road
Streatham
SW16 1BH
081 677 3031

11 Kingsway
Aldwych
WC2B 6YA
071 836 5951

16-17 George Street
Richmond
TW9 1JS
081 940 3671

----

89 The Broadway
Bexleyheath
DA6 7JN
081 301 0802

41-42 The Mall
The Stratford Centre
E15 1XE
081 534 5955

13 High Street
Walton-on-Thames
KT12 1BZ
0932 243262

Elephant & Castle
Shopping Centre
SE1 6SZ
071 730 8525

92 Notting Hill Gate
W11 3QB
071 727 9261

St Ann's Shopping Centre
St Ann's Road
Harrow
HA1 1AS
081 863 9374

201-205 High Street
Hounslow
TW3 1BL
081 577 3930

----

64 The Broadway
West Ealing
W13 0SU
081 579 3461

92-94 High Street
Eltham
SE9 1BW
081 859 3019

Centre Mall
Arndale Shopping Centre
Wandsworth
SW18 4TG
081 877 1979

9-10 Harben Parade
Finchley Road
NW3 6JG
071 722 4441

Broadgate
Western Mall
Liverpool Street Station
EC2M 7QA
071 628 1617

370-372 Chiswick High Road
Turnham Green
W4 5TA
081 995 9427

----

766 High Road
North Finchley
N12 9QH
081 445 2785

23 Winslade Way
Catford
SE6 4JU
081 690 1972

113 Kilburn High Road
NW6 6JH
071 328 3111

145-147 Cheapside
EC2V 6BJ
071 606 2301

Surrey Quays Shopping Centre
Redriff Road
SE16 1LL
071 237 5235

320 North End Road
Fulham
SW6 1NG
071 385 9585

6-8 Station Road
Hayes
UB3 4DA
081 848 9884

13-15 High Street
Weybridge
KT13 8AX
0932 852 043

92 Woodcote Road
Wallington
SM6 0NG
081 669 7739

93 High Street
Barnet
EN5 5UR
081 449 2144

----

889 Finchley Road
Golders Green
NW11 8RR
081 455 0036

117 Muswell Hill Broadway
Muswell Hill
N10 3RS
081 883 1706

5 Alderman's Hill
Palmers Green
N13 4YD
081 886 4743

29 The Broadway
Mill Hill
NW7 3DA
081 959 1316

82 Walm Lane
Willesdon Green
NW2 4RA

172 High Street
Beckenham
BR3 1EW
081 650 0538

4 Station Way
Cheam
SM3 8SW
081 643 5848

39 High Street
West Wickham
BR4 0LR
081 776 0306

112 High Street
New Malden
KT3 4FU
081 949 5907

76 High Street
Ruislip
HA4 7AA
0895 632108

153 Central Road
Worcester Park
KT4 7NL
081 337 1945

CHILDREN'S

MARCHPANE
16 Cecil Court
WC2N 4HE
071 836 8661
M-Sat 10.30-6.30

Collectable children's and
illustrated books with a particular
emphasis on the works of Lewis
Carroll. There is a good selection
of prints with a fine range of John
Tenniel Alice prints from 1872.
The shop is an enticing treasure
trove with second-hand and
antiquarian books to delight.
Interesting collectables and
oddities can always be seen in the
window such as 'Manual of the
Sten Gun.' If books fail to appeal
consider a limited edition Dalek,
battery operated with robot action
for £25.

**THE PUFFIN CHILDREN'S
BOOKSHOP**
1 The Market
Covent Garden
WC2E 8RA
071 379 6465
M-Sun 10-6.30

It would be inappropriate to have
anything but a children's
bookshop on the site of the first
Punch and Judy show, first held
in the 18th century. The full range
of Puffin titles is crammed into
three floors of selling space, with
much more besides. Children's
books from infant to teenager will
keep you and your charges out of
the Covent Garden crowds.

Merchandise from the gamut of
favourite children's characters
complements the colourful array
of books. Frequent events and
many signed copies add to the
attraction of the area.

DILLONS THE BOOKSTORE
37 Upper Berkeley Street
W1H 8AS
071 706 3040
M-F 9-7, Sat 9.30-5.30

A specialist bookstore also known
as Dillons Educational and
Children's. The specialisation is
self evident and the stock profile
is different to other dedicated
children's bookshops in that
Dillons concentrates heavily on
educational titles. Direct supply to
schools is a feature of the business
and they are as able to direct a
teacher to a suitable reading
course as they are a parent to a
GCSE revision aid.

**HAMLEYS BOOK
DEPARTMENT**
188-196 Regent Street
W1R 6BT
071 734 316
M-F 10-6, Thu 10-8, Sat 9.30-6

The mecca of toys in Regent Street
plays host to a book section. It
loses its impact squeezed between
the latest Sonic the Hedgehog and
Barbie in her wedding gown.
Books are arranged by subject and
you will find the favourites.

CHILDREN'S BOOKSHOP IN HARRODS
4th Floor - Harrods
Old Brompton Rd
SW1 7XL
071 730 1234
M-Sat 9-6, W 9.30-7

In the world of shopping Harrods ranks somewhere near the top. If you reach the book department without feeling overwhelmed by the sheer variety and size of this store you will enjoy a tranquil respite. The books are enticing and accessible, and help is forthcoming.

CHILDREN'S BOOK CENTRE
237 Kensington High Street
W18 6SA
071 937 7497
M-Sat 9.30-6.30, Th 9.30-7

The Children's Book Centre first opened in this area 20 years ago and has been at this location for 4 years. It is a bright and attractive shop, well frequented and has a tangible sense of fun. The huge range of books is arranged by age group and subject. The fiction range is extensive and there is a wide selection of work-books for children up to the age of ten. A TV set plays the latest videos and soft toys, educational games and books on tape compete with the books. Expert advice is to hand, school events organised and children's parties arranged.

JOHN LEWIS
Oxford Street.
Brent Cross Shopping Centre.
Kingston.
M-Sat 9-5.30, Th 9-8

Books sit side by side with toys in the children's department at the three department stores. Books are well displayed and easy to locate by age or title.

BOOKS FOR CHILDREN
97 Wandsworth Bridge Road
SW6 2TD
071 384 1821
M 10-6, Tu-F 9.30-6,
Sat 9.30-5.30

This bookshop prides itself on being a source of school texts. A decent range of children's books supplements the stock.

BOOKSPREAD
58 Tooting Bec Road
SW17 8BE
081 767 6377
M-F 10-5, Th 10-9, Sat 10-3

Located in a pleasing Edwardian house, by the red letter box, is an extensive range of books for children up to 14 years of age. The stock includes multi-cultural, non-racist, non-sexist and dual language books. Events are held regularly, from author visits to story telling sessions.

THE LION & UNICORN BOOKSHOP
19 King Street
Richmond
TW9 1ND
081 940 0483
M-S 9.30-5.30

Jennifer Morris runs one of the very few independent bookshops in the country devoted entirely to books for children. It is a superb shop and one of the best in the land. The stock comprises a complete selection of books: board books for babies, pre-school puzzles, classics, non-sexist & non-racist stories and information books for all ages. There is a wide range of books on tape and videos too covering old favourites, early learning, music and languages. It is a rare pleasure to be able to leave children busy at a play table in a book paradise whilst obtaining expert advice from helpful and knowledgeable staff. New parents, books for children with special needs, grandparents seeking a special gift - it is all here. A range of specialist services is provided for schools, libraries, parent groups and those who work with children professionally. Book exhibitions, class visits, school bookstalls, and late opening for distraction-free browsing and buying. The picture board behind the counter tells the story of the joys of bringing good books to children. It is covered with photographs of scenes from author visits and special events in the shop and there are smiling faces of children, parents, authors and staff on every picture.

CANONBURY BOOKSHOP
271 Upper Street
N1 2UQ
071 226 3475
M-Sat 9-7.30, Sun 10-4

Primarily a general bookshop with a specialist department in the basement devoted to children's books. There are books for children of all ages, with an innovative and appropriate range of educational and traditional toys.

RIPPING YARNS
355 Archway Rd,
N6 5AB
081 341-6111
M-F 10.30-5.30, Sat 10-5,
Sun 11-4

A bookshop since the '30s and christened Ripping Yarns in 1981 by Michael Palin and Terry Jones of Monty Python fame. Opposite Highgate tube and stocked with all manner of second-hand books, primarily adventure stories and illustrated children's titles, some interesting annuals and old comics. You may find a first edition or two. Books spill out onto the street encouraging browsers.

OWL BOOKSHOP
211 Kentish Town Rd
NW5
071 485 7793
M-Sat 9.30-6

Very much a general bookshop with a varied stock but housing an excellent children's department covering everything except school texts. The shop has a literary connection, albeit tenuous, being on the site of a department store mentioned by John Betjeman and the place where V S Pritchett's parents met when working in the store. The literary association continues by virtue of the many writers living nearby who have signed copies of their books. A friendly, quality bookshop run by knowledgeable and caring booksellers.

CHILDREN'S BOOKSHOP
29 Fortis Green Rd
Muswell Hill,
N10 3RT
081 444-5500
M-F 9.15-5.45, Sat 9.15-5.30,
Sun 12-5
Local co-operation is sadly something you don't see very often, but here is an example of a success. Opposite is the Muswell Bookshop, a general bookshop, and they share with the Children's Bookshop information, book signings and promotions. Here you'll find over 20,000 titles and while you browse and buy, your kids can play with toys and enjoy the pleasure of books. Their stock is well laid out, books for all ages supported by expert and friendly advice on what's best. They publish four newsletters annually on suggested and recommended reading, and the book events for children are very popular. Open on a Sunday too, it is a must.

WOMEN & CHILDREN FIRST
14 Greenwich Market
Greenwich
SE10 9HZ
081 853 1296
M-Sun 10-5.30

Located in the busy Greenwich market. It may not be able to offer the range of stock and services provided by larger children's bookshops but is a welcome respite from market shopping. Popular reading for all ages, and a selection of books on women's interests.

COMICS & SCIENCE FICTION

AMERICAN CARTOONS FANTASY GRAPHIC NOVELS HORROR IMPORTS

FORBIDDEN PLANET
71 New Oxford Street
WC1A 1DG
071 379 6042
M-W, Sat 10-6, Th-F 10-7

Forbidden Planet is the undisputed leader in this field. It has grown from a small shop in 1978 to a nationwide group. The London flagship occupies two floors and has three separate departments. The range of books on science fiction, fantasy and horror includes many hard-to-get imports and is the most comprehensive anywhere. Comics new, old and rare come from all over the world as does the bewildering range of related merchandise. Rare items behind the counter, where expert advise from fellow fanatics is always to hand, include an early Mickey Mouse comic for a mere £100. For true believers with as much money as dedication, try to resist a fine copy of the second Superman comic for a hyperspace £1200. More affordable and nearly as trendy would be a limited edition Marvel silk tie for £60. Some of the more exotic merchandise is resplendent in glass cases. Star Trek products seem curiously staid next to 'Enchantica', the Lladro of the fantasy world, with dragons and mystical beasts just waiting to find a good home on your living room mantelpiece. Uniquely, there is a special section for Small Press publications. Limited and signed editions are available along with an intriguing selection of TV Fantasy and Film books. Genres within genres.

GOSH! COMICS
39 Great Russell Street
WC1B 3PH
071 636 1011
M-Sun 10-6, Th-F 10-7

Opposite the British Museum and surrounded by literary, antiquarian and secondhand bookshops, Gosh! stands out in more ways than one. The Bloomsbury Booksellers Guide ignores Josh Palmanos' business yet it is as good a specialist as any. It started as a comic shop with the usual new and back issues, but it is the book side that has grown most innovatively and which sets it apart from the bland mediocrity evident elsewhere. Comics is interpreted in the widest sense and the variety of the book stock reflects this. There is an unrivalled selection of newspaper cartoon strips, in book form, especially from Europe and America. Even before the end of the 1992 Presidential election, *'Standing Tall in Deep Doo-Doo'*, a cartoon chronicle of the campaign and the Bush/Quayle years was hot on the shelves. At the other end of the scale the Barbar range of children's books is carried in the most appealing form, that is the foolscap size hardback. All the 38 Dr Seuss books in print are available from stock in hardback. Gosh! is aptly named - the variety of stock from cartoons to illustrated educational books for children will impress and surprise.

THE TINTIN SHOP
34 Floral Street
WC2E 9DJ
071 836 1131
M-Sat 10-6, Sun 1-6

'Blistering Barnacles!', a shop that since 1984 has specialised in books by Hergé and products derived from the artwork and characters. Some bookshops have a resident cat but here you expect to see Snowy lying behind the counter, poised for adventure. A location deep in tourist territory, steps from the tube, is just the place you expect to find all known books on the ginger quiffed hero, Hergé, and his other characters. If the books don't appeal, the goods based on them will: clothing, cards, prints, watches, calendars, diaries, models and jigsaws. For addicts unable to make the trip, use the mail order service.

STATESIDE COMICS AT VIRGIN
1st Floor Virgin Marble Arch
527-531 Oxford Street
W1
071 499 8839
M,W,F, Sat 9.30-7, Tu 10-7,
Th 9.30-8, Sun 12-7

Within this mammoth music superstore, Stateside comics carries mainstream Marvel and DC titles, specialising in the Silver and Golden age. It also stocks the very latest imports, graphic novels, trading cards and other comic-related merchandise.

STATESIDE AT HAMLEYS
188/196 Regent Street
W1 6BT
071 287 3097
M-Sat 9-7

Similar range to the Virgin store, inside the world famous toy shop, also including merchandise such as T-shirts, trading cards, holograms and posters.

STATESIDE IN NORTH LONDON
125 East Barnet Road
Barnet
EN4 8RF
081 449 2991
M-Th 10-7; F 10-8, Sat 9.30-6.30,
Sun 10-3

The first in the three shop Stateside chain offering the most advanced comics computer database in Europe. They will find you any back issue.

MEGA-CITY COMICS
18 Inverness Street
NW1 7HJ
071 485 9320
M-Sun 10-6, Th-F 10-7

Over 200,000 comics and graphic novels ranging from sci-fi to subversive! Located just off Camden's busy High Street, this well-lit and designed shop has knowledgeable staff. The catalogue is as thick as many paperback fantasy tales, but is more comprehensive and interesting. The regular signing sessions are popular and T-shirts, posters and collectors items are available.

ACME COMIC SHOP
391 Coldharbour Lane
SW9 8LQ
071 274 6697
M-Sat 10-6

Acme Press started this shop four years ago and it changed hands in 1991. Although there are hundreds of comics, graphic novels and other bumf it somehow lacks imagination and blends in with the crowd rather than stands out.

AVALON COMICS
143 Lavender Hill
SW11 5RA
071 924 3609
M-Th 10-5.45, F 10-7,
Sat 9.30-5.45

Comics galore, especially American, with new imports, back issues and collectors' items.

Graphic novels, second-hand science fiction, horror paperbacks, and associated merchandise completes the story. They welcome wants lists and offer a standing order service for new imports.

AT THE SIGN OF THE DRAGON
131 Sheen Lane
SW14 8AE
081 876 3855
M-Sat 10-6, W closed

Science fiction and fantasy books for enthusiasts and the curious in this general bookshop. Comics and graphic novels are available.

THEY WALK AMONG US
30 Union Court
Sheen Road
Richmond
TW9 1AA
081 948 8476
M-Sat 9.30-5.30, F 9.30-6

Although this shop is tucked away it is eagerly sought out by the faithful as it is the only comics specialist in the area. There is a full range of new American comics and graphic novels with some science fiction/fantasy books. The usual selection of peripheral merchandise, posters, T-shirts, badges, cards, videos and models is available. The wall behind the counter is decorated with rare issues such as the first Iron Man comic for £165.

READERS DREAM
100a Harlington Road West
Feltham
TW14
081 844 0780
M-F 9.30-6

Paperbacks only on science fiction and fantasy.

CALAMITY COMICS
160 Station Road
Harrow
HA1
081 427 3831
M-W 10-6, Th,F 10-7, Sat 9.30-6

Comics and graphic novels for the local enthusiasts.

FANTASY CENTRE
157 Holloway Road
N7 8LX
071 607 9433
M-Sat 10-6

Mainly second-hand books here in the fields of science fiction, fantasy and horror. There is a section of first editions and some new books. The Fantasy Centre has been around for 20 years, unlike many of the comic-oriented newcomers, so the stock and services are more complete than elsewhere. The paperbacks, especially the older ones with surreal cover illustrations, magazines and ephemera are better than average. Subject catalogues are issued regularly.

GRAPHICALLY SPEAKING
475 Bethnal Green Road
E2
071 613 0500
M-W, Sat 11-6, Th-F 11-7,
Sun 11-5

Started as a specialist library supplier of graphic novels, complete with an 'on approval' service, a good move to get this type of book into libraries. The book stock is currently restricted to comics and graphic novels but there are plans to add a science fiction section in the near future.

THE COMIC SHACK
720 High Road
Leytonstone
E11 3NN
081 539 7260
M-Th 9.30-5.30, F-Sat 9.30-6.30,
Sun 11-5.30

American comic books is the specialisation with science fiction and fantasy books as a sideline.

ATOMIC COMICS
1112 High Road
Chadwell Heath
Romford
RM6 4AH
081 597 8547
M-Sat 10-6, F 10-7

Founded in 1989 using the owners personal collection of comics and books as the opening stock. The usual range of new imports arrives monthly to satisfy local fans. Japanese and US animated videos lead the way amongst the trading cards, badges, role-

playing miniatures and some
original artwork.

SKINNY MELINK'S COMICS
66 Loampit Vale
SE13
081 318 0499
M-Th 11-6.30, F-Sat 11-7

Streetwise comic and graphic
novel shop with credibility.
Selling mainly new with the usual
smattering of second-hand and
collectors' issues.

COUNTRIES

AFRICA ASIA AUSTRALIA EASTERN EUROPE FRANCE GREECE IRELAND ITALY JAPAN MIDDLE EAST NEW ZEALAND SPAIN TURKEY

AFRICA BOOK CENTRE
38 King Street
WC2E 8JT
071 240 6649
M-F 11-5.30, Sat 11-5

Visit the Africa Centre to see the paintings and crafts in the ground floor gallery and head to the first floor for the bookshop. There is a wide range of books on all subjects relating to Africa, Black America, the Caribbean and Third World Development. Literature, art, languages, travel, music, history, politics, social studies, education and children's are the main subjects. Records, cassettes, cards and T-shirts are also available. New book lists and subject lists can be provided.

SOMA BOOKS
38 Kennington Lane
SE11 4LS
071 735 2101
M-F 10-5.30

A substantial range of books on Africa, the Caribbean, Black America and associated issues of race and education. General subjects are also covered and the children's section stands out with an innovative and carefully chosen range of multi-cultural, anti-sexist and non-racist books. Crafts, posters and cards include

many items of interest imported from Asia.

MAGHREB BOOKSHOP
45 Burton Street
WC1H 9AL
071 388 1840
M-Sat 9.30-6

The Maghreb comprises Algeria, Libya, Mauritania, Morocco and Tunisia. Books covering academic studies and Islam are available in Arabic and French. There are interesting studies on the slave trade and migration for those interested in this historic region.

GRASS ROOTS
71 Golborne Road
W10 5NR
081 969 0687
M-Sat 11-6.30

This co-operative stocks gifts, African crafts and books. Black politics, and related studies dominate.

NEW BEACON BOOKS
76 Stroud Green Road
N4 3EN
071 272 4889
M-Sat 10.30-6

An impressive range of books on Black Britain, Caribbean, Africa and Black America on subjects as diverse as cookery to radical politics and fiction. Within the multi-racial children's books are many joyous titles that you will not see in most general bookshops. Monthly booklists are available.

OPERATION HEADSTART
25 West Green Road
N15 5BX
081 802 2838
M-Thu 9.30-6.30, F-Sat 9.30-7

Previously known as Headstart Books and Gifts, this remains a centre for books, crafts and information an Africa, Black America, Caribbean and black issues worldwide.

ASIAN BOOKSHOP
112 Whitfield Street
W1P
071 387 5747
M-Sat 9.30-5.30

Books in Hindi, Urdu, Bengali, Gujerati and Punjabi, both fiction and popular general subjects. As well as a selection of dictionaries and English books from India, there is a good range of children's titles in languages of India. Books on tape are available in many languages and a stock catalogue can be consulted.

NEAL STREET EAST
5 Neal Street
WC2H 9PU
071 240 0135
M-Sat 10-7, Sun 12-6

Located in an old Covent Garden vegetable warehouse, this a shop specialises in crafts and products from the Far East, South East Asia and the Indian sub-continent. There is a good range of books covering the culture, beliefs and way of life of peoples indigenous to these parts of the world.

RUPOSHI BANGLALTD
220 Tooting High Street
SW17 0SG
081 672 7843
M-Sat 10-5.30

Bangladesh is brought to your doorstep in the form of a multi-media experience. The speciality is books and Ruposhi has plenty to choose from. Founded in 1974 as a resource centre for the Bangladeshi residents, it has blossomed to incorporate a type-setting service and a distributor of Bengali computer software. Books originate in Bangladesh, India and the UK and cover all subjects relating to language, literature and culture. Music, cultural artefacts and posters all contribute to this eastern experience.

JOHN RANDALL
47 Moreton Street
SW1V 2NY
071 630 5331
Tu-Sat 10-6, W 10-8

Some new books on South East
Asia, India and central Asia, and
the Middle East. The stock is
mostly antiquarian and second-
hand.

VIRDEE BROTHERS
26 South Road
Southall
UB1 1RR
081 571 4870
M-Sat 10-7.30

102 The Green
Southall
UB2 4BQ
081 574 4765
M-Sat 11.30-7.30

Mainly Hindi and Punjabi fiction
and poetry in both shops. There is
also a selection in Urdu and
Gujerati. Both shops have
children's books, language
learning materials and a large
range of music of the sub-
continent.

HOISANS BOOKS
25 Connaught Street
W2 2AY
071 262 7900
Tu-F 11-5

A specialist purveyor of books on
Central Asia, the Indian sub-
continent, and the Middle East.
Subjects represented include
religion, travel and history. Part of

the magic is provided by a fine
range of lithographs, miniatures
and manuscripts relating to the
specialisations.

FINE BOOKS ORIENTAL
46 Great Russell Street
WC1B 3PA
071 636 6068
M-F 9.30-5

Large antiquarian and second-
hand stock specialising in Japan,
the Far East, Middle East and
Asia. Photographs and postcards
complement the range of books.

ARTHUR PROBSTHAIN
41 Great Russell Street
WC1B 3PH
071 636 1096
M-F 9.30-5.30, Sat 11-4

Antiquarian and second-hand
books covering the language, art
and history of the Orient.

AUSTRALIAN GIFT SHOP
Western Australia House
115 Strand
WC2R 0AA
071 836 2292
M-F 9-5.30, Sat 9-1

A small selection of books on
Australia and books published in
the Antipodes. It is a good source
for Australian maps, gifts and
souvenirs, including the
ubiquitous Vegemite.

AUSTRALIAN BOOKSHOP
10 Woburn Walk
WC1H 0JL
071 388 6080
M-F 10-6, Sat 10-5

A comprehensive selection of books from and about Australia. All aspects of God's country are covered: history, social issues, Aborigines, fiction, the arts and flora and fauna. A selection of indigenous crafts and specially imported food products help create a home from home for Australians in London. Where else, apart from Earls Court on a Saturday night, will you find renditions of Wild Colonial Boy or Banjo Patterson's evocative poetry.

HAN-SHAN TANG LTD
8 Duke Street
St. James's
SW1Y 6BN
071 839 6599
M-F 10-5.30

The art of China, Japan, Korea and central Asia. Catalogues are published quarterly.

YING HWA
14 Gerrard Street
W1V
071 439 8825
M-Sun 11-7.30

Books in Chinese and in English on China, located in the heart of Chinatown.

GUANGHWA LTD
7-9 Newport Place
WC2H 7JR
071 431 3737
M-Sun 10-6

Books for students and children as well as a varied range of other subjects in Chinese and English. Chinese language learning aids, artefacts and prints all share space with the books.

COLLETS RUSSIAN & EAST EUROPEAN BOOKSHOP
40 Great Russell Street
WC1B 3PJ
071 580 7538
M-F 10-6.30, Sat 10-6

The first Collets bookshop was on the Charing Cross Road and opened in 1934. A glossy Waterstone's now occupies the site that was Collets European Book Centre and the shop on Great Russell Street is now Collet's only retail outlet. Here is an unparalleled selection of titles in Russian and English from and about Russia and Eastern Europe. Politics, history, literature, teaching aids, dictionaries and travel are comprehensively covered. There is a selection of periodicals, newspapers, music, videos and games from Russia. With markets in the East opening ever wider, a visit to peruse the business books could be invaluable.

ORBIS BOOKS(London) LTD
66 Kenway Road
SW5 0RD
071 370 2210
M-F 9.30-5.30, Sat 9.30-4.30

Established during World War II
to serve the Polish army in the
U.K. Stocking mainly Polish
books, but countries in Eastern
Europe, the CIS and the Baltic
states are also covered. A few
books in Czech, Slovak, Bulgarian
and Russian.

PMS BOOKSHOP LTD
240 King Street
W6 0RF
081 748 5522
Tu-F 10-6, Sat 12-6, Sun 12-4

This dedicated bookshop within
the Polish Centre in
Hammersmith stocks all things
Polish. The books, in Polish,
include education, history,
politics and culture. Books and
audio cassettes in English and
Polish are available for those
learning the language. Souvenirs
from Poland, toys, flags and war
memorabilia accompany Polish
daily newspapers, calendars and
magazines. This is a cultural
centre in which the bookshop is a
focal point.

**HUNGARIAN BOOK
AGENCY**
87 Sewardstone Road
Victoria Park
E2 9HN
081 980 9096
Th-Sat 11-5

Established in 1960 as the
Danubia Book Company, this
book service caters for the
Hungarian community in the U.K.
Primarily a mail order company,
they are the only importers of
Hungarian books into the
country. Some 2000 titles in
Hungarian covering language
textbooks and study aids,
literature, culture and music. A
few English titles on Eastern
Europe topics mingle with the
maps, newspapers, periodicals,
CD's, cassettes and cards. If you
want to visit the shop outside the
opening hours, phone for an
appointment.

UKRAINIAN BOOKSHOP
49 Linden Gardens
Notting Hill Gate
W2 4HG
071 229 0140
M-F 9-5.30, Sat 2-5

The Association of Ukrainians in
Great Britain is host to this
bookshop holding Ukrainian and
English titles in the popular
subjects. Visit the adjacent shop
for embroidery and other clothing
crafts of the Ukrainian people.

ANTHONY C. HALL
30 Staines Road
Twickenham
TW2 5AH
081 898 2638
M-Sat 9-5.30, W closed

Second-hand books on Russia and
her neighbours in Asia, Eastern
Europe and the Middle East.

LA PAGE BOOKSHOP
7 Harrington Road
SW7 3ES
071 589 5991
M-F 8.30-6.15, Sat 10-5

France is represented by this
bookshop and stationers, with
French speaking staff. Literature,
language teaching, reference and
children's books are the main
features. They have a extensive
selection of *bandes dessinees* titles.

THE FRENCH BOOKSHOP
28 Bute Street
SW7 3EX
071 584 2840
M-F 9-6, Sat 10-5

Students from the nearby Lycee
use this well-stocked bookshop
for reference books, French
bilingual books, paperback fiction
and graphic novels. French
literature is the focus among the
4000 titles and children's books
are also well represented. French
games and stationery are also
available.

ZENO BOOKSELLERS
6 Denmark Street
WC2H 8LP
071 836 2522
M-F 9.30-6, Sat 9.30-5

A family business dating back to
1944 when Father Kykkotis left
his monastery in Cyprus for
colder climes in London. The
bookshop stocks over 10,000 titles
in both Greek and English on
Greece and Cyprus. The subjects
include Byzantium, travel, history

and language learning. Greek
residents and visitors use this
bookshop regularly as do
universities, schools and libraries
around the world.

HELLENIC BOOKSERVICE
91 Fortress Road
NW5 1AG
071 267 9499
M-F 9.30-6, Sat 9.30-5.30

Two floors of books on Greece
and its islands, Cyprus and
Turkey. The classics are well
represented with books in Latin
and ancient Greek. All aspects of
Roman and Byzantium history
and religion compete with a
credible travel and children's
section. Music and learning aids,
cassettes and newspapers for the
Greek and Cypriot community
complete a popular centre for
residents and visitors alike.

BHAVANS BOOKSHOP
4A Castle Town Road
W14 9HQ
071 610 1575
M-Fr 10-7, Sat 10-4

Given that Mahatma Gandhi lived
a short walk away and attended
the church built by the local
council for the promotion of
culture, it is no surprise to find a
bookshop here reflecting the glory
of India. London is one of 70
branches of this worldwide chain,
based in Bombay. Music, dance
and Indian culture attract the eye,
language cassettes and Indian
classical music for the ear.

BOOKS FROM INDIA
45 Museum Street
WC1A
071 405 7226
M-F 10-5.30
Mr. and Mrs. Vidyarthi proudly boast that their bookshop grew out of a backpack way back in 1970. Now three floors covering all manner of books, music, stationery and crafts from and about the Indian sub-continent. It has grown into a major importer, distributor and publisher of Indo-centric products. There are 20,000 titles in 12 languages, from travel, language learning and culture to alternative medicine and homeopathy.

FOUR PROVINCES BOOKSHOP
244-246 Grays Inn Road
WC1X 8JR
071 833 3022
T-F 11-5.30, Sat 11-4.30

New and second-hand books on Ireland and Irish culture. In business for 10 years this shop specialises in history, sport, literature, music, travel and political and social studies. There are many Gaelic titles. Cassette tapes and T shirts are also sold.

GREEN INK BOOKS
8 Archway Mall
Junction Road
N19 5RG
071 263 4748
M-Sat 10-6

The emerald green of Ireland shines through just yards from Archway tube station. Probably the largest selection of books on and from Ireland outside of the country itself. The books are clearly categorised into literature, history, politics, travel and the other general subjects. Gaelic books for adults and children are stocked. Papers, magazines, music, videos, posters and crafts from Ireland contribute to a friendly atmosphere that is a home from home for the Irish in London.

OLD TOWN BOOKS
30 Old Town
SW4 0LB
071 498 0998
Tu-F 10-7, Sat 10-6, Sun 2-5

A small general bookshop with a genuine specialisation in Italy.

ACCADEMIA ITALIANA BOOKSHOP by MESSAGGERIE
24 Rutland Gate
SW7 1BB
071 225 3724
Tue-Sat 10-5, W 10-7

Messaggerie opened this bookshop in 1990 to serve the growing interest in books on Italy in Italian and English. Linked to a chain of eight bookstores in Italy, the shop is located in the basement of the Accademia Italiana Delle Arti e Arti Applicate near Knightsbridge tube. Italian fiction, poetry, art, tourist guides and language books, cassettes and videos are all sold. The English books are translations of Italian novels. Videos of Italian films without subtitles are available. Fellini as it was originally made.

JAPAN CENTRE BOOKSHOP
212 Piccadilly
W1V 9LD
071 439 8035
M-Sat 10-8, Sun 10-6

Europe's largest Japanese bookshop is a treat. As you enter, have a taste of sushi and sashimi and while you digest squid or salmon, make your way through the two floors of books on all aspects of Japanese culture. Upstairs are books on business, the ways and means of reaching the Japanese market or how to succeed in a Japanese owned company. Cooking, politics and origami are a few of the other subjects covered. A huge selection of Japanese novels occupies the rest of this floor and downstairs is a superb range of graphic novels and comics. The Japanese are known to be innovative illustrators and even if your Japanese is weak or non-existent, they are a feast for the imagination and easy to follow. A refrigerator of various foods can wrap up your visit, which will be memorable.

O.C.S. BOOKSHOP
2 Grosvenor Parade
Uxbridge Road
W5 3NN
081 992 6335
Tu-Sun 10-6

Japanese books and newspapers.

BOOKS NIPPON
64-66 St Paul's Churchyard
EC4M 8AA
071 248 4956
M-F 10-7, Sat 10-6

Books on Japan form part of a large shop with products from the land of the rising sun. Music, gifts, travel guides and books covering all subjects related to Japan.

BOSWELL BOOKS AND PRINTS
44 Great Russell Street
WC1B 3PP
071 580 7200
M-F 10-5

Despite the anachronistic name of this bookshop, Boswell stocks books on Japan. Have a look at the Japanese wood block prints.

AL HODA
76-78 Charing Cross Road
WC2H 0BB
071 240 8381
M-Sat 10-6

The range of books in Al Hoda is divided into three main areas: English, Arabic and Persian and Urdu. The subject range is akin to that in a general bookshop, with emphasis on educational materials and topics of particular relevance to the Middle East. This is the only bookshop in town to display the 'Arab Book of Political Humour' in the window.

IRANIAN BOOKSHOP
(KANOUNE KETAB)
2a Kensington Church Walk
W8 9BL
071 937 5087
M-Sat 9.30-12.30, 1.30-6

A stone's throw from Kensington
High Street, in a peaceful alley
with a handful of shops including
this small but well-stocked shop
specialising in books on Iran.
Most books are in Persian, but
some English books are available.
Subjects range from art to history,
literature to Islam.

AL-NOOR BOOKSHOP
54 Park Road
NW1 4SH
071 723 5414
M-Sat 10-7

Cramped shop specialising in
books on Islam and the Middle
East.

AL KASHKOOL BOOKSHOP
56 Knightsbridge
SW1X 7NJ
071 235 4240
M-Sat 10-7

Situated on this busy approach to
Harrods and next to the French
Embassy, books on all subjects
relating to the Gulf area in both
Arabic and English. Browse
through the antiquarian section
which includes a fine selection of
prints and lithographs.

**ALHANI INTERNATIONAL
BOOKS**
102 Crawford Street
W1H 1AN
071 402 7035
M-F 10-6

Books mainly in Arabic, but there
is a selection of titles in Swedish,
Malaysian and English.
Engineering is a speciality.

AL SAQI BOOKS
26 Westbourne Grove
W2 5RH
071 229 8543
M-Sat 10-6

This bookshop is housed in the
Kufa Gallery which promotes
Oriental art and culture. The
books cover all aspects of the
Arab world in Arabic and English
and include new and rare
volumes.

NASHRE KETAB
157 North End Road
W14 9NH
071 602 8990
M-Sat 10-6

Books and videos in Persian
relating to Iran and Afghanistan.
You will find some books in
English on these two countries.

DAR AL DAWA
32 Hereford Road
W2 4AJ
071 221 6256
M-Sat 9-7

Islamic and Middle Eastern
history are the feature of this
predominantly Arabic language
bookstore. However, the language
and reference section has a few
English titles.

KIWI FRUITS
6 Royal Opera Arcade
SW1Y 4UY
071 930 4587
M-F 9-5.30, Sat 10-4

For over thirty years, New
Zealanders have found a juicy
slice of home life in London.
Complementing their general
store in Covent Garden, this
bookshop concentrates on the art,
history, literature, poetry and
natural beauty of this twin island
paradise. The shop is behind New
Zealand house on Haymarket.

PAUL ORSSICH
117 Munster Road
SW6 6DH
071 736 3869
M-F 10-6

Spain is in focus in this bookshop
near Parsons Green tube. All
aspects of Hispanic studies
including Latin America and the
Philippines. Two catalogues are
published annually in Spanish,
and the display of antique maps
and Art Deco illustrations is
worth a long look.

TURKISH LANGUAGE BOOKS
81 Shacklewell Lane
E8 2EB
071 249 0367
M-Sat 10-6

Books in Turkish and English on
politics, the sciences and
literature. Turkish, Kurdish and
Cypriot books are all stocked as
are CD's, cassettes and videos.

CRAFTS & PASTIMES

BRIDGE CALLIGRAPHY CERAMICS CHESS COOKERY CRAFTS FASHION GARDENING MAGIC NUMISMATICS PRINTING

FALKINER FINE PAPERS
76 Southampton Row
WC1B 4AR
071 831 1151
M-Sat 9.30-6

Lettering and calligraphy take pride of place in this shop for printers, book restorers and papermakers. Titles on bookbinding, book conservation and marbling share space with supplies and materials for the trade.

CONTEMPORARY CERAMICS
William Blake House
7 Marshall Street
W1V 1LP
071 437 7605
M-Sat 10-5.30, Th 10-7

The retail outlet for members of the co-operative Craft Potters Association has been selling the work of the finest potters and ceramists in Britain since 1960. The stock of books on ceramics is extensive covering the history, aesthetics and technique of the craft. Potters' tools are on sale and the work of 80 potters on display fires the beginner's imagination and continually offers new pieces to collectors.

CHESS AND BRIDGE LTD
369 Euston Road
NW1 3AR
071 388 2404
M-Sat 9.30-6

Chess and bridge enthusiasts will do well to spend some time in this recently opened business. It is situated on the south side of Euston Road just two minutes walk east from Great Portland Street underground. Beginners and advanced players are welcome to inspect the wide selection of books solely devoted to chess and bridge. There is a good range of associated merchandise such as computer chess, software and card tables. Service and advice from the enthusiastic staff is suitably erudite rather than intellectually eccentric. They seem to have found a niche.

CAISSA BOOKS
A18-19 Grays in the Mews
1-7 Davies Mews
W1Y 1AR
071 409 7283
M-F 11-6

A market stall, once the only chess specialist in London, located in this popular antiques market. They publish books on chess and sell a range of new and second-hand titles with a few chess sets.

GOLDEN AGE
3 Denbigh Street
W11 2SJ
071 229 6765
M-F 9.30- 5.30

A model spitfire with a 12 foot wingspan hangs from the roof of this eclectic bookshop near Portobello Road. Collectables of the 19th and 20th centuries including toys, jewellery, ceramics, musical devices and silver are the subjects covered by books. Some models are on display, but for that purpose only.

BOOKS FOR COOKS
4 Blenheim Crescent
W11 1NN
071 221-1992
M-Sat 9.30-6

Once inside, like the *poisson* in the pan, it is extremely difficult to leave. Just off Portobello Road, the shop is packed from floor to ceiling with the widest range of food and wine books in Europe. In fact, Books for Cooks is the only bookshop dedicated entirely to culinary matters and sets a standard for all specialist retailers. The rear of the shop is taken up by a kitchen and small restaurant resulting in enticing smells mixing with the visual feast of fascinating books. Cookery courses are held on the premises and private dining is possible on the first floor. Everything from

the Malawi Cookbook to the latest on Cajun.
This internationally renowned business deserves the bookselling equivalent of Egon Ronay stars. You'll be pleased to know, however, that they do not cook the Penguins!

THE DOVER BOOKSHOP
18 Earlham Street
WC2H 9LN
071 836 2111
M-Sat 10-6

Books published by Dover are available here with a range of craft and activity books.

BOOKTREE
Merton Abbey Mills
Merantun Way
SW19 2RD
081 540 2694
W-Sun 10-5

A visit to this South London Craft Village yields a variety of attractions and a pleasant way to spend a slow Sunday. The Mill was once the site of the Liberty silk printing works and the waterwheel is one of few still operating. The Booktree carries a gamut of crafts: woodwork, embroidery, paper and flower crafts and drawing techniques with the materials to try it all yourself. The Craft Market sells ethnic foods and handmade goods every weekend and Bank Holidays.

R.D. FRANKS
Kent House
Market Place
Great Titchfield Street
W1N 8EJ
071 636 1244
M-F 9-5

Located in the heart of London's
fashion centre just behind Oxford
Circus, Franks stocks a wide
range of fashion books and
magazines. For anyone interested
in fashion, whether student or
home clothes maker, text and
reference books are displayed
with flair and expertise.

THE KEW SHOP
Royal Botanic Gardens
Kew
TW9 3AB
M-Sun 9.30-5.30

Located near the Orangery at the
main gate, books compete with all
manner of gifts and other Royal
Botanic Gardens products . Make
your way to the rear of the shop
and be transported into the world
of gardening, from the botanical
splendour of stately homes to
designs and ideas which will
transform your suburban postage
stamp. There are many superb
illustrated books to sit proudly on
your coffee table. For the more
serious student of botany, the
range of academic publications on
flora from around the world is
very impressive. A selection of
books covering bird life and a
sprinkling of books on natural
history and the environment adds
variety to the stock. For children,
the shelves near the exit are

stocked with books to inspire any
young gardener including
painting and drawing books for
the creative. Deciding whether to
go first to the shop and then to
saunter slowly around these
magnificent gardens, or the
reverse, is a choice you will find
enjoyable to ponder.

LLOYDS OF KEW
9 Mortlake Terrace
Kew
TW9 3DT
081 940 2512
M-F 10-4, closed W
Sat 10-5.30

The Royal Gardens at Kew are
within a few minutes stroll of this
gardening and botanical
bookshop. Books new and second
hand cover every aspect of
gardening and botany. The
comprehensive catalogue of
botanical titles listing over a
thousand items is available for £1.

GROWER BOOKS
50 Doughty Street
WC1N 2LS
M-F 8.30-4.30

Commercial growers use this
bookshop as a resource, but the
avid gardener can pick up a range
of useful titles on growing flowers
or arranging them in a vase.
Books on vegetables, weed control
and poisonous plants will keep
you rooted to the spot.

DAVENPORT'S MAGIC SHOP
7 Shopping Concourse
Charing Cross Station
Strand
WC2N 4HZ
071 836 0408
M-F 10.15-5.30, Sat 10-4.30

Davenport's is a truly unique shop devoted entirely to the fascinating world of magic and conjuring. Before the year 2000, this business will have celebrated its centenary. In some ways it is appropriate that it is partially concealed in a subterranean shopping arcade under a railway station. Telepathic powers would help you find your way here and the material is available to hone the technique so you can find your way home. Mystical apparatus and equipment dominates the shop but there are books on white magic, conjuring, ventriloquism and mind-reading. *Annemans's* publications on fully routined acts and programmes of magic such as *Mental Bargain Effects* and *Eleven Miracles of Mentalism* provide ready-made material for the magician. A studio accommodates regular talks and demonstrations from world famous exponents of the art. The London Society of Magicians meets here every fortnight and new members are warmly welcomed.

SPINK & SON
5,6 & 7 King Street
St. James's
SW1Y 6QS
071 930-7888
M-F 9.30-5.30

Established in 1666, this world-renowned fine art dealers maintains the largest stock anywhere of out of print and new books on numismatics. The book department is on the second floor. The Numismatic Circular, published since 1892, is issued ten times per year and lists all books for sale. Standard works of reference are published by Spink in the fields of coins, tokens, paper money, medals, orders and decorations of all types and from all countries. Not as intimidating as it might appear, all visitors and collectors are made welcome.

STANLEY GIBBONS
399 Strand
WC2R OLX
071 836 8444
M-F 8.30-5.30, Sat 10-4

World famous as the premier stamp collector and dealer, this shop has occupied this portion of the Strand for over 100 years. Worldwide catalogues, specialist titles, and out of print literature all on stamps make this shop a philatelist's heaven. Everything for the stamp collector, either expert or novice.

**COLLEGE BOOKSHOP
LONDON COLLEGE OF
PRINTING**
Elephant and Castle
SE1 6SB
071 735 8570
M-F 10.15-5

Books for students of printing and
graphic design. Not for the
browser.

**BRITISH LIBRARY
BOOKSHOP**
The British Museum
Great Russell Street
WC1B 3DG
071 323 7735
M-Sat 10-4.50, Sun 2.30-5.50

Despite the grandeur of many
landmark bookshops in London,
none but this one can claim to be
adjacent to the Magna Carta. The
bookshop was opened in 1988 to
provide a dedicated outlet for
British Library Publications and to
enable visitors to buy souvenirs
and scholarly works relating to
the collections. Turn right when
you enter the British Museum into
the Grenville Room. The shop is
small and one hopes will be much
larger when housed in the new
British Library, whenever it is
completed and if there is any
money remaining to provide a
bookshop. It might be compact
but the selection of books is
mighty. The specialisation is a
bibliophile's dream: books on
books, manuscripts, bookbinding,
papermaking, printing,
illustration and calligraphy
constitute the main sections.
There are also books on art,
history, reference and London.
The gift products include many
quality items and as well as the
cards and posters you will find
hand-made paper and quill pens.
Even if you bypass the shop, gaze
lovingly at the rare books and
manuscripts in glass cases.

ENVIRONMENT & NATURE

BOOKS FOR A CHANGE
52 Charing Cross Road
WC2H 0BB
071 836 2315
M-Sat 10-7

It would be easy to pulp and recycle the stock of some of the other bookshops on Charing Cross Road, but Books For A Change has titles of greater value and relevance. Peace, ecology and the environment, green development, third world issues and literature feature most strongly and indicate the *raison d'être* of this bookshop. Badges, posters, green stationery and clothing items carry the message beyond the written word.

THE COUNTRYSIDE BOOKSHOP
39 Goodge Street
W1P 1FD
071 636 3156
M-F 9.30-6.30, Sat 11-5

Near the junction with Tottenham Court Road, this bookshop covers a variety of outdoor activities. Two floors of books including gardening, conservation, horses and riding, fishing and crafts. A fine cookery section includes the popular titles as well as books on herbs. Downstairs houses ordnance survey maps with guide books on walking and camping in the UK.

WORLD OF DIFFERENCE
London Ecology Centre
21 Endell Street
WC2H 9BJ
071 379 8208
M-Sat 10-6

Where else in London could you enjoy a vegetarian meal, pick up a book on green issues and buy a humane mouse trap. This was London's first green technology shop for energy saving products. There is a small but interesting range of books on green issues, covering economics, politics, lifestyle, health and development. Titles of a technical nature accompany the innovative range of practical energy saving products. The mail order catalogue contains full descriptions of items such as solar power battery chargers, non-toxic paints and low energy light bulbs. The cafe offers a tasty selection of vego food for visitors to the gallery and bookshop and is a popular lunch venue.

I T BOOKSHOP
103-105 Southampton Row
WC1B 4HH
071 436 9761
M-F 9.30-6, Sat 11-6

Intermediate Technology Development Group (IT) was founded in the 1960s by E F Schumacher, author of *Small is*

Beautiful. Its aim is to enable people to develop and use productive technologies and methods which give them greater control over their own lives and which contribute to the long-term development of their communities. The IT bookshop is Britain's leading stockist of books on appropriate technology and development and is one of the few shops in the world dedicated solely to the promotion of these ideals. IT Publications publishes a wide range of handbooks, manuals, directories, case studies and three quarterly journals. The direct mail service and accompanying book catalogue serve both specialists and those interested in development issues all over the world. General subjects, travel, fiction and new age are also covered. The complementary products include crafts from around the world, world music and cards. The material in this bookshop will influence world development and is only the more visible aspect of IT activities.

THE BIRD AND WILDLIFE BOOKSHOP
2 - 4 Princes Arcade
SW1Y 6DS
071 287-1407
M-F 9.30-6, Sat 10-4

A compact shop in an attractive arcade off Piccadilly with a comprehensive and fascinating array of books on birds, nature and the environment. But this shop is not only for twitchers. Books on mammals, reptiles and insects are available. For those who can't travel to the other end of the country at the tweet of a bird to see a rare visitor, take an easier but equally satisfying journey to Princes Arcade. If you have a parrot, the book about caring for it is here. So is a variety of cassettes and CD's of bird sounds, and together with field guides there's everything you need for bird watching. Collectors and enthusiasts can browse through ornithological art, illustrated and reference books. So spend an afternoon outdoors with your binoculars, book and cassette. Look, listen and read.

CLIVE A BURDEN LTD
93 Lower Sloane Street
SW1W 8DA
071 823 5053
M-F 10-5.30

The hours at this bookshop are flexible, so it is best to phone ahead for an appointment to see the antiquarian and second-hand books on Topography and Natural History.

NATURAL HISTORY MUSEUM BOOKSHOP
Cromwell Road
SW7 5BD
071 938 9285
M-Sat 10-5.50, Sun 11-5.50

Two bookshops in one at this marvellous museum. The Geological Museum bookshop joins its cousin in providing an impressive array of books on natural history. There are

geological maps and guides as
well as a wide range of toys and
crafts. These are dwarfed by the
ever popular collection of
dinosaur-related items. Extinct?
Never!
Find the shop in Gallery 37.

**JG NATURAL HISTORY
BOOKS**
17 Streatham Vale
SW16 5SE
081 764 4669
M-F 10-6, Sat 10-5, W closed

Opposite Streatham Common
railway station is a fascinating
bookshop selling new and
second-hand books on natural
history. The specialisation is
reptiles and amphibians, with the
real thing in the associated shop
next door. Gemmology is also
covered. A mail order service is
provided (for the books, not the
subject matter) and specialist
book lists are available.

GENERAL

DILLONS THE BOOKSTORE
82 Gower Street
WC1E 6EQ
071 636 1577
M,W, Th, F 9-7, Tu 9.30-7,
Sat 9.30-6

Spending £2 million in the mid 80's on refurbishing a Grade II listed building has transformed a frog into a prince. This bookstore is the most impressive in London for its sheer size, organisation and presentation. Thirty thousand square feet of pure books is a visual feast. Every subject imaginable and some you haven't heard of make you reel from choice. On five floors, the books are arranged by subject, and helpful signage guides you through the maze. The art section for example is as comprehensive as most specialists, although it's difficult to find help if you need it. What is most appealing is that the sheer scale of this store does not overwhelm the buyer or browser. Enjoy.

VERMILION BOOKS
57 Red Lion Street
WC1R 4PD
071 242 5822
M-F 10-6

This bookshop stocks only review copies which it buys from a wide variety of newspapers and magazines. As a result the stock changes constantly and all books are sold at up to 35% off the published price. Given that review copies are as good as new, this is the shop to go to if you read a review and want the book. The owner has a very active wants list and will inform his customers when their book is available. As adventurous as the stock profile is the owner's library business. A van loaded with recently-reviewed books is driven to libraries all over the country where librarians who desire to add something new to their shelves can do so at a third less than the normal retail price.

HMSO BOOKS
49 High Holborn
WC1V 6HB
071 873 0011
M-F 8.15-5.15, Sat 9-1

Every Government publication you could ever wish for: White papers, Green papers, Acts of Parliament, Hansard, walking guides and the Highway Code.

SOUVENIR PRESS LTD
43 Great Russell Street
WC1V 3PA
071 637 5711
M-F 9.30-5.15

Located opposite the British Museum, the shop stocks primarily Souvenir Press titles, sociology, philosophy, psychology and literature.

PENGUIN BOOKSHOP
10 The Market
Covent Garden
WC2E 8RB
071 379 7650

Occupies an old greengrocer's shop in the original Covent Garden market building. It is a very attractive bookshop crammed with books to entice tourists and regulars. The business was once part of the Penguin Books empire but is now part of the Phoenix Bookshop Group. It still carries an impressive range of Penguins.

PENGUIN BOOKSHOP
2 Plaza House
191 Camden High Street
NW1 7BT
071 485 1328
M-Sat 10-8, Sun 11.30-5.30

A similar stock profile to the Covent Garden shop, with more room to browse in a pleasant shop opposite Camden Town tube station.

W & G FOYLE
119 Charing Cross Road
WC2H 0EB
071 437 5660
M-W, F, Sat 9-6, Th 9-7

'Foyles for Books' proclaims the huge banner hanging above the once proud heartland of bookselling in the capital. This at least is true! The travel department on the ground floor at first sight looks as good and as comprehensive as anywhere else.

Look closer, take your eyes away from the peeling paint and poor lighting to discover that in order to find, say, a book on Australia, you'll need to be conversant with publishers' imprints because every section is ordered by publisher. This is clearly not for the customer's benefit but to make life easy for staff and suppliers. The antiquated payment system has to be experienced to be believed(or disbelieved!). Foyles has every foible that the nearby branches of Waterstone's and Books *etc* have done much to eradicate from bookselling. By all means savour the character of a monster bookshop but be ready to enter the twentieth century by crossing the road to Books *etc*.

PIPELINE BOOKS
37 Neal Street
WC2H 9PR
071 240 3319
M-F 10-7.30, Sat 10-6, Sun 12-5

Neal Street is a busy thoroughfare for tourists and commuters alike. A few doors down, Food For Thought offers sustenance for the stomach and the selection in Pipeline offers food for the mind.

TEMPLE BAR BOOKSHOP
1 Essex Street
WC2R 3HU
071 379 4609
M-F 9-5.30

A smattering of books on a range of general subjects in a small, old style bookshop tucked away in the Temple.

FACT AND FICTION
110 Strand
WC2R
071 240 1884
M-F 9-7, Sat 11-5, Sun 12-5

Bargain books are the focus, plus current bestsellers, full price new books and basic popular titles in the general subject categories.

SELFRIDGES LTD
400 Oxford Street
W1A 1AB
071 629 1234
M-Sat 9.30-7, Th 9.30-8

A better than average book department in this Oxford Street superstore.

BBC SHOP
4-5 Langham Place
Upper Regent Street
W1A 4WW
071 927 4970
M-F 9-5.30, Sat 930-5.30

Home to the corporation's retailing arm. Packed with BBC publications and products, topical, educational and books, tapes and videos to bring back memories of your favourite programme. Cards, posters, all manner of gifts and the Radio Times are all here.

DISCOUNT BOOKS COMPANY
285 Oxford Street
W1M
071 495 0674
M-Sat 10-7, Th 10-8, Sun 11-5

Well situated for the constant flow of shoppers looking for cheap books. They won't be disappointed here.

LITERARY GUILD BOOKSHOP
87 Newman Street
W1P 4 EN
071 637 0341
M-F 10-6

For members only, though you are encouraged to join and choose from a selection of popular new books at knock-down prices. Travel, fiction, and some children's in a well laid out showroom.

GREENS THE BOOKCELLAR
17 Marylebone High Street
W1M 3PD
071 935 7227
M-F 9-6, Sat 9-3

Visitors to Marylebone High Street can appear on Greater London Radio, choose a holiday destination from Daunt Books across the road, and buy a newspaper and bestseller from Greens, all in a matter of a few yards. Greens dates from the 1930's and although the books are relegated to the basement, they stock a good general range from fiction to health. The ground floor is a well-lit general newsagents and even offers high quality film developing.

HATCHARDS
187 Piccadilly
W1V 9DA
071 439 9921
M-Sat 9-6

This London landmark was founded in 1797 by John Hatchard and holds all four Royal Warrants. It has a literary and historic pedigree second to none and its customers include book loving tourists from all over the world, the great and the good in this country and ex-pats overseas. The Abolition of Slavery Bill was signed by William Wilberforce on the premises. There are five floors of books comprehensively covering all general subjects. Fiction, biography, gardening (The Royal Horticultural Society was founded in this building), crafts and natural history are superbly stocked, and include the cream of new titles. If you are short of reading time they claim to have the largest selection of spoken word cassettes in the country. The rare books, first editions and fine bindings department recreates the ambience of Hatchards past and a book search service operates to find lost treasures of the book world.
Hatchards is now part of Dillons Bookstores but their considerable investment has resulted in this famous bookshop retaining its charm and appeal.

KER AND DOWNEY
14 Old Bond Street
W1X 3DB
071 629 2044
M-F 9-6

New and second-hand books concentrating on travel, maps, atlases and natural history.

READER'S DIGEST SHOP
22 Berkeley Square
W1X 6AB
071 409 5674
M-F 9-5.30
Here can be found the range of Reader's Digest books plus other publishers' series such as Time Life publications.

FOUNTAIN BOOKS
229 Chiswick High Rd
W4 2DW
081 994-9403

A local bookshop stocking a general range of popular subjects with a better than average children's and travel section. Titles by local authors always take pride of place in the window.

BOOK BARGAINS LTD
138-140 Charing Cross Road
WC2H
071 836 8391

135 Long Acre
WC2E 9AD
071 240 0456

A pair of bookshops offering a standard fare of bargains and publishers' remainders. The depth of stock is similar to the staff's knowledge of the opening hours. Sketchy.

ELGIN BOOKS
6 Elgin Crescent
W11 2HX
071 229 2186
Tu-Sat 10-6

Book reviews are displayed in this attractive general bookshop to attract buyers to the well chosen stock of new books. Fiction, poetry, drama and children's books stand out in the well balanced range.

BUSH BOOKS AND RECORDS
113 Shepherds Bush Centre
W12 8PP
081 749 7652
M-Sat 10-6

As the name suggests, this excellent shop has a dual function. Part of the shop is devoted to music, mainly classical, on tape and CD. The main area carries a wide selection of books on popular subjects. Fiction, travel and media studies are well covered- many BBC types are among the customers who frequent this good bookshop.

ARMY & NAVY
101 Victoria Street
SW1E 6QX
071 834 1234
M-Sat 9.30-6

Located on the second floor this open plan book department has a

particularly strong range of travel guides and books on London. The children's section is separate from the main department and offers a haven for the young ones.

BERGER AND TIMS
7 Bressenden Place
SW1E 5DE
071 834 9827
M-F 9-6

This business was founded in 1932 as a library supplier. That tradition continues as Berger and Tims supplies books to government, parliament, corporate and public libraries throughout the U.K. A varied stock of classics, modern fiction, reference, business and current affairs are carried in the large stock. The shop is a two minute walk from Victoria Station.

WEST LONDON BOOKS
15 Jerdan Place
SW6
071 385 8334
M-F 10-6.30, Sat 10-6

There are no full price books to be found here. Exclusively half-price bargains and remainders.

OPPENHEIM AND CO.
7/9 Exhibition Road
SW7
071 584 5641
M-Sun 8.30-6

The ground floor is taken up with remainders and reduced review copies. Upstairs is more of the same on transport.

PAN BOOKSHOP
158 Fulham Road
SW10 9PR
071 373 4997
M-F 9.30-9.30, Sat 10-10,
Sun 11.30-9.30

A well-established bookshop covering all the general interest subjects competently and attractively. Signed copies are a feature as is the comprehensive range of new paperbacks and hardbacks.

WORDS WORTH BOOKS
308 Streatham High Road
SW16 6HG
081 677 7872
M-F 9-7.30, Sat 9-6.30

116 Clapham High Street
SW4 7UH
071 622 5344
M-F 9-7.30, Sat 9-6.30

11 Butterfly Walk
SE5
071 277 1377
M-Sat 9-7.30

247 High Street
Orpington
BR6 0MY
0689 897757
M-Sat 9-5.30

This mini-chain started life in the late eighties in Streatham and is the creation of Tim Boon and Stephen Johnson, refugees from a large bookselling group. All four

shops carry an excellent range of bargain books as core stock and add general interest ranges in answer to the demands of their local customers. Each branch has something different to offer. Streatham uses the most up-to-date bibliographical services and specialises in speedy satisfaction of customer orders. New books, local history and black interest sections are worthy of note. This is the best all round bookshop in the area. The Clapham branch, in the middle of the High Street, is smaller but no less enthusiastic in its aim to bring books to the local community. The Camberwell shop is primarily a bargain specialist but there is a carefully chosen selection of new books and popular paperbacks. The Orpington out-post was relocated to better and larger High Street premises in early 1992 and now offers a broad range of new books as well as bargains and remainders. Whichever Words Worth bookshop you visit you will find good books mixed with a warm welcome and efficient service.

THE BOLINGBROKE BOOKSHOP
147 Northcote Road
SW11 6QB
071 223 9344
M-Sat 9.30-6

Owned by Pipeline Bookshops and supplied by their efficient and comprehensive wholesale business. This bookshop retains a strong local community image with an appealing range of books across the general spectrum. There is a strong bias towards the arts and fiction although there are few popular non-fiction areas which are not covered in some way.

BEAUMONT'S BOOKS
60 Church Road
SW13 0DQ
081 741 0786
M-Sat 9.30-6

Two floors housing a wide variety of books although no particular subject areas stand out.

BELL'S BOOKSHOP
10 Putney Exchange
Putney High Street
SW15 1TW
081 780 0854
M-Sat 9-6, Th 9-8

Well-designed antidote to its larger competitors. Bell's carries a solid range of basic stock in all popular non-fiction areas. The selection of literary fiction, children's and local books shows imagination and knowledge. Children's story-telling sessions are held weekly. There are plans to open more Bell's Bookshops to add to the original in Trowbridge, Wiltshire. This is good news for book buyers.

BECKETT'S BOOKSHOP
6 Bellevue Road
SW17 7EG
081 672 4412
M-Sat 10-6

Overlooking Wandsworth Common, a wide range of books with a reasonable children's section.

JOHN KEATS CORNER
Within Earlsfield Library
Magdalene Road
SW18 3NY
081 871 7755
M, Tu, Th 9.30-7, F, Sat 9.30-5

An appropriate location for this imaginative bookshop inside the public library. Mr. Wahid, the owner, has operated this business for five years and carries a modest range of paperbacks and children's books along with other general subjects and educational titles.

FIELDERS BOOKSHOPS
554 Wimbledon Hill Road
SW19 7PA
081 946 5044
M-Sat 9-5.30, Th,F 9-7

A stationery supplier on the ground floor but upstairs is a long established general book department. The travel and map section is reasonable and includes a good stock of Ordnance Survey maps.

RIVERSIDE BOOKSHOP
Hay's Galleria
Tooley Street
SE1 2HN
071 378 0051
M-F 9-6, Sat 10.30-5

Hay's Galleria is an attractive shopping complex overlooking the river near London Bridge. Popular tourist attractions, HMS Belfast and the London Dungeon are close by. The Riverbus service can bring you to this fine general bookshop where you will find an array of new books, a good range of contemporary fiction, local history books and a small specialist computer section.

THE BOOKCASE
158 Waterloo Road
SE1
071 401 8528
M-F 8-8, Sat 10-4

A pure bargain bookshop opposite the Old Vic theatre.

BOOKS OF BLACKHEATH
11 Tranquil Vale
SE3 0BU
081 852 8185
M-F 9.30-5.30, Sat 9.30-5

The ground floor is host to new books, upstairs are the bargains.

THE ARCADE BOOKSHOP
3 The Arcade
Eltham High Street
SE9 1BE
081 850 7803
M-Sat 9-5.30, Th 9-1

Taking advantage of the arcade surroundings, remaindered books find their way onto the pavement. Inside, children's books are a real strength.

THE BOOKSHOP DULWICH VILLAGE
1D Calton Avenue
SE21 7DE
081 693 2802
M-Sat 9.30-5.30

A large children's section in what is also a good local general bookshop. The stationery stock is imaginative with a nice selection of book plates, book marks, book ends and book shelves. This is also an Open University set text stockist.

DULWICH BOOKS
6 Croxted Road
SE21 8SW
081 670 1920
M-Sat 9.30-5.30

As with the previous shop, Dulwich books concentrates on children's books, but carries a range of titles from art to sport. The travel section deserves mention for its presentation and coverage.

CHENER BOOKS
14 Lordship Lane
SE22 8HN
081 299 0771
M-Sat 10-6

The stock here covers all the general subjects particularly biography, drama, literature, science fiction and history. The local history section is well supplemented by their own titles. Remainders and some second-hand books complete a nicely rounded package.

KIRKDALE BOOKSHOP
272 Kirkdale
SE26 4RS
081 778 4701
M-Sat 9-5.30

A short walk from Sydenham
Railway station, this bookshop
has been in business since 1966. It
is a charming shop which offers a
wide choice of new and second-
hand books rather than focusing
on a particular topic.

TOWER BOOKSHOP
10 Tower Place
EC3R 5BT
071 623 1081
M-Sun 9.30-6

Books on London struggle to find
space amongst all the souvenirs
aimed at visitors to the nearby
Tower.

THE BOOKCASE
26 Ludgate Hill
EC4M 7DR
071 236 5982
M-F 9 6

Once a pioneer in the bargain
books field. Just down the road
from St Paul's Cathedral and
offering a selected range of
bestsellers, books of local interest
and bargain books.

L SIMMONDS
16 Fleet Street
EC4Y
071 353 3907
M-F 9-5.30

A far cry from the brave new
world of High Street bookselling
this business has been run by the
Simmonds family since the end of
the second world war. The five
storey building is the narrowest
premises in Fleet Street and has a
history dating from 1522 when it
was occupied by William Gerard,
a scrivener. Simmonds Bookshop,
with its floor to ceiling wooden
shelving and metal racks is
dwarfed by Hammicks
Professional Bookshop opposite
but has a unique character in
general and academic bookselling.

PRIMROSE HILL BOOKS
134 Regents Park Road
NW1 8XL
071 586 2022
M-Sat 10-6.30, Sun 12-6

The splendour of Regents Park
and charm of Primrose Hill are
within walking distance of this
attractive late Victorian building
housing a two floor bookshop
overflowing with books. The
main subjects are fiction,
biography, art, travel, history,
children's and reference works.
New books comprise the majority
of the stock, but the basement
houses many second-hand titles
of interest, including review
copies. Choose from the quality
cards and avail yourself of the
photocopying service.

REGENT BOOKSHOP
73 Parkway
NW1 7PP
071 485 9822
M-F 9-6.30, Sat 9-6, Sun 12-6

Local authors including Beryl Bainbridge and Alan Bennett have signed copies available at this bookshop catering to a broad cross-section of tastes. It is an interesting shop with books on all topics and the new book displays always contain surprising items of interest.

THE BELSIZE BOOKSHOP
193 Haverstock Hill
NW3 4QG
071 794 4006
M-F 9.30-6.30, Sat 9.30-5.30

A pleasant local bookshop with a wide range of general books.

SWISS COTTAGE BOOKS
4 Canfield Gardens
NW6 3BS
071 625 4632
M-Sat 9.30-6.30

All the favourites in a well established local bookshop with a tangible character sadly missing in many similar shops. The arts and literature feature well alongside the eccentricity. The remaining subject areas are tuned to the demands of the local customers and range from psychology to Judaica. The physical characteristics of the shop are equally interesting- an unusual mezzanine facilitates a first floor gallery

THE BOOKSHOP ISLINGTON GREEN
76 Upper Street
N1
071 359-4699
M-Sat 10-10, Sun 12-5

The late opening hours make this an ideal place to collect suitable bedside reading. Upper Street has an atmosphere that encourages creativity and shops along the street compete for attention. Fiction, psychology, children's and computing are the specialities. Cards, calendars and cassettes round off what's on offer.

THE ANGEL BOOKSHOP
102 Islington High Street
N1 8EG
071 226 2904
M-Sat 9.30-6

Catering to their antique dealer neighbours, this bookshop has a fine antique reference section. Housed in an attractive 18th century building the wide range of books is in a most attractive setting.

HIGHGATE BOOKSHOP
9 Highgate High Street
N6 5JR
081 348 8202
M-Sat 10-6, Sun 12-5

A solid range of non-technical titles in a local bookshop offering a comprehensive range of stock.

HOLLOWAY STATIONERS AND BOOKSELLERS
357 Holloway Road
N7 0RN
071 607 3972
M-Sat 9-6

Books, primarily paperbacks, compete with stationery for space. All the popular subject areas are here from new age to social studies.

CROUCH END BOOKSHOP
60 Crouch End Hill
N8 8AG
081 348 8966
M-F 9-6, Sat 9.30-6

Pretty location for this local bookshop overlooking a walled garden. The mix of stock covers new and second-hand books very much based on the arts. fiction and children's titles.

MUSWELL HILL BOOKSHOP
72 Fortis Green Rd
N10 3HN
081 444-7588
M-F 9.30-6, Sat 9.30-5, Sun 12-5

A superb local general bookshop founded 20 years ago. North Londoners don't have far to travel to find good books: this shop co-operates with The Children's Bookshop directly across the road, on promotions, book signings and children's parties. Both shops manage to succeed together and maintain their individual characters. Fine signage guides you through the latest novels, signed copies by local authors,

travel, art and the popular range. The staff are helpful, and the shop is browser-friendly. They pride themselves on frequent and successful book signings and readings and maintain a mailing list to notify customers of these events. Look out for the fine selection of local Hampstead and Highgate history.

BOOKSAVE
63 Chase Side
N14 5BU
081 886 9889
M-Sat 9-5

The boast here is that there is a book for everyone. The range consists exclusively of discount and bargain books. You'll need the ladders supplied to reach the floor to ceiling shelving. Booksave supplies hospitals, residential homes and special interest clubs.

STOKE NEWINGTON BOOKSHOP
153 Stoke Newington High Street
N16 0NY
071 249 2808
M-Sat 9.30-5.30

A bookshop that encourages browsing and buying with a varied range of quality books. It has a good reputation as a general bookshop built up by serving the local community over the last five years. It is strong in fiction, healthcare, childcare, travel and biography and service.

MORGANS
1287 High Road
N20 9HS
081 445 2692
M-Sat 9-5

Books of all shapes, sizes and content. One for the local community.

GRAHAM WYCHE
1 Chaseville Parade
Chaseville Park Road
N21 1PG
081 360 1318
M-F 9-6

Books for business, from computing to management, including HMSO publications.

TURNERS BOOKSHOP
46 Chipstead Valley Road
Coulsdon
CR5 2RA
081 660 1432
M-Sat 9-5.30

Fiction and non-fiction for adults and children, popular general subjects with some bargain books. A large range of books for supply to schools and libraries from this educational showroom.

THE IBIS BOOKSHOP
109 High Street
Banstead
Surrey
0737 353260
M-S 9-5.30

Small in size but big in reputation and service, this shop has served the local community for over 50 years. Originally a lending library, it is the only bookshop in the local area as WH Smith was seen off many years ago. New books, especially hardbacks, feature strongly.

BAINES BOOKSHOP
3 Lower Square
St. Nicholas Way
Sutton
SM1 1EA
081 661 1677
M-Sat 9-5.30

This bookshop is conveniently situated in the civic centre, housing the local library and adult education establishment. The subject range is sweeping and best in the arts and the humanities. Academic and language books are stocked to serve students at the local college.

BROADWAY BOOKSHOP
51 The Broadway
Cheam
SM3 8BL
081 643 7048
M-Sat 9.30-5.30

A shallow range of stock squeezed into a small but attractive building with low ceilings, cubby holes and narrow stairs.

DEES OF STONELEIGH
14 The Broadway
Stoneleigh
Epsom
KT17 2HU

081 394 0763
M-Sat 9-6

One of five bookshops serving the book buyers of Epsom. A competent range of stock with a nice selection of children's books.

THE SURREY BOOKSHOP
11 King's Shade Walk
Epsom
KT19 8EB
0372 740272
M-Sat 9-5.30, Th 9-8

Just a couple of years away from celebrating 20 years of general bookselling in Epsom. The shop is small but the service makes up for this with a speedy service for customer orders.

REGENCY BOOKSHOP
45 Victoria Road
Surbiton
KT6 4JL
081 399 2188
M-Sat 9-5.30

Offers all you would expect from a suburban general bookshop. Helpful service and well ordered stock in a welcoming atmosphere.

CANNINGS
181 High Street
New Malden
KT3 4BL
081 942 0450
M-Sat 9-5.30

One of many bookshops which started life as a lending library. This long established link is retained as Cannings supplies many schools and libraries in the London area. Apart from WH Smith, it is the only dedicated bookshop in the immediate area.

BOOKS & CO
Bentalls Shopping Centre
Kingston
Surrey
M-W, F, Sat 9-6, Th 9-9

The Discount Book Company operates this bargain bookshop in the new Bentalls Centre. They buy remainders from publishers at keen prices that they promise to pass on to the customer. Prominent notices in the shop state that they do not buy just because of the price and the quality of stock in this exceptional bargain bookshop supports this claim with the slogan '....we buy quality books we are proud to sell....' The design is as glossy and bright as the Dillons Bookstore two levels above but as yet Dillons do not offer to exchange books found elsewhere at a lower price. Books & Co do.

SERENDIP BOOKSHOP
35 Walton Road
East Molesey
KT8
081 941 5848
M-Sat 9.30-5.30

The only bookshop in East Molesey, with a well chosen selection of new publications and children's books.

THE SWAN BOOKSHOP
12 Church Road
Teddington
TW11 8PB
081 977 8920
M-Sat 9-5.30, W 9-5

Many years of bookselling
experience help to produce a
bookshop offering a selective
range of new hardbacks and
popular non-fiction subjects,
primarily in the form of
affordable paperbacks.

THE OPEN BOOK
10 King Street
Richmond
TW9
081 940 1802
M-F 9.30-6, Sat 9.30-7

A window display full of the pick
of recent publications greets the
visitor to this shop. There are
many signed copies amongst the
choice selection of new titles and
the literary paperback fiction
section reflects the ethos behind
the shop. Skylights and plants
add to the welcoming feel.

LANGTON'S BOOKSHOP
44 Church Street
Twickenham
TW1 3NT
081 892 3800
M-Sat 9.30-5.30

A family run business in an
attractive shop with the usual
range of books. Service is
knowledgeable if a little erratic.

KEW BOOKSHOP
1-2 Station Approach
Kew
TW9 3QB
081 940 0030
M-Sat 9.30-6

Conveniently located outside Kew
underground station offering a
popular range of general subjects,
maps, cards and gift wrap.

WEYBRIDGE BOOKS
28 Church Street
Weybridge
KT13 8DX
0932 842498
M-Sat 9.30-5.30

In business for over 10 years with
a general range of books,
postcards, prints and calendars
competing with WH Smith for
local business.

THE BOOKSHOP
13 Station Approach
Virginia Water
Surrey
GU25 4DP
0344 842463
M-Sat 9-5.30

An attractive double fronted
building in a pleasant parade of
shops close to Virginia Water
station. The business is owned by
the author Bryan Forbes and has
been established for 25 years. It
offers all you would expect from
an excellent example of a local
general bookshop serving
discerning customers. There is a
feeling of space with an array of
books lying face up on tables and

display units. New books and children's books are especially well represented as is art, with a good selection in a glass fronted bookcase. Service is attentive and knowledgeable and with a demand for books outside the range the shop is able to carry, emphasis is given to a swift order service for any book in print.

THE HAYES BOOKSHOP
6 Glebe Avenue
Ickenham
UB10 8PB
0895 637725
Tue-Sat 9.30-5.30

Charles and Betty Glover have been in bookselling a long time and having considered then rejected retirement, much to the relief of book buyers who have benefited from their wealth of experience, continue on in this welcoming shop. Books new and old line the walls and there is something to appeal to all tastes among the well ordered sections.

THE BOOKSHOP
51 High Street
Ruislip
HA4 7BD
0895 678269
M-F 9.15-5.30, Sat 9.15-5

Centrally located on the High Street, a modest bookshop offering general books, cards, videos and giftwrap to local shoppers. WH Smith provides opposition on the book front but does not compete with this specialist business supplying

books to educational establishments in the area.

HAMMOND ROBERTS
136 Field End Road
Eastcote
HA5
081 868 5786
M-Sat 9-5.30

A coy bookshop with a surprisingly good selection of general and academic books.

CORBETT'S BOOKSHOP
56 Bridge Street
Pinner
HA5 3JF
081 866 8517

102 Marsh Road
Pinner
HA5 5NA
081 866 3956
M-Sat 9.15-5.15

Together, the two branches of this long established business monopolise the book market in Pinner. Marsh Road is the more specialist, concentrating on educational books including children's, business and school textbooks. Bridge Street is a good all-round general bookshop.

NORTHWOOD BOOKSHOP
46 Green Lane
Northwood
HA6 2QB
0923 826999
M-Sat 9.15-5.30, W 9.15-1

Located in a busy shopping area with easy parking, this local bookshop meets the needs of discerning bookbuyers. Under the current ownership for over 10 years the stock is a well balanced mix covering the range of general subjects. Additional services include a fax and photocopying facility and picture framing.

CHORLEYWOOD BOOKSHOP
4 New Parade
Chorleywood
WD3 5NJ
0923 283566
M-Sat 9-5.30

A deservedly flourishing village bookshop expertly run by Messrs Ayers and Coleman. It offers all you would expect from a bookshop keen to play a full role in the local community.

MUIRS BOOKSHOP
198 High Street
Barnet
EN5 5SZ
081 440 8398
M-Sat 9-6

Over 20 years as a bookshop but bang up-to-date with a fully computerised stock control system and a strong service-oriented culture. The general and academic ranges are well covered by over 12,000 titles. In addition to Barnet bookbuyers, libraries and schools enjoy the efficient service.

ELAINES
67 Darkes Lane
Potters Bar
EN6 1BJ
0707 54032
M-Sat 9-5.30

A bookshop for the browser located near the British Rail station. An assorted bag of subjects in stock coupled with a good selection of commercial and general stationery and partyware.

BOOKWORLD
157 High Street
Potters Bar
EN6 5BB
0707 53452
M-F 9.30-5.30, Sat 9-5.30

Opposite the bus garage on the High Street is where you'll find this small general bookshop with a fair selection of paperbacks.

THE BOOK CENTRE
26 Fawkon Walk
Hoddesdon
EN11
0992 467497
M-Sat 9-5.30, Th 9-10

It may be off the London beat but local residents appreciate the value of this bookshop midway between the capital and Cambridge. It is handsomely fitted and clearly laid out with an appealing selection of especially chosen to satisfy the local market. A book search service is offered and books published in America are imported to add variety.

ROUND ABOUT BOOKS
368 Mare Street
E8 1HR
081 985 8148
M-Sat 7.30-6

The early opening times indicate
that this shop is a newsagent first
and bookshop second. Local
history and paperback fiction
dominate.

OWEN CLARK
129-133 Cranbrook Rd
Ilford
IG1 4QB
081 478 0324
M-Sat 9-5.30

Art books are well represented
alongside the commercial
stationery and drawing and
painting products. Open
University texts are stocked and
educational establishments are
supplied.

VILLAGE BOOKSHOP
475 High Road
Woodford Green
IG8 0XE
081 506 0551
M-Sat 9.15-5.30

A small village bookshop run by
two ex-teachers who offer a
modest collection of general titles.

WAITE AND SONS
9 The Broadway
Woodford Green
IG8 0HL
081 504 2019
M-Sat 9-5.30, Th 9-1

A very small general stock one
minute from the local station.

THE BOOKSHOP
150 High Road
Loughton
IG10 4BE
081 508 9855
M-Sat 9-5.30

Serving Loughton with a variety
of popular subjects and paperback
bestsellers.

JAMES SMITH BOOKSELLERS
Vicarage Field Shopping Centre
Ripple Road
Barking
IG11 8DQ
081 591 9090
M-Sat 9-6, Th 9-7

Established in 1926, the present
owner is married to the great
grand-daughter of the founder.
The business continues to pride
itself on exporting books to all
corners of the globe. The business
has a City background having
traded in the Holborn area until
1991. The expertise was relocated
to Barking along with the stock.
Computer books are a genuine
specialisation and the wide range
of general stock is supplemented
by a full selection of academic
texts in the Autumn.

EPPING BOOKSHOP
71 High Street
Epping
CM16 4BA
0992 575849
M-Sat 9-5.30

Well displayed books covering the popular titles in hard or paperback.

SWAN LIBRARIES BOOKSELLERS
27 Corbets Tey Road
Upminster
RM14 2AR
0708 222930
M-Th 9-5.30, F 9-6, Sat 9-5.30

In 1937 this business was founded as a library supplier and grew up as a general bookshop in the fifties. It now offers a large selection of general books.

COUNTY BOOKSHOPS
Unit 13 Glades Shopping Centre
High Street
Bromley
BR1 1DD
081 466 0155
M-Sat 9-6, Th 9-9

Bargains and remainders on offer in the shopping centre patrons.

BECKENHAM BOOKSHOP
42 High Street
Beckenham
BR3 1AY
081 650 9744
M-Sat 9.30-5.30, W 9.30-1

Although it has the standard profile of a local general bookshop, it offers a good alternative to WH Smith.

THE BOOK CELLAR
191 Pett's Wood Road
Orpington
BR5 1JZ
0689 872518
M-Sat 9-5.30, W 9-1

Most popular subjects are covered with a good selection of children's books, including reading schemes not normally available from stock elsewhere. Second-hand books, picture framing and greetings cards complete a compact but enterprising package.

F&R FREEDMAN
10 High Street
Caterham
CR3 5UA
0883 348881
M-Sat 9-5.30, W 9-1

Perched at the top of Caterham Hill and opposite the community centre. A full range of book services are provided: new books, second-hand books, stationery, educational supply and booksearch. Frank and Rosalyn Freedman present an excellent general bookshop with a local reputation to match. Although the shop is small, it always has in stock unusual books of interest. The booksearch service is long established and unlike others it actually works! Caterham residents will be glad that it is not necessary to travel to London to find a good bookshop.

LANGUAGES

THE EUROPEAN BOOKSHOPS LIMITED
4 Regent Place &
5 Warwick Street
W1R 6BH
071 734 5259
M-Sat 9.30-6

Two bookshops concentrating on
European languages and English
Language Training, within a very
short walk of each other and
minutes from Piccadilly Circus.
The shop in Regent Place is the
more specialised language shop.
There is a comprehensive range of
books, cassettes and videos on
learning and teaching English.
Warwick Street has a wide
selection of novels in European
languages, children's books, travel
guides and magazines. Official
European Community
publications, and current books of
use to those who want to know
more about the EEC, are also
stocked.

GRANT & CUTLER
55-57 Great Marlborough St
W1V 2AY
071 734 2012
M-Sat 9-5.30, Th 9-7

Over 100,000 books in a multitude
of languages from French to
Swahili. The books are organised
by country and in each section
you will find a wide choice on
popular general subjects, in the
language of the country.
Literature, language teaching and
learning books are widely
stocked. Free catalogues are
available and there is also a
selection of technical language
dictionaries. Grant & Cutler deals
with the leading European
publishers and offers an efficient
special order service for
customers wishing to obtain
books published in other
countries. It is the country's
premier foreign language books
specialist.

SKOLA BOOKS
27 Delancey Street
NW1 7RX
071 388 0632
M-F 10-3

A tiny collection of EFL and
English language training books
and dictionaries. Predominantly a
wholesale business operating a
mail order service for primary
and secondary schools.

KELTIC LTD
25 Chepstow Corner
Chepstow Place
W2 4TT
071 229 8560
M F 10-5.30, Sat 10-5

Teachers are employed by Keltic
and will recommend the correct
books and materials from the
stock of 6000 titles for teaching
and learning English as a foreign
language. The subject matter
naturally attracts customers who

make full use of the international mail order service and institutional department supplying educational establishments all over the world. Regular mailings will keep students and teachers up-to-date on new publications and the Keltic Complete Guide to EFL Materials, published annually, is a valuable reference source.

ESPERANTO BOOKSHOP
140 Holland Park Avenue
W11 4UF
071 727 7821
M-F 9.30-6

The international language, Esperanto, was created in 1887 and is intended to be a neutral, easy to learn second language. If you feel the need to broaden your language skills, Esperanto books, videos and audio materials are here to help. You can then return to read the imported books in Esperanto.

LINGUAPHONE LANGUAGE CENTRE
124-126 Brompton Road
SW3
071 589 2422
M-Sat 9.30-6

All the familiar Linguaphone language learning courses and a selection from other leading publishers. In addition, before popping into Harrods opposite, you can take an aptitude test to gauge your language learning ability.

LCL INTERNATIONAL BOOKSELLERS
102-104 Judd Street
WC1H 9NF
071 837 0486
M-F 9.30-5.30, W, Sat 9.30-2

Over 100 languages are represented by dictionaries and books for learning complemented by an equally impressive range of cassettes and videos. Primarily a supplier direct to educational establishments, but callers will find a helping hand to guide them to the material best suited to their language learning needs.

BOURNEMOUTH ENGLISH BOOKCENTRE
106 Piccadilly
W1V 9FL
071 493 5226
M-F 10-6.30

English language teaching service for teachers and students. Audio and video cassettes complete the ELT package.

NW BOOKSHOP
Community School
North Wharf Road
W2 1LF
071 402 9636
M-F 8.45-5.30

Foreign languages and school textbooks with a second-hand section offering a cheaper option to literacy and fluency.

EUROCENTRE BOOKSHOP
21 Meadow Court Road
Lee Green
SE3 9EU
081 318 5633
M-F 1-2.10, 4-4.30, W closed

English as a foreign language is
the focus of this small bookshop
catering for students within the
Eurocentre.

BENEDICTS BOOKSHOP
92 Lillie Road
SW6 7SR
071 385 4426
M-F 9.30-5.30

A small stock of new and second-
hand books on linguistics and
language teaching. The teaching
materials, for all languages,
include learning packs, tapes and
videos.

LITERATURE

BERNARD STONE
THE TURRET BOOKSHOP
36 Great Queen Street
WC2
071 405 6058
M-Sat 10-6

Walk past this intriguing
bookshop and you will have
missed one of London's lesser
known literary landmarks.
Having recently moved to this
location from 42 Lamb's Conduit
Street, the lifesize model of
Sigmund Freud (by Lyn Kramer)
remains intact and only hints at
the eccentricity within. The
collection of poetry from the USA
and Britain is superb. Not only
can you find books and literary
periodicals, but you can attend
the regular poetry readings, book
launches and signings. With a free
flow of wine, these provide rich
entertainment and attract
dedicated followers more
interesting than the glitterati at
the Groucho. The work of many
up and coming young poets is
championed here and there are
associations with Durrell, Henry
Miller, the Liverpool poets,
Ginsberg and the Beats and many
Irish poets. It is Fiona Pitt-
Kethley's favourite bookshop.
Bernard Stone, the owner,
specialises in works by Ralph
Steadman: books, signed posters,
and if you're especially honoured,
a glimpse of an original as unique
as this fine bookshop.

ULYSSES
31 Museum Street
WC1A 1LH
071 637 5862
M-Sat 10.30-6, Sun 12-6

Formed in 1991 out of Check
Books, Peter Joliffe and Peter Ellis.
Close to the British Museum and
even closer to the other Ulysses
shop opposite, foreign travel,
topography and history are the
specialisations. The emphasis is
on quality and passing the time of
day with fellow dealers who
prowl the area looking for
customers. The catalogues are
excellent and the prices high.

ULYSSES
40 Museum Street
WC1A 1LH
071 831 1600
M-Sat 10.30-6, Sun 12-6

Massed ranks of modern first
editions and literature, the
majority behind glass in grand
floor to ceiling bookcases, with
prices to match. Contemporary
authors are as well represented as
old standards. Catalogues of
illustrated and modern first
editions are regularly issued.

DICKENS HOUSE MUSEUM
48 Doughty Street
WC1N 2LF
071 405 2127
M-Sat 10-5

The Dickens House Museum is the only remaining house in London once lived in by the great man himself. It was originally opened by the Dickens Fellowship in 1925 and is a valuable source of income to the charity which owns the museum. There is a small range of stock, both antiquarian and modern, by and about Dickens and his times. It is a popular London attraction and there is also a selection of videos, tapes, posters, cards and assorted souvenirs.

BERTRAM ROTA
9/11 Langley Court
Covent Garden
WC2E 9RX
071 836 0723
M-F 9.30-5.30

More akin to a private library than a bookshop, but unlike a library, you can, wallet permitting, buy books here. The collection of first editions of English and American literature is unrivalled in London and glass cases display interesting and rare items of literature. Private Press books feature strongly. The serious collector can also find corrected proofs, manuscripts, historic and literary autographs. The catalogues are regular and always offer a choice selection.

THE BLOOMSBURY WORKSHOP
12 Galen Place
WC1A 2JR
071 405 0632
M-F 10-5.30

A gallery and bookshop specialising in work by the celebrated Bloomsbury Group who lived and worked in the area in the first part of the century. Virginia Woolf, E M Forster, Leonard Woolf, Roger Fry, Vanessa Bell, Maynard Keynes, Duncan Grant, David Garnett, Lytton Strachey and Clive Bell are among the writers and artists whose first editions, paintings and drawings they have available. Galen Place is off Bury Place close to Bloomsbury Square.

BELL, BOOK & RADMALL
4 Cecil Court
WC2N 4HE
071 240 2161
M-F 10-5.30, Sat 10-4.30

A real specialist in first editions of modern English and American literature. Glass fronted cabinets house many scarce books and collectors will unfailingly see a book they covet in the window. Prices are high but the stock has quality and is invariably in fine condition. Catalogues are issued.

MURDER ONE
71/73 Charing Cross Road
WC2H 0AA
071 734 3483
M-W 10-7, Th-Sat 10-8

You will find three distinct departments here: Murder One, Heartlines and New Worlds. It is the crime, science fiction and fantasy and romance bookshop. A more realistic order would be fantasy, romance then crime!

They aim to stock all books in print in this country plus a host of imports from America and the range of stock, both new and second-hand is extensive. The other products include murder mystery dinner party games. Furtive glancers with turned up collars, together with trekkies and less than new romantics pay homage here.

G. HEYWOOD HILL LTD
10 Curzon Street
W1Y 7FJ
071 629 0647
M-F 9-5.30, Sat 9-12.30

This prestigious location in the heart of Mayfair is the site of a bookshop packed to the rafters with a wide range of subjects, but concentrating on literature and a choice selection of new books. The history is as literary as the new, second-hand and antiquarian books, fighting, in a genteel sort of way, for space on the wooden shelves and display tables. It was founded in the thirties and has been referred to in the memoirs of leading persons of letters of the period. Nancy Mitford worked here during the Second World War. The current cadre of customers probably includes raincoat clad gents from a nearby office occupied by a secretive Government Department. Children's books are downstairs and you are bound to find an interesting annual or two along with all the classics of children's literature.

CHARLOTTE ROBINSON BOOKS
35 Great Pulteney Street
W1R 3DE
071 437 3683
M-F 11-6

The ground floor, complete with original panelling, of a pleasing Georgian house two minutes walk from Piccadilly Circus. There is a quality stock of around 5000 titles, majoring in the fields of modern first editions, children's, illustrated books and a special collection of literature of the Great War. Six to eight specialist catalogues are issued every year.

JOHN SANDOE BOOKS
10 Blacklands Terrace
SW3 2SP
071 589 9473
M-Sat 9.30-5.30, W 9.30-7.30

A few minutes walk from Sloane Square is a fine general bookshop which has served the demanding local community since the late fifties. The stock concentrates exclusively on literature and the arts in an attractive three storey building. The paperback sections of literary fiction, poetry and classics are particularly worthy and blend wholly with the always appealing displays of a wider than average range of new hardbacks.

POETRY BOOK SOCIETY
21 Earls Court Square
SW5 9DE
081 994 6477
M-F 9.30-5.30

Founded by T S Eliot in 1953 and
dedicated to the cause of
contemporary poetry in Britain.
The premises is an office
administering the poetry book
club. A quarterly newsletter is
produced.

VILLAGE BOOKSHOP
46 Belsize Lane
NW3
071 794 3180
M-Sat 11-5.30

A large stock of antiquarian and
second-hand books occupies
every space in this long
established bookshop. A similar
number of titles is held in storage
so the range is wide and prices
reasonable. Literature and art
dominate and there is always a
good selection of modern first
editions. The unique feature is the
section of German books, many
from the last century.

MIND BODY SPIRIT

MYSTERIES NEW AGE CENTRE
9-11 Monmouth Street
WC2H 9DA
071 240 3688
M-Sat 10-6

This lilac painted double fronted shop bills itself as London's Psychic and New Age Centre. There are three facets to this shop: books, equipment and services. The host of paranormal, psychic and spiritual apparatus is all embracing: tarot cards, dowsing, crystal balls, pyramid energy, incense, pendulums, aural research, biorhythms, natural healing and remedies. The range of books to accompany the above is well ordered and easy to peruse. Psychic readings are available every day and courses are held on tarot, astrology, palmistry and spiritual guidance.

WATKINS BOOKS
19 Cecil Court
WC2 4EZ
071 836 2182
M-Sat 10-6 W 10.30-6

The largest bookshop in Cecil Court with two floors devoted to what is now widely known as New Age or Mind, Body and Spirit. Watkins was founded almost 100 years ago but still has something new to offer. The overall theme is definitely esoteric and there is the finest range of books on natural therapies and holistic health. Psychology, eastern religions and philosophy are covered equally well. There is a second-hand books section downstairs.

ATLANTIS BOOKSHOP LTD
49a Museum Street
WC1A 1LY
071 405 2120
M-F 10-5.30, Sat 11-5

New age and occult enthusiasts are well catered for here. A large stock of new and second-hand books on witchcraft, astrology, spiritualism, psychic phenomena and the paranormal sits easily alongside a selection of tarot cards and crystal balls.

WHOLEFOOD BOOKS
24 Paddington Street
W1M 4DR
071 935 3924
M 8.45-6, Tu-F 8.45- 6.30,
Sat 8.45-1

Predominantly a health food store, but with a complementary range of books on health, alternative therapies, vitamins, organic farming, wholefood cookery and natural childbirth. The books are in the corner and you have to make your way past the enticing enviro-friendly food products and organic fruit and vegetables. It is satisfying to buy a book, choose a recipe, buy the ingredients and enjoy the result.

HEALTHWISE BOOKSHOP
The Family Planning Association
27-35 Mortimer Street
W1N 7RJ
071 636 7866
M-Thu 9.30-5, F 9.30-4.30

Condoms, for both sexes, and books in harmony. Dispensing information and books on sex, contraception, education, health, AIDS and HIV together with the Association's own publications.

MERCURIUS
291 Portobello Road
W10 5TD
081 960 6463
M-Sat 10-6

A wide range of alternative books on astrology, magic, eastern religions, mythology and occult.

COSMIC BOOKSHOP
15 Blenheim Crescent
W11
071 221 8784
M-Sat 11-6

Astrology features strongly in this bookshop for devotees of the mysteries of the universe.

GENESIS BOOKS
188 Old Street
EC1V 9BP
071 250 1868
M-F 11.30-7, Sat 11-3

The East West Centre is home to this bookshop in which the book selection reflect the activities of the centre. Shiatsu massage ,

natural healing and macrobiotic cookery classes are on offer. The stock of books is equally impressive, a strong selection on alternative medicine, natural healing and astrology. If you are looking for a specific area, booklists are available on iridology, herbalism and vegetarianism. Audio and video cassettes on yoga and other relaxation therapies complement the books. After a visit to the centre there is little doubt that you will emerge revitalised.

JAMBALA BOOKSHOP
247 Globe Road
E2 0JD
081 981 4037
M-W, F 11-6, Th 12-6, Sat 10-6

An ideal location for an alternative bookshop, round the corner from the London Buddhist Centre, next to a vegetarian restaurant and close to Bethnal Green tube. There is a wide range of general books although it is selective with a strong alternative bias. Women's studies, mythology and natural health is well covered with good children's and ecology sections.

ACUMEDIC CENTRE
101-105 Camden High Street
NW1 7JN
071 388 5783
M-Sat 9.30-5.30

Acumedic is a health centre of international repute specialising in acupuncture and chinese herbal therapy. It is part of a world-wide organisation offering a comprehensive range of specialist facilities and has been providing a new kind of health service to the Camden community for over 10 years. The bookshop covers the whole spectrum of health: not only all the authorised guides to acupuncture and oriental medicine but a selective range on osteopathy, homeopathy, herbalism, gemmology and healthy food and living. Books on physical exercise and sport are also included from Tai Chi to popular sports. The health shop and professional medical showroom provide acupuncture equipment, homeopathic supplies and natural beauty products. The clinic is where healthy living, East and West, comes together. The specialist clinics include skin, pain, well-woman, asthma, allergies, weight loss, children's and anti-smoking.

CHANGES BOOKSHOP
242 Belsize Road
NW6 4BT
071 328 8242
M-F 10-6, Sat 10-5

Specialising in psychology and psychotherapy in its widest interpretation. Accompanying the classics in this field are books on creative therapies involving art and music. Tea and coffee will soothe the nerves whilst browsing through this well thought out collection of books.

INSPIRATION
28 Devonshire Road
Chiswick
W4 2HD
081 994 0074
M-Sat 10-6

West London's New Age Centre for new and second-hand books, products and services. The books cover all the popular fields and amongst the products you can discover Rain Sticks, Mayan Music Balls and Glo Stars. Services include tarot reading, channelling and workshops. Take classes in meditation and psychic development when life cries out for a new dimension.

PSYCHIC SENSE BOOKSHOP
1 Antique City Market
98 Wood Street
E17 3HX
081 520 4032
M-Sat 9.30-5, closed Th

Mainly second-hand but some new books. Especially astrology, spiritualism, paranormal and the occult. They have been in business for over ten years and offer book search and a mail order service. In addition to the books, there are other associated products such as Guatemalan worry dolls to whom you can pour out your troubles in order to alleviate stress and anxiety.

L N FOWLER & CO
1201 High Road
Chadwell Heath
Essex
081 597 2491
M-F 9-5

Fowlers was founded in the City
in the 1880's where it remained
for nearly 100 years before
moving to the present site in
Chadwell Heath. Publishing
books on phrenology was the
original specialisation and today
it is the leader on astrology with
almost 3000 titles dedicated to this
subject on display in a compact
showroom. Fowlers is primarily a
distributor and publisher for
leading astrology specialists in the
USA such as CRCS, Divorce, Yogi
Publications and White Eagle. To
appreciate the depth of expertise
at Fowlers consider the fact that
they supply the specialist
bookshops in London and all over
the country. A sub-specialisation
on homeopathy is being
developed with standard
reference works such as the *A-Z of
Aromatherapy* and *Herbal Remedies
for Dogs*.

MUSEUMS & GALLERIES

**BRITISH LIBRARY
BOOKSHOP**
The British Museum
Great Russell Street
WC1B 3DG
071 323 7735
M-Sat 10-4.50, Sun 2.30-5.50

Despite the grandeur of many landmark bookshops in London, none but this one can claim to be adjacent to the Magna Carta. The bookshop was opened in 1988 to provide a dedicated outlet for British Library Publications and to enable visitors to buy souvenirs and scholarly works relating to the collections. Turn right when you enter the British Museum into the Grenville Room. The shop is small and one hopes will be much larger when housed in the new British Library, whenever it is completed and if there is any money remaining to provide a bookshop. It might be compact but the selection of books is mighty. The specialisation is a bibliophile's dream: books on books, manuscripts, bookbinding, papermaking, printing, illustration and calligraphy constitute the main sections. There are also books on art, history, reference and London. The gift products include many quality items and as well as the cards and posters you will find hand-made paper and quill pens. Even if you bypass the shop, gaze lovingly at the rare books and manuscripts in glass cases.

BRITISH MUSEUM
Great Russell Street
WC1B 3DG
071 323 8587
M-Sat 10-4.50, Sun 2.30-5.50

On entering this august institution turn right for the British Library Bookshop and left for the British Museum Bookshop. The emphasis is firmly in line with the major collections of the museum. Archaeology, classical history, ancient Egypt, Greece, medieval studies and ancient civilisations are the major areas. There is a small but selective range of educational children's books. A range of gifts, souvenirs and cards caters for the hordes of tourists attracted to the museum.

DICKENS HOUSE MUSEUM
48 Doughty Street
WC1N 2LF
071 405 2127
M-Sat 10-5

The Dickens House Museum is the only remaining house in London once lived in by the great man himself. It was originally opened by the Dickens Fellowship in 1925 and is a valuable source of income to the charity which owns the museum. There is a small range of stock, both antiquarian and modern, by and about Dickens and his times. It is a popular London attraction and there is a selection of videos, tapes, posters, cards and assorted souvenirs.

LONDON TRANSPORT MUSEUM SHOP
The Piazza
Covent Garden
WC2E 7BB
071 379 6344
M-Sun 10-5.45

Simply the best and most reliable service operated by London Regional Transport. The museum houses a collection of historic buses, trams, trolley buses and underground trains with a fascinating range of ephemera and art. The shop reflects the museum contents and carries around 500 titles on road and rail transport in general with a special emphasis on London past and present. Transport art books are a speciality. The shop has a treasure trove of gift ideas based on London Transport's unique poster images. Amongst the Underground souvenirs are silk ties and bow ties overprinted with the network map.

PHOTOGRAPHERS GALLERY BOOKSHOP
5 & 8 Great Newport Street
WC2H 7HY
071 831 1772
Tu-Sat 11-7

The Photographers Gallery was founded over twenty years ago and following a refit and redesign in late 1992, offers the largest space devoted to photography in London. There are twenty four exhibitions a year in four galleries, an education programme, a print sales room, library (members only), cafe and a bookshop. It has London's leading specialist photography bookshop with publications on every aspect of the art. The mail order service keeps you in touch whilst away on assignment and the broad selection of posters, cards and magazines is one of the best in any arts venue. The shop layout is both innovative and clear, thanks to the design skills of Nick England. You will experience no difficulty in finding and enjoying books by British, American and European photographers, photo journalism, new work, landscape, architecture, history, theory and technique.

NATIONAL PORTRAIT GALLERY BOOKSHOP
St Martin's Place
WC2H 0HE
071 306 0055
M-F 10-4.45, Sat 10-5.45,
Sun 2-5.45

Situated within the Gallery to the left of the foyer at the main entrance, or enter direct through the side entrance. The extensive range of books and merchandise reflects the magnificent art collections of the gallery. National Portrait Gallery publications, British art and portraits, art history and biography are the major areas of expertise. There is a selection of literature and children's educational books, including tapes and videos. Posters, postcards, cards and stationery feature the famous images within the Gallery. The range of crafts is of interest to the art lover and tourist alike, with bags, jigsaws, bookends, mugs and other gift items.

THE COLISEUM SHOP
English National Opera
St Martin's Lane
WC2N 4ES
071 240 0270

London's opera bookshop, two doors from the London Coliseum. There is a range of 500 books solely devoted to the world of opera. In addition to the books is a wide selection of CD's, tapes, videos and opera related merchandise.

POLLOCKS TOY MUSEUM
1 Scala Street
W1P 1CT
071 636 3452
M-Sat 10-5

The museum was founded in the fifties with the toy theatre collection retrieved from Benjamin Pollock, the last of the Victorian toy theatre printers. It is adjacent to a toy shop and minutes from Goodge Street underground. The shop can be visited without entering the museum but don't miss one of the most unusual and fascinating collections in London. There is a small but attractive range of books on dolls, toys and collectables with some children's books. The real treat is the cut and assemble and pop-up books on

children's theatre and classic characters such as Punch and Judy.

MUSEUM OF MANKIND BOOKSHOP
6 Burlington Gardens
W1X 2EX
071 323 8045
M-Sat 10.30-4.30

The study of ethnography, the scientific description of human races and cultures, is featured in this bookshop, which is part of a fascinating and educational museum. There are titles covering non-western civilisations and books relating to the variety of exhibitions at this museum for all ages.

ROYAL ACADEMY OF ART BOOKSHOP
Piccadilly
W1V ODS
071 439 7438
M-Sun 10-5.30

Small range of current art books, featuring exhibition catalogues, art history and artists. There is a complementary range of cards, calendars and gift items.

MUSEUM OF LONDON
150 London Wall
EC2Y 5HN
071 600 3699 ext 267
Tu-Sat 10-5.40, Sun 12-5.40

The shop is within the museum but outside the ticket barrier, so it is not necessary to pay just to visit this interesting shop. It is located in the City, close to the Barbican Centre and five minutes walk from St Paul's. There is a comprehensive collection of books relating to the history of London and its people, including Museum of London publications. The books cover all aspects of London life, from maps and guides to specialist titles on the collections in the museum. Children's requirements are met handsomely with a well chosen set of educational and activity books. Gifts, stationery and music with a London theme tempt the visitor.

THE ROYAL SHAKESPEARE COMPANY SHOPS
Barbican Centre
EC2Y 8DS
071 628 3351
usually 5.45-9.15 on performance days, matinee days 12.30-9.15

There is a main bookstall at level three stalls left, and two satellites, at level four. The opening hours and location may be confusing, but the specialisation on the theatre and Shakespeare has clarity. All aspects of the theatre are covered with a large range of Shakespeare texts and criticism. The Royal Shakespeare Company branded merchandise is better than that on offer at similar venues and can also be obtained from the mail order department at the main shop in Stratford.

ZWEMMER AT THE WHITECHAPEL GALLERY
80 Whitechapel High Street
E1 7QX
071 247 6924
Tu, Th, Sun 11-5, W 11-8

The Zwemmer empire continues at this well known art venue. The concentration is firmly 20th century art - Bloomsbury to Pop art, architecture and design. Special displays always back up current exhibitions providing background titles, tie-ins and catalogues. There is a good selection of magazines, posters and cards.

DESIGN COUNCIL BOOKSHOP
28 Haymarket
SW1Y 4SU
071 839 8000
M-Sat 10-6, Sun 1-6

The Design Council showroom is a fine example of taking a national talent and presenting it to visitors for interest and to generate new ideas. There is a host of superb designers in this country and one reward is for their work to be shown here. The bookshop complements the displays by presenting a complete range of associated books and publications in an innovative setting. Design management, technical design, packaging products, landscape, history, furniture, architecture and education are all covered. Cards, stationery and gifts are also available.

ICA BOOKSHOP
Nash House
12 Carlton House Terrace
SW1
071 930-493
M-Sun 12-10

Art, media, design, women's studies, culture and fiction with a wide range of design and art magazines. Become a member or pay for the day and enjoy the bookshop, gallery, movie theatre, vegetarian restaurant and bar.

TATE GALLERY SHOP
Millbank
SW1 4RY
071 834 5651
M-F 10.30-5.45, Sat 10-5.45,
Sun 2-5.45

The Tate boasts three selling areas. The Gallery shop is to the right of the gallery, off the rotunda; the Clore sales desk which is on the ground floor of the Clore gallery and the Exhibition sales desk which is only open to coincide with special exhibitions. The range of books reflects the collections at the Tate and includes all aspects of art throughout the ages. British painting from 1570 to the present and foreign 20th century painting and sculpture are the main specialities. There are always displays of catalogues, books and other items relating to special exhibitions and events in the Gallery. Prints, posters, slides, cards and gifts are included in the repertoire.

NATIONAL ARMY MUSEUM
Royal Hospital Road
SW3 4HT
071 730 0717
M-Sun 10-5.30

Pleasantly located adjacent to the Royal Hospital in Chelsea. The shop carries a small range of books on all aspects of military history and soldiering through the ages and operates as a gift shop to visitors to this fascinating museum.

DILLONS THE BOOKSTORE
The Science Museum
Exhibition Road
SW7 2DD
071 938 8127
M-Sat 10-6, Sun 11-6

Hordes of visitors and tourists pass through this bookshop within the museum. The focus is on all aspects of science and technology, both popular and specialist. General subjects are well represented and the children's section is biased towards practical activities and basic science topics. The bookshop is closer to a general Dillons than a specialist shop but still offers an interesting range of books reflecting the collections within the museum.
Unfortunately, the museum's own shop, adjacent to the bookshop, is disappointing.

NATURAL HISTORY MUSEUM BOOKSHOP
Cromwell Road
SW7 5BD
071 938 9285
M-Sat 10-5.50, Sun 11-5.50

Two bookshops in one at this marvellous museum. The Geological Museum bookshop joins its cousin in providing an impressive array of books on natural history. There are geological maps and guides as well as a wide range of toys and crafts. Find the shop in Gallery 37.

VICTORIA & ALBERT MUSEUM SHOP
Cromwell Road
SW7 2RL
071 938 8434
M 12-5.30, Tu-Sat 10-5.30, Sun 2.30-5.30

After a walk around this stupendous museum, spend some time in this equally excellent shop just on the left as you enter the museum. The books cover the study, conservation and preservation of the major collections in the V & A: textiles, ceramics, furniture, metalwork, sculpture and the arts and crafts of the Far East, Indian and Islamic cultures. The books form only part of what is a gift givers delight, as the range of products inspired by the sumptuous collections will attract the most jaded culture vulture. If you can't decide what to buy take a V & A gift voucher.

MUSEUM OF THE MOVING IMAGE BOOKSHOP
National Film Theatre
South Bank
SE1 8XT
071 928 3535
M-Sun 10-6

A museum hugely popular with visitors to London, children and all those interested in drama, TV and the media. The shop carries a variety of merchandise to attract the souvenir buyer and the books cover the specialist areas comprehensively, from animation to special effects and writing screen plays. British Film Institute publications are also available.

ROYAL NATIONAL THEATRE BOOKSHOP
Ground Floor Foyer
South Bank
SE1 9PX
071 928 2033
M-Sat 10am-11pm

An expansive bookshop in more ways than one. There is a permanent location opposite the stalls entrance to the Lyttelton and two outlets in the stalls foyers of the Olivier and Cottesloe. The core stock of 2500 titles concentrates on the theatre (excluding ballet and opera) and the bookstalls focus on books and items related to the current repertoire. There are play texts, especially those of current London productions, critiques, biographies and reference books. The remainder of the stock is carefully chosen to reflect the taste and interests of the clientele and consists of literary fiction and film and TV tie-ins. Souvenirs are on sale with many quality National Theatre branded products.

WATERSTONE'S
Royal Festival Hall
South Bank Centre
SE1 8XX
071 620 0403
M-Sun 11-10

This specialist bookshop reflects the artistic and literary activities at the South Bank. The opening hours themselves are a revelation it is open eleven hours a day, every day except Christmas Day. It is situated in the midst of the Festival Hall and carries a good range of fiction, new books, literature and books on the applied arts. The bookshop plays an active role in the life of the centre and frequently hosts readings and events linked to the South Bank programme.

HAYWARD GALLERY SHOP
Hayward Gallery
South Bank Centre
Belvedere Road
SE1 8SX
071 928 3144
M-Sun 10-6, W,Th 10-8

A specialist stock on art: artists from A-Z, photography, art reference, sculpture and contemporary art. There is always a comprehensive selection of publications related to current exhibitions and this covers the culture, art and literature of the

main topic. The other products include a wide selection of cards, posters and calendars connected to the exhibitions and the selection of associated diaries is a real feature.

IMPERIAL WAR MUSEUM
Lambeth Road
SE1 6HZ
071 416 5000
M-Sun 10-6

An attractive shop located inside one of London's top tourist attractions. Over 2000 books are stocked on twentieth century military history and conflict. The emphasis is firmly on the two major conflagrations but contemporary military conflicts and issues are also covered. There is a comprehensive selection of educational titles on the two World Wars. The range of gift products retains a military theme, with cassettes and videos also.

DESIGN MUSEUM BOOKSHOP
Butlers Wharf
Shad Thames
SE1 2YD
071 403 6933
Tue-Sun 11.30-5.30

A small shop inside the entrance to the Design Museum. There is a wide selection of Design Museum publications, exhibition catalogues, posters and postcards all with a designer theme. A mail order service is available, as is a stock list, on request.

PERFORMING ARTS

CINEMA DANCE FILM DRAMA
MUSIC OPERA THEATRE

THE CINEMA BOOKSHOP
13-14 Great Russell Street
WC1B 3NH
071 637 0206
M-Sat 10.30-5.30

A small shop off Tottenham Court Road packed to the wings with books new and old on the cinema. The range of signed photographs, posters and memorabilia makes this a Mecca for film buffs.

A ZWEMMER OUP MUSIC & BOOKS
26 Litchfield Street
WC2H 9NJ
071 379 7886
M-F 9.30-6, Sat 10-6

Expert service and expertly chosen stock awaits the aficionado. The complete range of Oxford University Press music, Faber, Novello and all other publishers in this field is held in pull-out wooden trays lining the wall. The book stock has a classical bias but jazz, blues and contemporary music is also represented.

THE COLISEUM SHOP
English National Opera
St Martin's Lane
WC2N 4ES
071 240 0270

London's opera bookshop, two doors from the London Coliseum. There is a range of 500 books solely devoted to the world of opera. In addition to the books there is a wide selection of CD's, tapes, videos and opera-related merchandise.

TRAVIS AND EMERY
17 Cecil Court
WC2N 4EZ
071 240 2129
M-F 10-6, Sat 10-1

Exclusively music '...the only one in London' proclaims the sign in the window. There are new and second-hand books on all aspects of music and specialist catalogues are issued. The collection of sheet music is extensive with prints and photographs as a variation to the theme.

STAGE DOOR PRINTS
1 Cecil Court
WC2N 4EZ
071 240 1683
M-F 11-6, Sat 11.30-6

This is largely a print shop specialising in performing arts but there is a modest range of interesting books on opera, music, ballet, theatre and film. The range of ephemera and memorabilia offers much of interest and there is always a selection of autographed photographs of legendary Hollywood stars. Victoriana features strongly and the sets of Edwardian cards and valentines from the Victorian age add to the theatrical atmosphere.

DANCE BOOKS
4 Cecil Court
WC2N 4EZ
071 836 2314
M-Sat 11-7

Founded in the mid sixties by John O'Brien, an ex Ballet Rambert dancer, so no shortage of expertise and first hand knowledge here. The shop is attractively decorated with dance prints and the stock is well organised. All forms of dance and human movement are covered by the well chosen range of new and second-hand books, with some bargains to be found. The selection of dance videos is noteworthy.

PLEASURES OF PAST TIMES
11 Cecil Court
WC2N 4EZ
071 836 1142
M-F 11-2.30, 3.30-5.45

The opening hours are not quite as eccentric as some of the stock but time your Saturday visit for the first of the month otherwise an appointment will be required to obtain access to this delightful shop. David Drummond, an actor who has been operating here since the late sixties, claims that '...his interest in the theatre manifested

itself Frankenstein like to the detriment of his performing career.' Over 5000 books on the performing arts and juvenilia pre 1940s with a bias towards Victorian and illustrated books. There is a wide selection of playbills, cards and picture postcards and items can be hired by accredited bodies.

RAY'S JAZZSHOP
180 Shaftesbury Avenue
WC2H 8JS
071 240 3969
M-Sat 10-6.30

Look for the bright red painted frontage with a black cat on the fascia above the shop on the corner of Shaftesbury Avenue and Monmouth Street. Ray was manager of Collets Jazz and Folk Record Shop for over twenty five years until Collets closed it and sold the jazz business to Ray. The shop is a landmark of the London jazz scene and sells mainly records, CDs, tapes and 78 rpm jazz and blues. The book stock is small but there is a wealth of knowledge and experience to help you find that crucial volume.

DRESS CIRCLE
57 Monmouth Street
WC2H
071 240 2227
M-Sat 10-6

The burgundy coloured frontage of this attractive shop is reminiscent of the lush velvet drapes in a West End playhouse. Showbiz is the name of the game here. Records, CDs and tapes of musicals and film soundtracks, memorabilia, theatre posters, sheet music and scores, scripts, tickets and books on all things theatrical. Listen to the music, read the dirt on the stars and buy tickets for the show, all at Dress Circle.

BBC WORLD SHOP
Bush House
Strand
WC2 4PH
071 257 2576
M, Tu, F, 9.30-6, W 10-6, Th 9.30-7

The BBC World Service started this shop as an information centre for listeners and in the last ten years it has grown into a profitable contributor to BBC coffers. It is at street level at the entrance to Bush House facing Kings College. Here is the full range of BBC publications with a superb collection of videos and tapes providing a nostalgic trip through the TV and radio highlights of years gone by. Current programmes are covered equally well. The World Service is a life-line for many people around the world and here you can obtain, free of charge, leaflets in the languages of countries in which programmes are received, detailing the all important frequencies for reception. A selection of short-wave radios puts the average High Street electrical shop to shame. The mail order service looks after customers around the globe. This is a fine example of a part of the

BBC that provides an invaluable service but unless you have cause to search for it you may never know it exists.

VIRGIN MEGASTORE
Book Department
28-30 Oxford Street
W1N 7AP
071 631 1234
M-Sat 9.30-8, Sun 11-7

The Megastore concept is one that Virgin pioneered and has subsequently mastered. Once you're wandering in the multi-media environment it's difficult to leave without buying something to read or listen to. The bookshop caters for the music lover: music books, from biographies to group profiles and illustrated coffee-table books. You will not find a better set anywhere on contemporary music. A selection of music magazines, many from overseas, a groovy section on the Beat Generation, hip fiction and popular culture completes a well-thought out book department. Upstairs is The Fantastic Store, a small area devoted to comics, graphic novels, posters and cards.

FRENCH'S THEATRE BOOKSHOP
52 Fitzroy Street
W1P 6JR
071 387 9373
M-F 9.30-5.30

French's has been publishing plays since 1830 and the bookshop developed around the turn of the century. Carrying over

4000 play titles and 2000 books on the theatre you are assured of finding the play of your choice. The sections are well labelled making a search through the shelves a straightforward task and a pleasurable experience. French's also sells study guides and notes. If you are producing or writing a play, the collection of sound effects, dialect recordings and CD's is unique and invaluable.

POLLOCKS TOY MUSEUM
1 Scala Street
W1P 1CT
071 636 3452
M-Sat 10-5

The museum was founded in the fifties with the toy theatre collection retrieved from Benjamin Pollock, the last of the Victorian toy theatre printers. It is adjacent to a toy shop and minutes from Goodge Street underground. The shop can be visited without entering the museum but don't miss one of the most unusual and fascinating collections in London. There is a small but attractive range of books on dolls, toys and collectables with some children's books. The real treat is the cut and assemble and pop-up books on children's theatre and classic characters such as Punch and Judy.

VINTAGE MAGAZINE SHOP
39 Brewer Street
W1R 7HF
071 439 8525
M-Sat 10-7

Deep in the heart of Soho, Vintage offers a small selection of cinema and theatre books, but they concentrate mainly on vintage magazines and stage and film posters. There is a selection of music press dating from the 70's that makes for interesting and nostalgic reading. Posters, cards and calendars complement the main stock.

BOOSEY & HAWKES MUSIC SHOP
295 Regent Street
W1R 8JH
071 580 2060
M-F 9-6, Sat 10-4

A business with an illustrious history in the music world. In 1990 the interior was destroyed by fire, and reopened in the following year fully restored to its 1930's art deco splendour, originally designed by Anna Zinkeisen. It is the only company in the world to combine instrument manufacturing with a leading music publishing business. The shop carries every piece of music in the Boosey & Hawkes catalogue currently in print, as well as all Peters Edition titles. There is a wide selection of printed music and music books from all the leading publishers. The stock is more eclectic than it once was, and although it concentrates on classical music and education there is an enhanced section on popular and contemporary music. Also on sale is a comprehensive selection of periodicals, stationery, gift items and accessories.

SCHOTT MUSIC SHOP
48 Great Marlborough Street
W1V 2BN
071 437 1246
M-F 9-5, Sat 10-2

This world renowned business was founded in Germany in the late 17th century, and opened in London in 1835. They have been at this location since 1909 and the focus of their business remains music publishing. The retail showroom offers a magnificent collection of printed music, books on music, an early music shop and a huge selection of recorders and recorder music for all levels.

QUARTET BOOKSHOP
45-46 Poland Street
W1V 4AU
071 437 1019
M-Sat 10-6

Situated in the heart of Soho and appropriately specialising in cinema, photography and jazz. It started life in the mid eighties as a general shop and although a silver screen emphasis has now developed, the general areas are still appealing with contemporary fiction, health and biography to the fore.

CHAPPELL OF BOND STREET
50 New Bond Street
W1Y 9HA
071 491 2777
M-F 9.30-6, Sat 9.30-5

A large selection of classical and popular music, displayed by instrument.

MUSEUM OF THE MOVING IMAGE BOOKSHOP
National Film Theatre
South Bank
SE1 8XT
071 928 3535
M-Sun 10-6

A museum hugely popular with visitors to London, children and all those interested in drama, TV and the media. The shop carries a variety of merchandise to attract the souvenir buyer and the books cover the specialist areas comprehensively, from animation to special effects and writing screen plays. British Film Institute publications are also available.

ROYAL NATIONAL THEATRE BOOKSHOP
Ground Floor Foyer
South Bank
SE1 9PX
071 928 2033
M-Sat 10am-11pm

An expansive bookshop in more ways than one. There is a permanent location opposite the stalls entrance to the Lyttelton and two outlets in the stalls foyers of the Olivier and Cottesloe. The core stock of 2500 titles concentrates on the theatre (excluding ballet and opera) and the bookstalls focus on books and items related to the current repertoire. There are play texts, especially those of current London productions, critiques, biographies and reference books. The remainder of the stock is carefully chosen to reflect the taste and interests of the clientele and consists of literary fiction and film and TV tie-ins. Souvenirs are on sale with many quality National Theatre branded products.

WATERSTONE'S
Royal Festival Hall
South Bank Centre
SE1 8XX
071 620 0403
M-Sun 11-10

This specialist bookshop reflects the artistic and literary activities at the South Bank. The opening hours themselves are a revelation- it is open eleven hours a day every day except Christmas Day. It is situated in the midst of the Festival Hall and carries a good range of fiction, new books, literature and books on the applied arts. The bookshop plays an active role in the life of the centre and frequently hosts readings and events linked to the South Bank programme.

KENSINGTON MUSIC SHOP
9 Harrington Road
SW7 3ES
071 589 9054
M-F 9-5.30, Sat 9-4

A sister shop to the Barbican Music Shop it was not prepared to divulge any details on the shop. If the service is along similar lines, try one of the many other excellent shops for books and printed music.

BARBICAN MUSIC SHOP
Cromwell Tower
White Cross Street
EC2Y 8DD
071 588 9242
M-F 9-5.30, Sat 8.45-4

Here can be found a wide range of books on classical and popular music and a comprehensive selection of scores. There are many titles on how to play instruments and more serious tomes for students of music from the nearby Guildhall School of Music and Drama.

THE ROYAL SHAKESPEARE COMPANY SHOPS
Barbican Centre
EC2Y 8DS
071 628 3351
usually 5.45-9.15 on performance days, matinee days 12.30-9.15

There is a main bookstall at level three stalls left, and two satellites, at level four. The opening hours and location may be confusing, but the specialisation on the theatre and Shakespeare has clarity. All aspects of the theatre are covered with a large range of Shakespeare texts and criticism. The Royal Shakespeare Company branded merchandise is better than that on offer at similar venues and can also be obtained from the mail order department at the main shop in Stratford.

THE FOLK SHOP
Cecil Sharp House
2 Regent's Park Rd
NW1 7AY
071 485 2206
M-F 9.30-5.30

A few books to be found on folk songs, musicians and the music. Additionally, there is a choice of books on customs and folk lore. A collection of musical instruments decorates the shop walls accompanied by a fine range of world music on tape, record and CD. The building houses the English Folk Dance and Song Society so there is resident expertise and in-house services which include mail order, catalogues, a magazine and library facilities.

OFFSTAGE THEATRE AND FILM BOOKSHOP
37 Chalk Farm Rd
NW1 8AJ
071 485-4996
M-Sun 10-6

Located near the busy Camden market, this specialist bookshop houses a wide range of new and second-hand books on the performing arts. Not quite as established as The Mousetrap it has, however, been in existence for 10 years. Drama, the media, film, criticism, biographies and stagecraft are well represented. A fascinating range of memorabilia with a large selection of theatre programmes provides good dreaming potential. Offstage also stocks technical books on make-up, lighting, sound and production. Whether you are a student of the arts or an avid theatre goer you will find something of interest here. The shop also provides access to a 50 seater basement which is available for fringe productions, rehearsals, and workshops. The best specialists always offer more than just books and knowledge and this artistic emporium can claim a starring role.

UPPER STREET BOOKSHOP
182 Upper Street
N1 1RQ
071 359 3785
Tu-Sat 9.30-6

A general second-hand bookshop with a bias towards the performing arts amongst the general stock.

POLITICS & SOCIAL SCIENCES

GAY'S THE WORD
66 Marchmont Street
WC1N 1AB
071 278 7654
M-F 11-7, Sat 10-6, Sun 2-6

A comprehensive and innovative bookshop covering all subjects relating to homosexual, lesbian and feminist society. Novels, magazines, newspapers and information are all dispensed with knowledge and enthusiasm. Tea and coffee is available while you arrange to receive the regular newsletter.

THE ECONOMISTS BOOKSHOP
Clare Market
Portugal Street
WC2A 2AB
071 405 8643
M-F 9.30-6, W 10.30-6, Sat 10.30-1.30

Occupying the middle ground of LSE territory, students need go no further for books on politics, economics and social sciences. Although it is now owned by Dillons Bookstores, this bookshop has retained its street credibility. Apart from the full range of new titles there is always a wide selection of second-hand course texts and basic reading for students.

INDEX BOOKCENTRE
28 Charlotte Street
W1P 1HJ
071 636 3532
M-F 9-7, Sat 10-5

The shop occupies the ground floor of a Georgian terrace a few minutes walk south of Goodge Street underground. The stock is a mix of general subjects with art and design, paperback fiction and media studies featuring prominently. Socialism, both new and second-hand books, is the main theme with a notable section on Labour History. With the demise of Collets in Charing Cross Road, Index is the only socialist bookshop in central London.

KARNAK HOUSE
300 Westbourne Park Road
W11 1EH
071 221 6490
M-F 10-5

A modest stock covering academic subjects, politics, social sciences, children's and Black studies. There is a small range of general books.

PATHFINDER BOOKSHOP
47 The Cut
SE1 8LL
071 401 2409
M, W. F 12-2, 5-7, Tu, Th 5-7

Sat 10-7

The premises has been a distribution point for Pathfinder Press for twenty years and has been a bookshop since 1990. It is one of forty such outlets around the world and is a five minute walk from Waterloo, opposite the Young Vic theatre. The ethos behind Pathfinder is crystallised by the quote from Castro, 'The truth must not only be the truth.....it must also be told.' These prophetic words appear on a mural on the wall of the Pathfinder building in New York. Displays of the mural, featuring portraits of revolutionary leaders whose writings and words are published by Pathfinder, can be seen in the bookshop. Colour posters and cards of the mural portraits of Malcolm X and Nelson Mandela are available. The shop is staffed by volunteers and provides essential reading for those who want to understand and change the world. The stock is small at around 2000 titles and covers socialist politics and books on the struggle for freedom and social justice. Some titles are available in Spanish, French, Farsi, Turkish, Hindi and Urdu. They promote books by Guevara, Trotsky, Marx, James Connolly and others. Pathfinder is the main publisher of the writings of Malcolm X and is one of the few places to find recent speeches by Mandela. So-called radical bookshops are coming to terms with the break up of the Soviet Union and Pathfinder is responding by importing the classics of socialism by its former

leaders as fast as they are being pulped in the former USSR. The premises is used for weekly political meetings, bookstalls are organised for events, from demonstrations to freshers fairs, and a readers club offers discounts off all Pathfinder titles and selected other books.

DEPTFORD BOOKSHOP
55 Deptford High Street
SE8 4AA
081 691 8339
M-Sat 9.30-5.30, Th 9.30-1.30

The Deptford Bookshop is a true community bookshop, supported by Lewisham Council. The profits fund the Deptford Literacy Centre which provides numeracy and literacy classes for adults. They stock a wide range of paperbacks specialising in children's books, multi-cultural fiction, non-fiction and women's issues. The selection of picture paperbacks for children is by far the best in South-East London. The free story telling sessions every Saturday morning are very popular. Parents and teachers can obtain advice on selecting appropriate books and help is on hand to set up libraries, classroom collections and bookstalls.

BOOKPLACE
13 Peckham High Street
SE15 5EB
071 701 1757
M-Sat 10-6, closed Th

This is a non profit-making local community bookshop. Children's books with a multi-cultural focus feature strongly. Books on Black issues and women's interest reflect the needs of the local community. The range of services on offer match the philosophy behind the shop and its stock and include: library supply, literacy and creative writing classes, creche facilities and an innovative publishing programme for locals.

LABOUR PARTY BOOKSHOP
150 Walworth Road
SE17 1JT
071 234 3339
M-F 9.30-5, closed 12-1 for lunch

Located inside the Labour Party HQ and specialising in socialism, politics, disarmament, equality and trade unions. There is a basic selection of general paperbacks and new books, especially those by or about Labour figures. Booklists are available occasionally and for the truly dedicated try the official party merchandise.

121 BOOKSHOP
121 Railton Road
SE24 0LR
071 274 6655
W-Sat 1-5, Sun 3-5

Anarchism and the class struggle in all its glory. There are books and publications on squatting and exercising your civil rights. Pick up advice on how not to pay the poll tax or where to put a roof over your head, in the cafe which is occasionally the scene of lively and topical debate.

JOHN BUCKLE BOOKS
170 Wandsworth Road
SW8
071 627 0599
M-Sat 10-6

Second-hand books on popular general subjects and a range of new books on political topics.

TIMBUKTU BOOKS
378 Coldharbour Lane
SW9
071 737 2770
M-Sat 9.30-7

A small selection of books on all matters of Black interest from poetry to politics.

INDEX BOOKCENTRE
10-12 Atlantic Road
SW9 8HY
071 274 8342
M-Sat 10-6

A sister branch to Charlotte Street and the best bookshop in the area. Socialist politics and history is again the main theme. The range of general subjects is comprehensive and affordable, with paperbacks in the majority. Black writers, Africa and Caribbean topics are well covered. Local schools and libraries are supplied and this is reflected in the selection of text books and educational titles.

EAST END BOOKSHOP
THAP Books
178 Whitechapel Road
E1 1BJ
071 247 0216
M-F 10-5.30, Sat 10-5

In this long established bookshop serving Tower Hamlets you will find 12,000 titles on local history, Bengali language, women, black and worker writers and children's books. The Bengali books are of great value to the local community as is the range of carefully chosen reference guides and educational books. Two other areas of special interest are the superb range of non-sexist and anti-racist children's books and books on East London. A bookstalls service brings relevant books to schools, colleges, workshops and conferences. Providing adult literacy facilities is a key function of the bookshop and writing workshops and events are held. Story telling sessions entertain the children and a newsletter disseminates all the information you need to make use of this excellent resource.

FREEDOM PRESS BOOKSHOP
84b Whitechapel High Street
in Angel Alley
E1 7QX
071 247 9249
M-F 10-6, Sat 10-4

Anarchist politics rule OK? Located at the offices of Freedom Press who have for the past 100 years been publishers and distributors of the alternative social and political press. The philosophy of anarchism and its practical application to the problems of modern society are covered by such titles as '*The Future of Technics and Civilisation*' and '*History of the Makhnovist Movement.*'

CENTERPRISE BOOKSHOP
136 Kingsland High Street
E8 2NS
071 254 9632
M-Sat 10.30-5.30, Th 10.30-7.30

Serving Hackney in the way that the East End Bookshop serves Tower Hamlets. It opened over twenty years ago with the Hackney Reading Centre and Advice Centre. Books of a radical nature are well represented alongside children's, educational books, Black issues, women's issues and general fiction. The bookshop supports a very active local publishing scene and there is an equally inventive programme of arts and literature events. Cards, cassettes, T-shirts and crafts are also available.

NEWHAM PARENTS CENTRE
745-7 Barking Road
E13 9ER
081 552 9993
M-F 9.30-5.30, Sat 9.30-5

An educational centre run by local people for local people. The overall purpose of this venture is to produce and make available a wide range of material on education. This is interpreted in its widest sense and covers women's interests, understanding other cultures, languages and an excellent children's section including play materials. There are general books on the arts, activities and standard reference books.

HOUSING CENTRE TRUST
20 Vestry Street
N1
071 253 6103
M-F 10-5.30

A few minutes walk north of Old Street station. A specialist range of books and publications on all aspects of housing: architecture, design, planning, finance, sheltered housing and management of housing associations. It is primarily a service to members of the Trust but is happy to provide information and advice to other interested parties.

PORCUPINE BOOKCELLAR
Basement
5 Caledonian Road
N1 9DX
071 837 4473
M-F 10-6.30, Sat 10-5

A general range of second-hand books on general subjects and politics. Booklists are available on political and economic history. Amongst the general subjects you will find women's studies and fiction, books on printing and some modern first editions.

HOUSMANS BOOKSHOP
5 Caledonian Road
Kings Cross
N1 9DX
071 837 4473
M-Sat 10-6

Above the aptly named Porcupine Bookcellar and a short distance from Kings Cross station. As an antidote to the military specialists, there is a substantial section here on pacifism and anti-militarism. In the politics section you can find books on anarchism alongside a large selection of political magazines and journals. The general books reflect the overall radical theme and include feminism, gay issues, the environment and contemporary fiction.

NEW ERA BOOKS
203 Seven Sisters Road
N4 3NG
071 272 5894
Tu-F 10-5.30, Sat 11.30-4.30

A small stock on Marxism, Leninism, anti-imperialism and development in the third world. They import and distribute books from China and a trade list is available of all Chinese titles. Chinese handicrafts are also sold.

COMPENDIUM BOOKSHOP
234 Camden High Street
NW1 8QS
071 485 8944
M-Sat 10-6, Sun 12-6

A Pandora's box of delights in Camden for the browser and

buyer alike. A smorgasbord of choice- Compendium is either the starter or dessert. A superb selection of New Age books, from the occult to health, and an excellent large section on women's studies and current social issues. Philosophy, politics and world religions are all on the menu. Elderly citizens can find books on their concerns. Join the politically aware, the right-on and the social workers to enjoy a radical bookshop that knows its subject and how to sell books.

BOOKMARKS
265 Seven Sisters Rd
N4 2DE
081 802 6145
M, Tu, F, Sat 10-6, W, Th 10-7

Founded in the sixties as a mail order service for the International Socialists, it opened as a bookshop in the early seventies and has since trebled in size. A wide range of books on socialist politics, lesbian and gay issues, trade unionism, Marxism, social sciences and Black interest. The Bookmarx Club offers the best socialist books at reduced prices, ranging from current issues and socialist fiction to history and Marxist theory. A children's book catalogue is available listing a selection from picture books to teenage fiction. The prevailing criteria are multi-culturalism and anti-sexism, a welcome starting point for challenging traditional reading for children. It is not necessary to be a left of centre political animal to obtain this useful list, compiled with the help

of Michael Rosen. The accompanying range of pamphlets, journals and political postcards demonstrates that Bookmarks has more to offer than the average radical bookshop. The layout is clear and books are easy to find. Bookmarks is also the bookselling and publishing arm of the Socialist Workers Party.

KILBURN BOOKSHOP
8 Kilburn Bridge
Kilburn High Road
NW6 6HT
071 328 7071
M-Sat 9.30-5.30

Located opposite Kilburn High Road railway station and three minutes walk from Kilburn Park underground. It opened in 1980 and has built up an enviable reputation as a good local bookshop with a healthy radical zeal. The community feel is supported by the large sections of Irish books, Black studies, lesbian and gay interests. The stock is largely paperback but there is always a selection of new hardbacks, particularly fiction.

THE WILLESDEN BOOKSHOP
Library Centre
High Road
NW10 4QU
081 451 7000
M-Sat 10-6

A sister shop to the Kilburn Bookshop and although it is not strictly a political specialist, it has a similar bias to its parent. It is located within a large library and arts complex on the site of the old Willesden Library. In addition to the bookshop there is an art gallery, cinema, cafe and exhibition space. Children's books and the associated topics of education and books for teachers are the main specialisations. The general stock reflects the themes in the Kilburn Bookshop and matches the needs of the multitude of visitors to the centre.

RELIGION & THEOLOGY

BUDDHISM CATHOLICISM CHRISTIANITY
EASTERN RELIGIONS ISLAM JUDAISM

**THE LONDON BUDDHIST
CENTRE**
51 Roman Road
E2 0HU
081 981 4032
M-F 10-5

Within the Buddhist Centre is this
bookshop stocking Buddhist texts
in English translations. Works
from the Zen, Mahayana and
Tibetan schools can be found.
There is a selection of incense,
candles, Buddhist images,
meditation cushions and stools.

WISDOM BOOKS
402 Hoe Street
E17 9AA
081 520 5588
M-Sat 9.30-5.30

Wisdom Books is primarily a mail
order and book distribution
operation. Wisdom Publications
was founded in 1978 under the
spiritual guidance of two Tibetan
Lamas. The purpose was to keep
Tibetan Buddhism alive during
the oppressive Chinese
occupation of Tibet and to
promote Buddhism in the west.
The publishing business is now
based in the USA and the Hoe
Street location is a showroom and
distribution point. You have to
ring the door bell to be admitted
to the first floor bookshop and
once inside you can select from
one of the most comprehensive
collections in London of books on
Buddhism.

ST PAULS
Morpeth Terrace
SW1P 1EP
071 828 5582
M-F 9.30-5.15, Sat 10-6

Adjacent to the imposing
Westminster Cathedral a short
walk from Victoria station. The
Society of St Paul took over the
Cathedral bookshop in 1991 and
expanded into the adjoining
conference centre to form what is
probably the largest religious
bookshop and multimedia centre
in the country. A circular
illuminated sign above the stairs
leading down to the cavernous
bookshop proclaims that St Pauls
is not just a commercial venture.
This is clear and there are many
bookshops that would envy the
space and fittings devoted to all
Catholic and Christian topics.
Church requisites and religious
articles are also stocked, from
gowns to candles. The depth of
stock does not yet match the size
of this operation and it is clear
that some of the ranges are still
being developed.

FAITH HOUSE BOOKSHOP
THE CHURCH UNION
7 Tufton Street
SW1P 3QN
071 222 6952
M-F 9.30-5

The Church Union was founded in 1859 and continues to uphold the Catholic faith in the Church of England. Religious books, especially liturgical, musical and catechetical, are stocked for Anglican and Roman Catholics. General Christian titles are also carried.

PADRE PIO BOOKSHOP
264 Vauxhall Bridge Road
SW1V 1BB
071 834 5363
M-F 10-5.30, F 10-6.30

Dedicated to Padre Pio, the stigmatised monk. There is a large range of Roman Catholic publications, particularly devotional teaching. Daily prayers of divine mercy and intercession from 3-4pm.

CATHOLIC TRUTH SOCIETY
BOOKSHOP
25 Ashley Place
Westminster Cathedral Piazza
SW1P 1LT
071 834 1363
M-F 9.15-5, Sat 9.15-1

Dedicated to serious theology and books for the Catholic faith as well as providing a range of church requisites and cards.

ST. PAUL MULTIMEDIA
199 Kensington High Street
W8 6BA
071 937 9591
M-Sat 9.30-5.30

Books on the ground floor cover the wide range of Christian literature, mainly Roman Catholic. The first floor houses a spectacular array of appropriate music and material on tape, CD and video.

CENTRE FOR PEACE
BOOKSHOP
326 High Road
Ilford
IG1 1QP
081 478 3517
M-Sat 9.45-5, Sun open before and after Mass

Located in the Cardinal Heenan Centre, books on theology and related subjects.

A R MOWBRAY
Dillons Bookstore
28 Margaret Street
W1N 7LB
071 580 2812
M-Sat 9-6, Th 9-7

Mowbray's was once considered to be one of the most interesting general bookshops in London but it is for its long history as a specialist religious outlet that it is best known. When bought by Dillons Bookstores in the late eighties it could only claim to be a bookshop with a growing reputation for eccentric service and under-investment. Re-named and refitted as a Dillons Bookstore it has secured a new lease of life and is rebuilding its reputation as a specialist business. The founder's portrait hangs proudly behind the counter in the Religious Department where the shelves are packed with books on all religious subjects. There are few places that can compete with this depth of stock. Church requisites of all types are available although the furniture business fell by the wayside a long time ago. It seems incongruous to see communion wafers displayed behind a glass panel next to own-label wine in a West End bookshop. Regular events are well attended and the customer base using the mail order service is world-wide.

ST MARTIN-IN-THE-FIELDS
The Crypt
Trafalgar Square
WC2N
071 839 8362
M-Sat 11.30-7.30, Sun 11-6

The entrance is off Duncannon Street, to the south of the church and on the east side of Trafalgar Square. Go down the steps and you will find the shop next to the cafe and the London Brass Rubbing Centre. There is a small and therefore shallow selection of books on religion and theology. The gifts, cards and wrapping paper are somewhat more interesting.

SCRIPTURE UNION BOOKSHOP
11 Mason's Avenue
Harrow
HA3 5AH
081 861 3259
M-Sat 9-5.30

The Scripture Union first opened a Christian bookshop in London in 1925 and now has a chain of 22 shops around the country. The theme has remained constant. Stocking over 8000 titles of all types of Christian books, bibles, prayer and children's books. In addition they have a wide range of Christian music on CD and cassette, cards, posters and gift items. There are regular book signings by well-known Christian writers and thinkers.

Other London addresses:
16 Park St, Croydon
14 Bond St, Ealing
5 Wigmore St, W1
14 Eton St, Richmond

S P C K
CHARLES HIGHAM
Holy Trinity Church
Marylebone Road
NW1 4DU
071 387 5282
M-F 9-5

The S.P.C.K. (Society for the Promotion of Christian Knowledge) has two shops at this one location. The church houses both. The larger shop specialises in religion and theology: bibles, sermons, doctrines, spirituality and all associated subjects. In addition to the general Christian books is a selection of bargain books, music on CD and tape, candles, cards and a full range of church requisites. Walk through the rear door and you enter the Church proper. Charles Higham, a second-hand and antiquarian specialist of repute can be found here. The concentration is centered on second-hand and antiquarian theology, church architecture, history, patristics and mysticism.

CHRISTIAN BOOKS & MUSIC
Kensington Temple
Kensington Park Road
W11 3BY
071 727 8684
M-F 10-7, Wed 10-8, Sat 10-6.30

Christian literature in general, especially charismatic and evangelical publications. Videos, music and cards coexist with a large stock of bibles and some children's books. A short walk from Notting Hill Gate tube.

CHURCH HOUSE BOOKSHOP
31 Great Smith Street
SW1P 3BN
071 222 5520
M-F 9-5, Th 9-6

Theology and spirituality with a Church of England emphasis. Large selection of books, cassettes and cards. A video hire library is included in the shop.

KING'S BOOKS
28/30 Queen's Rd
SW19 8LR
081 947 2982
M-Sat 10-5, W 10-1

The realisation of a vision by local Christians resulted in this bookshop attached to a modern church in Wimbledon. They sell Christian books, church music and other related items.

THE RUSSIAN ORTHODOX CATHEDRAL BOOKSHOP
67 Ennismore Gardens
SW7 1NH
071 584 0096
Only open before and after services

The bookshop is inside the Cathedral of the Assumption and All Saints. Orthodox Christianity is the dominant subject.

PROTESTANT TRUTH SOCIETY BOOKSHOP
184 Fleet Street
EC4A 2HJ
071 405 4960
M-F 9-5.30

The Society was founded in 1889 and has been in Fleet Street since 1947. This bookshop stocks primarily Protestant reformed and evangelical literature, greetings cards and social stationery.

LONDON CITY MISSION BOOKSHOP
175 Tower Bridge Road
SE1 2AH
071 407 7585
M-F 9.30-4.30

The mission was founded in 1835 and the book room originated out of a need to supply bibles and Christian literature to missionaries in the London area. This tradition continues.

THE BIBLE BOOKSTORE
744 Romford Road
E12
081 553 0335
M-F 9.30-8

29/30 Graville Arcade
(Brixton Indoor Market)
Coldharbour Lane
SW9
071 737 5583
M-F 9.30-6

Both stores are outlets for the World Vision for Christ and were founded on this mass crusade. Both shops stock around 1500 titles, mainly on religion, with some general reference books and dictionaries.

DAYBREAK BOOKS
68 Baring Road
SE12 0PS
081 857 1188
Tue-Sat 9-5.30

An evangelical Christian bookshop that goes beyond the boundaries of the church. Book parties can be held in your house, an idea that really brings books and faith into your living room.

CLC BOOKSHOP CHRISTIAN LITERATURE CRUSADE
26/30 Holborn Viaduct
EC1A 2AQ
071 583 4835
M-F 9.30-5.30, Th 9.30-6,
Sat 9.30-5

Two floors of books and music covering evangelical and charismatic Christian literature. The tapes and CD's feature popular Christian artists and groups. Chancery Lane is the nearest tube station.

PENDLEBURY'S BOOKSHOP
Church House
Portland Avenue
N16 6HJ
081 809 4922
M-Sat 9.30-5

From a small theological bookroom, Pendlebury's has grown to be the largest second-hand theological bookshop in the country. Over 40,000 titles occupy four vestries in this picturesque church in North London. Included in this vast stock are collectable volumes, fine bindings, secular and general theology. The catalogue is very informative.

SCM BOOKROOM
26-30 Tottenham Road
N1 4BZ
071 249 7262
M-F 9-5

Although the business is predominantly mail order, visitors are welcome to browse the compact range of Christian religion and theology books from all the major theological publishers, as well as those by SCM press. SCM will also organise bookstalls at appropriate events.

CORNERSTONE
638 High Road
N12 0NL
081 446 3056
M-Sat 9.30-5.30, F 9.30-6.30

Cornerstone was established as a resource centre for local churches to promote the Christian faith through the sale of books and related items. All subjects relating to Christianity are covered. It is a registered charity with the added efficiency of a computer stock control system.

THE MUSTARD SEED
21 Kentish Town Road
NW1 8NH
071 267 5646
071 267 5646
M-Sat 10-7, Sat 10-5

Surrounded by leafy plants in an ideal setting, this bookshop specialises in the creation debate. Christian apologetics are at home here with a wide selection of books and tapes on this major

issue, one minutes walk from Camden Town tube station.

CHRISTIAN BOOKSHOP
111 Cecil Road
Enfield
EN2 6TR
081 363 8517
M-Sat 9-5.30

Their acronym ASK (Accessible, Stockholding, Knowledgeable) gives the flavour of this customer driven shop. Close to Enfield town centre it stocks all the popular titles as well as a good selection of books covering Christianity throughout the world. All manner of bibles from old editions to new translations find space alongside music cassettes and children's stories.

MARANATHA CHRISTIAN BOOKSHOP
22 Windsor Street
Uxbridge
UB8 1AB
0895 255748
M-Sat 9-5.30

Daily readings, a children's play area and a cup of coffee make sure your visit is a pleasant one. A short walk from the tube station, this shop concentrates on Christian literature, commentaries, devotional aids, bibles and children's books. In addition to dried flowers, music and crafts, there is a photocopying and fax service.

CANAAN CHRISTIAN BOOKCENTRE
121 High Street
Staines
TW18 4PD
0784 457194
M-Th 9.30-5, F 9-5.30, Sat 9-5

Supported by local churches, the stock is varied, from bibles to hymn books, some commentaries and biographies. Have a light meal from the coffee shop. Church bookstalls are supplied and a bi-monthly newsletter keeps customers informed of new books and issues.

OASIS CHRISTIAN CENTRE
23 Wallington Square
Surrey
SM6 8RG
081 773 1428
M-Sat 9-5.30, W 9-1.30

Located in the centre of Wallington, serving the local community with a High Street Christian bookshop. Books, CD's, cassettes, videos and craft items are for sale. The range of children's books is impressive.

OASIS CHRISTIAN CENTRE
2 Burwood Parade
Guildford Street
KT16 9AE
0932 569405
M-Sat 9-5.30, W 9-2

General Christian bookshop serving the residents of Chertsey.

HIGHWAY CHRISTIAN BOOKSHOP
277 Ewell Road
Surbiton
KT6 7AB
081 399 8363
M-Sat 9-5.30

Adequate parking for visitors where religious books, bibles and second-hand books are all available. Schools and libraries are supplied.

FRONTLINE CHRISTIAN BOOKSHOP
2A Newmarket Way
Hornchurch
RM12 6DS
M-Sat 9-5

Located inside the Havering Christian Fellowship Centre in Hornchurch, along with a pleasant cafe. There is a small range of Christian books, bibles, music and stationery.

HAVERING CHRISTIAN BOOKSHOP AND CENTRE
80 Victoria Road
Romford
RM1 2LT
0708 727625
M-Sat 9-5.30

Over 5,000 books, music, videos and gifts with a colour photo copying service too. There is a tea room on the premises.

BOOKS ON ISLAM
14 Blackstock Rd
N4 2DW
071 359 7596
M-Sat 10-6, F closed 12-2

A dedicated Islamic bookshop
with 700 titles on all aspects of
Islam with mostly Sufi books. The
Holy Koran in its traditional form
and English translations are a
feature along with Hadith
(sayings of the Prophet) all in
English. Gifts and items necessary
for practising the Islamic faith,
such as prayer rugs and
perfumes, are also available.

MUSLIM BOOKSHOP
233 Seven Sisters Rd
N4 2DA
071 272 5170
M-Sat 10-6, Sun 11-5

Stop in to buy or browse and ask
for help to find books on Islam
and related subjects. There are
books in Arabic and English and a
good stock of related products,
from maps to clothing.

ISLAMIC BOOK CENTRE
120 Drummond Street
NW1 2HL
071 388 0710
M-F 10-6, Sat 10-7, Sun 11-7

Books in English, Arabic and
other languages of the Moslem
world, all on every aspect of
Islam.

DAR AL-TAQWA
7a Melcombe Street
NW1 6AE
071 935 6385
M-Sat 9-6

Religious books on the Islamic
faith and the Middle East in
Arabic and English. Language
learning books, dictionaries and
children's books as well as crafts
and music.

JEWISH MEMORIAL COUNCIL BOOKSHOP
Woburn House
Upper Woburn Place
WC1H 0EP
071 387 3081
M-Th 10-5.30; F 10-4 summer,
10-2 winter

The bookshop is on the second
floor above a most informative
museum on Jewish culture and
history. Serving the Jewish
community for over 70 years, the
Council and its bookshop stocks
books in English and Yiddish,
covering the range of Judaica.
They also sell religious service
and Jewish Holiday texts as well
as Hebrew dictionaries, books for
children and books on Israel.

THE HEBREW BOOK AND GIFT CENTRE
18 Cazenove Road
N16 6BD
071 254 3963
M-Th 10-6, F 10-1.30, Sun 10-3
A well-equipped bookshop with a
large selection of Talmudic
studies and books in both English
and Hebrew, including fiction.

The staff speak Hebrew and will show you the range of Cantorial and Chassidic tapes. Gifts and cards are also sold.

MESOIROH SEFORIM BOOKSHOP
61 Oldhill Street
N16 6LU
081 809 4310
M,W 9.30-7; Tu,Th,Sun 9.30-9.30

Predominantly a publisher of Hebrew books, Mesoiroh sells children's and educational books in both English and Hebrew. Religious articles are available alongside a photocopying and printing service.

JOHN TROTTER BOOKS
13 Sentinel Square,
Brent St,
NW4
081 203 6350

MANOR HOUSE BOOKS
80 East End Rd,
N3
081 349 9484
M-Th 10-4, Sun 10-1

Both shops specialise in Judaica comprising new, second-hand and antiquarian books. Mr. Trotter claims to have the largest stock of rare and second-hand books in Europe relating to Judaism. The Brent Street shop is the larger, better laid out shop, with a wide range of books on all Jewish subjects, the Middle East, its peoples and the history of the area. The Manor House shop is

small and has a good selection of Primo Levi's work.

J. AISENTHAL
11 Ashbourne Parade
Finchley Road
NW11 0AD
081 455 0501
M-Th 9-6, F 9-3, Sun 9.30-1.15

Serving the Jewish community in Golders Green with books on all aspects of Judaica in English and Hebrew. A good stock of related products for all aspects of Jewish life.

MENORAH PRINT & GIFT CENTRE
227 Golders Green Road
NW11 9ES
081 458 8289
M-Th 9.30-6, F 9.30-1, Sun 10-1

Books on Israel and Judaica as well as gifts centred around the Holidays and festivals.

JERUSALEM THE GOLDEN
146-148 Golders Green Road
NW11 8HE
081 455 4960
M-F 9.30-6 (summer),
9.30-4 (winter), Th, Sun 9.30-10

Two rooms divided into children's and adult books. Serving the community with a good selection of bibles and dictionaries, and books covering religious education. The largest selection in Europe of Hebrew music and videos is available for the enthusiast. The collection of silverware is interesting.

CHAPTER TWO
199 Plumstead Common Road
SE18 2UJ
081 316 4972
M-F 9.30-5.30, Sat 10-1.
Closed W

The speciality is bibles and commentaries, continuing a tradition going back to the early years of the last century. The Plymouth Brethren and dispensational theology is the focus, along with accurate translations of the bible. Second-hand books are also sold and they sell world-wide to over 100 countries.

FRIENDS BOOK CENTRE
Friends House
173/5 Euston Road
NW1 2BJ
071 387 3601
M-F 9.30-5.30, Tu 10.30-5.30

The door to this shop is behind the number 73 bus stop opposite Euston Station. Quakerism is the speciality, but books on liberal Christianity, peace and world religions are also covered. Peace and co-operative games, green and development books give this shop a serene air. There is a wide range of cards and peace orientated merchandise with a selection of second-hand titles on Quakerism. A full list is available.

SWEDENBORG SOCIETY
20-21 Bloomsbury Way
WC1A 2TH
071 405 7986
M-F 9.30-5

The Swedenborg Society was founded in 1810 in honour of the Swedish scientist and theologian whose mystical ideas became the basis of a religious movement. For the last 70 years Swedenborg's writings, related books and biographies have been sold from this listed building. There is also a reference and lending library on the premises.

SECOND-HAND

SKOOB BOOKS
15 Sicilian Avenue
WC1A 2QH
071 404 3063
M-Sat 10.30-6.30

Skoob has been in the renowned
Sicilian Avenue for over ten years
and has assumed the mantle of
the best and largest academic
bookshop in London. This
accolade came initially from the
London weekly magazine Time
Out and has stuck ever since.
Unlike cafes that receive rave
reviews then slip effortlessly into
mediocrity, Skoob earned its
claim to fame then built on it to
the extent that it is widely known
and accepted as the best. The
specialisation is in literature,
literary criticism, philosophy,
history, art, music, social sciences,
business and economics. The
stock has real depth yet remains
accessible and selective. The ethos
is right, the execution effective
and the customers loyal and
satisfied. A bookish visitor or
student in London should not
miss Skoob.

**SKOOB TWO/SKOOB
ESOTERICA**
17 Sicilian Avenue
WC1A 2QH
071 405 0030
M-Sat 10.30-6.30

Added to the original Skoob in
the mid eighties. Second-hand
and antiquarian books with an
academic theme and esoteric bias.
Science and technology, classics,
oriental studies and all religions
are stocked as adventurously as in
the parent shop.

UNSWORTH, RICE & COE
12 Bloomsbury Street
WC1B 3QB
071 436 9836
M-Sat 10-7, Sun 12-6

This shop opened on April fool's
day 1992 but the real fools are
those who miss out on the low
prices of scholarly and academic
books. It is a bright and modern
shop with orange walls and blue
shelving. The stock is second-
hand and remainders with some
antiquarian books in three glass
fronted cabinets. 'Post it' notes
stuck on the front cover of the
books with the price in red ink
reinforce the feeling of value for
money. No furtive searching for
pencil on endpaper here. History
and the humanities is the central
theme: history & archaeology,
classics, philosophy & social
sciences, literature, languages and
the arts. The combination of cheap
books and quality reading is
appealing and offers the best
value in the area.

WORLD OF BOOKS
39 Woburn Place
Russell Square
WC1H OJR
071 436 0027
M-Sun 11-7 summer; 10-6 winter

A large stock of general books
with an emphasis on biography
and militaria.

MARCHMONT BOOKSHOP
39 Burton Street
WC1H 9AL
071 387 7989
M-F 11-6.30

General second-hand books with
an emphasis on literature and the
arts. Some modern first editions,
contemporary poetry and review
copies.

HENRY PORDES BOOKS
58-60 Charing Cross Road
WC2H 0BB
071 836 9031
M-Sat 10-7

Sellophane-covered books line the
windows and indicate that the
stock of literature and art is better
than that on show in immediate
neighbours' emporiums. The rest
is a mixture of general second-
hand, some antiquarian and many
remainders trying to look like
bargains.

QUINTO BOOKSHOP
48a Charing Cross Road
WC2H 0BB
071 379 7669
M-Sat 9-10, Sun 12-8

An interesting and varied
collection of second-hand titles
with a reasonable section of
modern first editions. Better than
average fare for regular Charing
Cross Road browsers.

ANY AMOUNT OF BOOKS
62 Charing Cross Road
WC2H 0BB
071 240 8140
M-Sun 10.30-7.30

Second-hand books, thoroughly
weeded of any potential 'finds',
with a bias towards literature and
modern first editions. Many
cheap books and leather by the
yard for those who need it.

CHARING CROSS ROAD
BOOKSHOP
56 Charing Cross Road
WC2H 0BB
071 836 3697
M-Sun 10.30-9.30

Fast-moving stock, some dross,
some OK over a wide range of
general subjects. Charing Cross
Road was once the undisputed
centre of bookselling in London.
With the exception of some shops
in Cecil Court the interesting
second-hand and antiquarian
bookshops have all gone away.
What remains is a market place
for dealers and finders to hive off
the best of the steady stream of
incoming stock so the remains can
be flogged from tatty shops with
only a historical claim to fame.

THE CLEARING HOUSE
10 Cecil Court
WC2N 4HE
081 946 9677
M-Sun 8-midnight

Probably the longest opening
hours and cheapest books of any
bookshop in London. Books in
boxes on outside tables go for
£1.50 a hardback and 25p a
paperback, as do books from the
extensive range of general stock
inside. Miles away from the ultra
bargains is the specialisation in
literature, particularly P G
Wodehouse.

BAYSWATER BOOKS
27a Craven Terrace
W2 3EL
071 402 7398
M-Sat 11-7

Roger Noble owns what he
describes as the smallest
bookshop in London, and
possibly the country. It started life
with a firm intention to specialise
in poetry but commercial survival
forced an extension of the stock
into other general areas of fiction,
the arts, biography and comic
books. The opening hours are
flexible as the owner is a
dedicated book seeker on behalf
of his customers and is often
elsewhere. The stock is largely
second-hand with some
antiquarian.

NOTTING HILL BOOKS
132 Palace Gardens Terrace
W8 4RT
071 727 5988

M-Sat 10.15-6, Th 10.15-1

Second-hand paperbacks spill
onto the pavement, but inside the
stock inclines towards art,
literature, history and academic
subjects. Paperbacks, remainders,
and second-hand books dominate
with some review copies. Good
for browsing.

MUSIC & VIDEO EXCHANGE
56 Notting Hill Gate
W11 3HT
071 229 8420
M-Sun 10-8

One bookshop that is ready to
proclaim that they never refuse to
buy books. The stock reflects this,
in both condition and range.
Inexpensive paperbacks
predominate with a cheap
selection of literary and genre
fiction. Records and cassettes are
also sold.

J CLARKE-HALL LTD
7 Bride Court
EC4Y 8DU
071 353 4116
M-F 10.30-6.30

A disappointing shop in a small
arcade off Bride Lane. The stock
includes a mixture of second-
hand and antiquarian books with
a selection of review copies at low
discounts. One bright spot is a
specialisation in the works of
Samuel Johnson. A specialisation
in book design and printing has
been claimed but I scoured the
shelves for books on bookbinding
in vain.

POPULAR BOOK CENTRE
87 Rochester Row
SW1P 1LJ
071 834 3534
M-F 10-5, Sat 10-4

Cheap and well worn reading in
the form of bargains and
paperbacks.

RESPONSE BOOKSHOP
300 Old Brompton Road
SW5 9JF
071 370 4606
M-F 9.30-4.30, Sat 9.30-1

A worthy second-hand bookshop
founded in 1978 to raise money
for local community development
projects. There is a small coffee
bar at the back of the shop. All the
books are donations and there is
no buying by the shop. As a result
the stock profile and quality
varies but bargains are to be
found with the knowledge that
the price paid is going to a good
cause. Take your unwanted books
here.

CONSTANT READER
BOOKSHOP
627 Fulham Road
SW6 5UQ
071 731 0218
M-Sat 10.30-6.30

A general stock with no special
focus.

GLOUCESTER ROAD
BOOKSHOP
123 Gloucester Road
SW7 4TE

071 370 3503
M-F 8.30-10-30pm, S-S 10.30-6.30

An adventurous second-hand
bookshop of ten years standing. It
is clearly a cut above the norm
with long opening hours and a
real desire to sell good books and
please customers (a basic enough
aim in retailing but not always
evident in second-hand
bookshops). The stock covers all
the popular general areas with the
arts, history and literature
sections standing out. Prints and
postcards are sold and catalogues
are issued.

JOHN THORNTON
455 Fulham Rd
SW10 9UZ
071 352 8810
M-Sat 10-5.30

Two floors of second-hand and
antiquarian books backing onto a
private garden. The number of
titles in stock is around 10,000, a
large proportion of which is
theology. The range of general
stock is wide with prices from 50p
to £500. John Thornton has a shop
in Sissinghurst, Kent where he
specialises in gardening and
Victoria Sackville-West.

NATIONAL SCHIZOPHRENIC
FELLOWSHIPBOOKSHOP
5 Victoria Crescent
SW19
081 542 2665
M-Sat 10-4

A general second-hand bookshop
off Wimbledon Broadway with all

profits going to the National Schizophrenic Fellowship. The landlords are currently looking for a substantial increase in rent so it is not certain how long this bookshop will continue its good work here. All books are donated and they are sold at prices much cheaper than average. There is a large collection of books and publications on engineering and associated technical subjects.

MY BACK PAGES
318 Elephant & Castle
Shopping Centre
SE1
071 252 6889
M-Sat 10-6

Douglas Jeffers opened this bookshop, the first of the My Back Pages empire, in 1990 after practising the craft of second-hand bookselling in London's markets. A single subject specialisation cannot be identified here although academic topics, social sciences, paperback fiction, cinema and art dominate. Black history and literature is represented along with a few Irish titles in the same areas. The stock is extensive, affordable and with four shops to feed you will always see something new. They buy lots over the counter or will collect.

MY BACK PAGES
8-10 Balham Station Road
SW12 5SG
081 675 9346
M-F 10-8, Sat 10-7

Filled a gap in this part of London for a general second-hand bookshop. It is 100 yards from Balham tube and railway stations, and is 10 yards from a free car park. The hardback fiction section is good and it is possible to find the odd first edition at bargain prices if not in the best condition. Paperbacks are in the majority and all general subjects are covered.

MY BACK PAGES
106 Mitcham Road
SW17
081 672 6635
M-Sat 10-6.30

Two rooms of books with a profile not dissimilar to the Balham shop. There is a selection of new books but this is likely to be reduced as the owner finds it hard to operate on the measly margins mega publishers deign to give to small bookshops. There is no shortage of paperback fiction for 50p.

MY BACK PAGES
286-288 Streatham High Road
SW16
081 677 4925
M-Sat 10-6

The fourth and most recent shop in the chain adds much to the bookselling scene in Streatham. The painted fascia is more vibrant and bookish than the designer led light boxes of the so called up-market bookstores. It is a multi-coloured Miro style painting of cameos of recognised literary figures from Tin-Tin to Shakespeare. The stock is wide ranging and caters well to the local market by carrying good sections on Black history and literature and women's issues. Modern first editions do not include the cream but are eminently affordable. A feature of this chain is the variety in the paperback stock: it's not just discarded old Penguins and romance novels. Mini-specialisations come and go according to the availability of stock. Collectable paperbacks such as early Pans can be found. The sixties section on America and the 'Beats' is hip and timely and makes you wonder what the frontage would look like after a glass of cool-aid.

ALPHA BOOK EXCHANGE
193 Streatham High Road
SW16 6EG
081 677 3740
M-Sat 10-7

The ancient sign in the window proudly proclaims ' the cheapest reading in London.' This shop is all about low cost reading as it is an old style book exchange dealing primarily in paperback fiction. There is a healthy trade in magazines: back issues and current. Try buying a book from a 'new' bookshop and asking for a half credit when you return it !

SWANS BOOKSHOP
5 Tooting Market
Tooting High Street
SW17 0RH

081 672 4980
M, Tu, Th 9-5, F, Sat 9-5.30
A real traditional London second-hand bookshop. It has been at this site for almost 25 years and was opened by the owner's father. The grandfather started the business 80 years ago with a barrow in Deptford Market which was followed by a stall then a shop in which the father worked all his life before opening in Tooting. The stock, although second-hand, is not as old as the business and there is always something of interest in the wide range of subjects carried. The turnover of stock is fairly brisk and a half-price exchange scheme recycles old favourites.

PLUS BOOKS
19 Abbey Parade
Merton High Street
SW19 1DG
081 542 1665
M-Sat 9.30-6

Paperbacks and magazines galore in this second-hand bookshop that has been selling and exchanging all types of fiction for over 30 years.

CROYDON BOOKSHOP
304 Carshalton Road
Carshalton
SM5 3QB
081 643 6857
Tu-Sat 10.30-5.30, Tu, F closed for lunch 1-2

A huge selection of general non-fiction and fiction all at reasonable prices. The business has good and active sources for fresh stock so there is always something new.

THE RICHMOND BOOKSHOP
20 Red Lion Street
Richmond
TW9 1RW
081 940 5512
F & Sat only 9.30-6

A large but selective range of modern second-hand books, almost exclusively hardbacks. The opening hours are restrictive and border on the hobbyist but do not deter the weekend regular who is determined to seek out quality second-hand books. The Humanities and Arts are the main specialisations in floor to ceiling shelving. Current review copies are always available and the illustrated art section stands out. The fiction section (it's called literature here) is interesting in that the position of books constantly changes as the books are rotated within the alphabetical order. This ensures that customers get to see the range of stock rather than staring in familiar bewilderment at the same books visit after visit. The regular sales provide an opportunity to pick up a few bargains but generally prices are high, even for recent review copies, and whilst this works in leafy Richmond they wouldn't sell as many books in Streatham.

W & A HOUBEN
2 Church Court
Richmond
TW9 1JL
081 940 1055
M-Sat 10-6

Located in a pedestrian alley in central Richmond. They offer a good mix of new and second-hand books specialising particularly in the arts, social sciences and the humanities. The academic side is strengthened by a comprehensive range of text books.

WHITEHALL BOOKSHOP
43 The Broadway
Cheam
SM3 8BL
081 643 8272
M-Sat 9.30-5.30, W 9.30-1.30

Peter Batten, co-owner of Whitehall Bookshop, is an ex-professional jazz musician whose interest in literature has resulted in the subject specialisations within this small bookshop. There is an emphasis on Irish writers, particularly Joyce, Yeats and Beckett. He is in the process of building a collection on jazz. There is always a wide choice of illustrated art books. If your interest is in these areas make your needs known as the active book finding service and throughput of stock means that some books do not linger on the shelves.

W.A. FOSTER
183 Chiswick High Road
W4 2DR
081 995 2768
M-Sat 10.30-6

An attractive shop that claims to be the oldest in Chiswick, still with the original bow window. It has been providing second-hand and antiquarian books to local book buyers for over twenty years. One thing that does stand out about this bookshop is that only books in very good to fine condition are stocked. As a result, the sections of art and illustrated books and fine bindings are particularly good.

FAIRCROSS BOOKS
166 Thames Street
Strand on the Green
W4 3QS
081 994 1912
M-Sun 12-5

A great place to browse amongst the antiques and a wide ranging stock of antiquarian, second-hand and bargain books housed in two rooms.

OSTERLEY BOOKSHOP
168A Thornbury Road
Isleworth
TW7 4QE
081 560 6206
M-Sun 10-5.30

A traditional style second-hand bookshop located in the old Osterley railway station. A short walk from the Piccadilly line station and close to the entrance to Osterley Park. The stock is wide ranging in general and academic topics including a small section of modern first editions. The shop is crammed full of books and it is difficult for customers to adhere to the sign pleading 'keep books tidy.' The shop atmosphere is conducive to the sort of browsing that can sometimes reveal a long searched for treasure amongst the cheap paperbacks. Cards, and some intriguing 1930s-1950s designer socks, scarves and linen items for 50p each all add to the clutter.

BONAVENTURE
259 Archway Rd
N6 5BS
081 341-2345
W-Sat 11-6

A small shop that has seen better days and not as adventurous as the name might suggest. It specialises in second-hand travel books but also has a general selection.

R A BOON BOOKSELLERS
251 Holloway Road
N7
071 700 0243
M-Sat 9.30-5

Boons is opposite the University of North London and subsequently the range of second-hand books has an academic and technical flavour. Theology, especially Catholicism, history, literature and the arts are the favoured areas.

ROBBIES BOOKSHOP
118A Alexandra Park Road
Muswell Hill
N10 2AE
081 444 6957
M-Sat 9-5.30, closed Th

Previously the Paperback
Bookstore of Burnt Oak. It is an
unpretentious shop that
concentrates on paperbacks with a
good selection of collectable
vintage books, Penguins, Pelicans
and Puffins. The general ranges
offer inexpensive hardbacks and
they are always interested in
buying books.

VORTEX BOOKSHOP
139-141 Stoke Newington
Church Street
N16 0UH
071 254 6516
M-F 11-6, Sat 10-6, Sun 12-6

Part of a large complex
incorporating a cafe and art
exhibition space, both more
interesting than the bookshop
dealing in the humanities and
more general topics.

CIRCA
144 Stoke Newington
Church Street
N16 0NY
071 249 9775
M-Sat 12.30-6

Second-hand literary fiction and
academic titles, especially politics
and social issues, form the
nucleus of the stock. Some review
copies and recently published art
books appear at bargain prices.

Alongside the books is a selection
of modern designer jewellery,
china and cards.

COMYNS BOOKS
61 Stirling Way
N18 2UE
081 807 3427
M-F 9.30-6, Th closed

Cheap and cheerful selection of
magazines and popular
paperback fiction to read and
exchange.

WHETSTONE BOOKS
368 Oakleigh Road North
Whetstone
N20 0SP
081 368 8338
M-F 9.30-3.30, Sat 9.30-5

A traditional small second-hand
bookshop heavy on cheap
paperback reading and no
particular focus.

ARCHIVE BOOKS
83 Bell Street
NW1 6TB
071 402 8212
M-Sat 10-6

General old books with a large
range of sheet music. Lots of
cheap books but a lazy sort of
shop of limited appeal.

WALDEN BOOKS
38 Harmood Street
NW1 8DP
071 267 8146
Th-Sun 10.30-6.30

Off Chalk Farm Road and opposite the bus garage. A general stock with an emphasis on the arts and literature with paperbacks prominent.

KEITH FAWKES
1-3 Flask Walk
NW3 1HJ
071 435 0614
M 10-5, Tu-Sat 10-5.30

Three display windows beckon the browser and collector to this fascinating emporium of second-hand and antiquarian books. English literature is a favoured topic with many choice items. The main body of stock covers many subjects from sheet music to popular paperbacks and always offers something of interest.

GABRIELS BOOKSHOP
47 Walm Lane
NW3 4QU
081 451 2047
M-Sat 10.30-6.30

This long established shop once specialised in Spanish books but now deals only in general second-hand books. There is no particular emphasis in the stock profile.

FITZJOHNS BOOKS
27A Northways Parade
College Crescent
NW3 5DS
071 722 9864
M-Sat 11-6

A short distance from Swiss Cottage underground and offering an eclectic selection of second-hand stock in psychology, the sciences and academia.

HOLLOWAY BOOK EXCHANGE
1 Midland Crescent
Finchley Road
NW3 6ND
071 794 9255
M-F 11-7, Sat 10-6

This shop was opened on the back of bookstalls in Holloway Road, which still operate, and is aimed primarily at collectors and dealers. The stock covers paperbacks, hardback fiction and collectable pulp and vintage film memorabilia. There is therefore a lot of prints and magazines.

FORTUNE GREEN BOOKSHOP
74 Fortune Green Road
NW6 1DS
071 435 7545
W-Sat 10.30-5.30

Once only open on Saturdays, the loyal literary clientele can now browse and buy four days a week. It is an eccentric shop with a character you can feel. As well as perusing a nice range of books on literature, history, politics, art and women's interests, you can find out about all manner of literary events and local groups.

TWO JAYS BOOKSHOP
14 Whitchurch Lane
Edgware
HA8 6JZ
081 952 1349
Tu, W, F, Sat 10-5

A large selection of books on all
subjects from classics through
history to sport. The cinema
section attracts film fans and they
are always willing to buy fresh
stock.

BOOKMARK BOOKSHOP
67 High Street
Edgware
HA8 7DD
081 905 6993
Tu, Th F, Sat 9.30-5

Sports, football (books and
programmes) and science fiction
stand out amongst the generality.

EDWARD TERRY
26 Chapel Road
Ilford
IG1 2AG
081 478 2850
M-Sat 9.30-5.30

Second-hand and bargain books
galore on all subjects. Some local
Essex history books and a
collection of National Geographic
magazines.

**THE BOOKSHOP
BLACKHEATHLTD**
74 Tranquil Vale
SE3 0BN
081 852 4786
M-Sat 9.30-4.30

A comprehensive stock of second-
hand books, but there are some
new paperbacks. Local history is
well represented as is travel,
military and maritime. You may
find some modern first editions in
this bookshop crammed with
books.

STUDIO BOOKS
2 Montpelier Vale
SE3 0TA
081 318 9666
Tu-Sat 11-6

A little hard to locate but well
worth the effort. The shop is at the
first floor rear of 2 Montpelier
Vale and access is obtained via the
mews opposite Blackheath
station. There are almost as many
books in store as there are on
display so ask if you cannot see a
specific title. The stock covers a
wide range, with an academic
bias, and is particularly strong on
politics, technology, fiction,
Pelicans and Penguins.

SPREAD EAGLE BOOKSHOP
8 Nevada Street
Greenwich
SE10 9JL
081 305 1666
M-Sun 10-5.30

Located in an old coaching house
opposite Greenwich Theatre and
established as a bookshop in 1957.
There is close to 20,000
antiquarian and second-hand
books with good ranges of
topography, history, performing
arts, literature and maritime. The
stock is very much non-technical

and wants lists are welcomed. Printed ephemera and curios add to the appeal of an interesting emporium.

COFFEE HOUSE BOOKSHOP
139 Greenwich South Street
SE10 8NX
081 692 3885
M-Sat 10-5.30, closed Th

A small stock of second-hand books, mainly paperbacks, with a leaning towards fiction and pop music. In addition to the books, there is a jumble of magazines, comics, postcards, sheet music, records, tapes, coins and jewellery.

MARCET BOOKS
4A Nelson Road
Greenwich
SE10 9JB
081 853 5408
M-Sun 10.30-5.30

In an alley leading to the craft market. Maritime subjects and travel feature strongly in a pleasing shop conducive to browsing.

GREENWICH BOOKSHOP
37 King William Walk
SE10 9HU
081 858 5789
M-Sat 10.30-5.30, Sun 10-6

Second-hand books, new books cards and bargain books to tempt visitors to the Maritime Museum and the Cutty Sark.

POPULAR BOOK CENTRE
284 Lewisham High Street
SE13 6JZ
081 690 5110
M-Sat 9.45-4.45

A traditional old paperback exchange with the customary selection of cheap fiction and magazines.

COLLECTED WORKS
3 Melbourne Terrace
SE22 8RE
081 299 4195
M-Sat 10.15-6.15, W 10.15-1

Antiques, collecting, literary and genre fiction, history and art in this interesting shop. Glass, ceramics and antiques are on show and for sale.

BROMLEY BOOKSHOP
39-41 High Street
Bromley
BR1 1LE
081 313 0242
M-Sat 10-5

You will find this small bookshop at the rear of the High Street by an antique shop. The stock is mainly non-fiction with magazines and old postcards. They are located in a book buying area and maybe as a result there is always something new and interesting in the range carried.

SPORT

BOXING CRICKET FOOTBALL
GOLF HORSES

SPORTSPAGES
Caxton Walk
94-96 Charing Cross Road
WC2H 0JG
071 240 9604
M-Sat 9.30-7

Sportspages claims to be Britain's premier sports bookshop and to take sport seriously. To see the vast range of books and videos on all sports is to witness that this claim cannot be disputed. The area devoted to baseball alone is larger than the average sports section in a general bookshop. The shop blackboard is reminiscent of a betting shop with current results of sporting contests from around the world chalked up for all to see. A television in the corner plays tapes from the enormous selection and you are as likely to see black and white scenes of the glory days of Welsh rugby as you are World Series baseball. The collection of football fanzines is unrivalled as is the range of magazines. Fitness, physiology, training, how to play, writing on sports.......it is all here along with enthusiastic and authoritative help from sports fanatics. Signing sessions and author events by sports personalities are a feature at this mecca for fans. It is impossible to walk past without seeing devotees buying, browsing or staring misty eyed at the framed print of Stanley Matthews in mid body-swerve.

BOOKS ON SPORT
LILLYWHITES
Ground Floor
Piccadilly Circus
SW1Y 4QF
071 915-4000
M-F 9.30-7, Sat 9.30-6

Within this internationally known sports store selling a huge range of sports clothing and equipment there is a sports bookshop on the ground floor. It stocks a range comprehensive enough to rival Sportspages from archery to yachting. Sporting calendars and a staggering collection of over one thousand videos complete this sporting delight. The fitness section is particularly strong.

THE LORD'S SHOP
Marylebone Cricket Club
Lord's Cricket Ground
NW8 8QN
071 289 1611
M-F 10-5 off season
M-F 10-5 and every match day in season

Cricket, cricket and more cricket. As good a range of new cricket publications from around the world as you will find anywhere, along with Lord's and MCC merchandise from sun hats to key rings. Combine a visit to the shop with a look at the Lord's Museum.

J W McKENZIE BOOKSELLER
12 Stoneleigh Park Road
Ewell
KT19 0QT
081 393 7700
M-F 9-5, Sat 10-1

Pleasures of life can be hard to find and this cricket specialist, tucked away off a busy suburban road, in the deep so to speak, is no exception. You need to be a connoisseur and collector to seek out and appreciate J W McKenzie, a cricket book specialist for over 20 years. It is the only shop of its kind and has customers all over the world united by a love of cricket. Whether you are looking for a county history, an obscure collection of cricket writing or the rarest of antiquarian volumes from the earliest days of lore you will find the answer here. To acquire an understanding of the depth of specialisation and knowledge pick up The Bibliography of Cricket from year dot to 1980. It is heavier than Ian Botham's bat, listing every book published on cricket. It was compiled with the help of Mr McKenzie who also publishes the occasional limited edition and 3-4 fascinating catalogues every year.

SARAH BADDIEL GOLFIANA GALLERY
B12 Grays Antique Market
Davies Mews
W1Y 1AR
071 408 1239
M-F 10-6

One of the stalls in the market with second-hand books on golf, motoring and juvenilia. Golf is the speciality with a small range of ephemera, clubs, and prints. Tin and diecast toys sit alongside the books on motoring.

ROWLAND WARDS
At Holland & Holland
31 Bruton Street
W1X 8JS
071 499 4411
M-F 9.30-5.30

Holland & Holland are gun makers established in the last century. A bookshop is accommodated amongst the weaponry and associated paraphernalia. The stock is a small but selective range of new and antiquarian books. The subjects covered are shooting. field sports, big game hunting and places to go to hunt animals.

FARLOW'S OF PALL MALL
5 Pall Mall
SW1Y 5NP
071 839 2423
M-F 9-6, Sat 9-4

Primarily concerned with the supply of equipment and attire for country pursuits, shooting and fishing. There is a collection of appropriate books to assist the hunter to locate, bag and deal with the catch.

TURF NEWSPAPERS
19 Clarges Street
W1Y 7PG
071 499 4391
M-F 9-5, Sat 9-12

Just a few minutes walk from Green Park off the north side of Piccadilly. It was founded in 1944 as a headquarters for bookstalls operating at racecourses in South East England. Horse racing and breeding are the main subjects with allied topics also covered, along with table mats, prints and videos of races. There is a mail order facility and subscription service for newspapers and periodicals.

THE HORSEMAN'S BOOKSHOP
1 Lower Grosvenor Place
SW1W 0EL
071 834 5606
M-F 9-5.30, Sat 9-1

The stock here is both specialised and comprehensive and covers all subjects equine. Established in 1926 the business pedigree is impressive as is the intention to carry all current books in the country, and the main ones from overseas. Although the majority of books are new, there is a selection of second-hand and antiquarian books, mainly obtained in response to a specific customer request. Amongst the loyal customers is HM The Queen

and HRH The Duke of Edinburgh as the shop holds a Royal Warrant. Riding, racing, breeding, driving, polo, equestrian and veterinary books are here with cards, calendars and gifts.

SPORTING BOOKSHOP
4, 5, 6 Antique City Market
98 Wood Street
Walthamstow
E17 3HX
081 521 9803
M-Sat 9.30-5, Th closed

An interesting choice of second-hand and antiquarian books on a wide range of sports. Football books and programmes, cricket and boxing are the main specialisations. Curiously there is a selection of film magazines.

TRANSPORT & MILITARY

AVIATION BUSES MARITIME MILITARY
MODELLING MOTORING RAILWAYS TRAMS

THE AVIATION BOOKSHOP
656 Holloway Rd
N19 3PD
071 272 3630
M-Sat 9.30-5.30

Close to Archway tube, this shop
specialises exclusively in
Aviation, the only such shop in
Europe. The business was started
in 1948 and is well established as
an authority on all topics
aeronautical. They stock both new
and second-hand books along
with a vast range of magazines,
technical plans, videos, posters
and photographs. The interior is
decorated with expertly made
model aircraft and attracts visiting
enthusiasts from all over the
world. A complete catalogue of all
new books is produced twice
annually, the second-hand stock is
too large to list. Mail order and
booksearch facilities complete a
finely tuned package of services.

IMPERIAL WAR MUSEUM
Lambeth Road
SE1 6HZ
071 416 5000
M-Sun 10-6

An attractive shop located inside
one of London's top tourist
attractions. Over 2000 books are
stocked on twentieth century
military history and conflict. The
emphasis is firmly on the two

major conflagrations but
contemporary military conflicts
and issues are also covered. What
sets this shop apart from other
militaria specialists in London is
the comprehensive selection of
educational titles on the two
World Wars. The range of gift
products retains a military theme,
with cassettes and videos also.

FRANCIS EDWARDS
13 Great Newport Street
WC2H 7JA
071 379 7669
M-Sat 9-9, Sun 12-8

A small stock of antiquarian and
second-hand books on military
and maritime subjects amongst a
more general range of books.

CAPTAIN O M WATTS
45 Albermarle Street
W1X 4BT
071 493 4633
M-F 9-6, Thu 9-7, Sat 9-5

A shop selling equipment and all
items to do with yachting and
boating. The small selection of
books on sailing covers technical
matters, navigation and boat
building.

G L GREEN NAVAL & MARITIME BOOKSHOP
104 Pitshanger Lane
Ealing
W5 1QX
081 997 6454
By appointment only

Ironically the sea is more open than this specialist and is generally more welcoming. If you do book an appointment here you will see an extensive range of over 5000 books, journals, magazines and postcards on all matters naval and maritime. A booksearch service is offered and catalogues are issued monthly. Computer generated quotations can be provided on requested books.

BROWN & PERRING
36-44 Tabernacle Street
EC2A 4DT
071 253 4517
M-F 9-5.15

They are specialist navigation chart agents and stock Admiralty publications along with other books on commercial maritime pursuits.

KELVIN HUGHES
145 Minories
EC3N 1NH
071 709 9076
M-F 9-6

Established in the first half of the last century as a service to those involved in commercial shipping and sailing. Clothing and equipment dominates and there is a selection of maritime books and charts.

THE LONDON YACHT CENTRE
13 Artillery Lane
E1 7LP
071 247 0521
M-F 9-6, Sat 9-1.30

Founded in 1957 as a general yacht chandlers and now one of the leaders in the country. It is only two minutes walk from Liverpool Street station and carries an extensive range of yachting hardware, electronic equipment and clothing. There is a selective range of associated publications on technical aspects of yachting and cruising, charts and pilots.

ANTHONY J SIMMONDS
23 Nelson Road
Greenwich
SE10 9JB
081 853 1727
M-Sat 10-6 also Sun in Nov, Dec

Other bookshops in the area have a section of maritime books but this shop specialises exclusively in new, second-hand and antiquarian books on the subject of naval and maritime history, yachting and voyages. It is appropriately located between the Naval Museum and the local parish church in a fine listed building. The stock is varied and ranges from 50p to £5000 and you can be assured of expert and friendly service. Two specialist catalogues are produced every year and sent to customers world wide, many of whom discovered the shop on a visit to the museum.

NATIONAL ARMY MUSEUM
Royal Hospital Road
SW3 4HT
071 730 0717
M-Sun 10-5.30

Pleasantly located adjacent to the Royal Hospital in Chelsea. The shop carries a small range of books on all aspects of military history and soldiering through the ages and operates as a gift shop to visitors to this fascinating museum.

GORDON ROAD BOOKSHOP
36 Gordon Road
Enfield
EN2 0PZ
081 366 0722
Tu, Th-Sat 10-5

Has developed a specialisation in mainstream second-hand military books since the acquisition of stock in 1990 from the now closed Arms & Militaria bookshop. There is also a wide range of second-hand books, especially affordable paperbacks, on other general subjects.

W E HERSANT LTD
THE CHOLMELEY BOOKSHOP
228 Archway Road
N6 5AZ
081 340 3869
M-Sat 10-1, 2-5 closed Thu

A military and naval specialist of 70 years standing selling new and second-hand books a few minutes walk from Highgate tube. They can also be seen at military and wargaming events.

ISO PUBLICATIONS
137 Westminster Bridge Road
SE1 7HR
071 261 9588
M-F 9.30-5.30, Sat 10-3

A small scruffy shop stuffed with all manner of books on mass destruction, weaponry and war. In other words, all things military, aviation and naval. The first thing you notice is lots of signs saying 'no bags past here', a sure reflection on the type of browser attracted by this specialisation. There is a good selection on modelling and model engineering. ISO is also a publisher of military books.

CHATERS
8 South Street
Isleworth
TW7 7BG
081 568 9750
M-Sat 9-5.30

This premises has been a bookshop for over 60 years and started life selling second-hand fiction. In the late fifties it began to deal solely in all forms of transport and entered the next decade as a specialist dedicated to motoring and motorcycling. Clive Stroud, the current manager, succeeded his father who made the business. The expert continuity shines through. They aim to have in stock every book in print and most of those that are no longer available new. All UK published books are carried with a large American selection and other European titles where the home grown is not sufficient. The range of videos is unrivalled and the best in Europe. The out of print section on the first floor accommodates over 200 feet of shelving packed with the best stock anywhere. Behind the scenes can be found back issues of motoring magazines dating from the very first issues at the turn of the century. Look at bound volumes of early Motorsport and smell the racing oil. The basement storeroom contains technical treasures in the form of workshop manuals and handbooks. Chaters repeatedly comes to the rescue by providing the missing link to restorers and owners and the motoring press frequently use the basement as a reference source. The area in which this shop differentiates itself from its competitors is in the other services it provides. All stock records are held on computer, and have been collected for over 35 years. The book search service is therefore all embracing and in the rare event of not being able to meet a customer demand from stock, the request is held on the waiting list and as soon as the book becomes available the customer is notified. A same day service operates for mail and fax orders and is actively used by the world wide customer base. The regular catalogues of new and in-print books are eagerly awaited

by motoring aficionados. A complete list of out of print books is available for a nominal charge. Circuit shops operate at Brands Hatch, Oulton Park and Silverstone on race days. Other major motoring events, such as the Essen Show, are attended by the mobile bookstall courtesy of a Mercedes van.

MOTOR BOOKS
33, 34, 36 St Martins Court
WC2N 4AL
071 836 5376/6728/3800
M-W, F 9.30-5.30, Th 9.30-7,
Sat 10.30-1, 2-5.30

Started at number 33 in the late fifties to service motoring enthusiasts. Aviation, military, railways and maritime subjects have been added over the years as shops next door to the original have been acquired. They claim to be world leaders in current books on motoring, railways, maritime, military and aviation. Ten minutes in the shop with John Lello, the manager for over 35 years, will do much to convince you of this proud boast. It is the only place that you will find every current workshop manual and has been a prime mover in the production of reprints of long unavailable technical manuals. The range of railway books and videos is enormous and includes the largest selection on American railways in one place outside and inside the USA. There is a genuine 50,000 books here and although the specialist catalogues cover a lot of ground, a personal visit will astound the enthusiast with the bewildering range.

THE BOOKING HALL
7 Charlotte Place
W1P 1AQ
071 255 2123
M-F 11-3, 4-7, Sat 11-5

In a small pedestrian area between Charlotte Place and Newman Street just minutes from Goodge Street tube. The Booking Hall is known to dedicated railway fans who can find over 2000 titles on their passion. Railways of the British Isles is the main area of expertise along with the London Underground, Buses and Trams. Both new and second-hand books are stocked. The selection of ephemera is fascinating with leaflets, timetables and old magazines. A station board and nameplate may be seen occasionally. The owner was previously involved in the model railway business and the film industry, hence the videos and second-hand model items.

LONDON TRANSPORT MUSEUM SHOP
The Piazza
Covent Garden
WC2E 7BB
071 379 6344
M-Sun 10-5.45

Simply the best and most reliable service operated by London Regional Transport. The museum houses a collection of historic buses, trams, trolley buses and underground trains with a fascinating range of ephemera and art. The shop reflects the museum contents and carries around 500 titles on road and rail transport in general with a special emphasis on London past and present. Transport art books are a speciality. The shop has a treasure trove of gift ideas based on London Transport's unique poster images. Amongst the Underground souvenirs are silk ties and bow ties overprinted with the network map.

IAN ALLAN TRANSPORT BOOKSHOP
45 Lower Marsh
SE1 7RG
071 401 2100
M-Sat 9-5.30

Ian Allan is a train spotter whose passion led him into becoming a leading specialist publisher and bookseller. Their 50th anniversary was celebrated in 1992. Transport on the road, on track and rail, in the air and on the water is covered here in its entirety. The inevitable overlap into matters military is also handled comprehensively. Whether your need is for the 'London Underground Handbook' or 'Industrial Estates Within the M25', you'll be sure to find it here. There are model trains, cars, magazines, catalogues and a notice board to disseminate information to the faithful. The range of railway videos is worthy of note as is the selection of railway station names 'fridge magnets.

WORLD OF TRANSPORT
37 Heath Road
Twickenham
TW1
081 891 3169
Tu-Sat 9.30-5.30

A transport specialist in more
ways than one. The shop is close
to the railway station and covers
air, road and rail transport to the
tune of 4000 titles as well as
videos on the same topics.
Individual subject catalogues are
produced and a world wide mail
order service operates. In addition
to books, they have expanded into
the travel industry by arranging
accommodation, flights, car hire
and travel insurance.

THE SMOKEBOX
3 Cromwell Road
Kingston
KT2 6RF
081 549 9700
Tue-Sat 10.30-6

A small bookshop aptly named as
it feels like the inside of a
matchbox, one with the spent
matches stuffed back inside. The
second-hand stock of books and
magazines is all over the place, in
terms of display and aspects of
transport. Unless you're the most
determined enthusiast you'll need
to rely on the resident expertise to
find whatever you're looking for.

LENS OF SUTTON
4 Westmead Road
Sutton
SM1 4JT
081 642 0981
M-Sat 11-6, Wed- 11-2

A corner shop, in business since
1929, between Sutton and
Carshalton. A comprehensive
range of over 5000 books and
periodicals on buses, trams and
railways. Titles as diverse as
'Steam in Australia' to 'Railways
through the Chilterns' hark back to
the glorious days of steam and
trams when Southern Region and
the M25 had not even been
dreamed of. To complement the
specialist books there is a number
of Dinky, Matchbox, and Corgi
models of cars, trucks and buses.

FALCONWOOD TRANSPORT AND MILITARY BOOKSHOP
5 Falconwood Parade
The Green
Welling
DA16 2PL
081 303 8291
Th-Sat 9.30-5.30

Second-hand books and
magazines galore on aviation,
motoring, railways and maritime
transport. There is also a range of
military titles, mainly 1914 on.
Catalogues are issued
periodically. This shop can be
difficult to find without the use of
an A-Z or local knowledge. It is in
a small shopping parade off the
A2.

TRAVEL

THE TRAVELLERS BOOKSHOP
25 Cecil Court
WC2N 4EZ
071 836 9132
M-F 11-7, Sat 11-6.30

A voyage of discovery for the armchair traveller and intrepid explorer alike. The layout, over two floors, is a little confusing, like the surface of the globe. The mix of antiquarian books for collectors, new travel guides and maps works well. There is a huge range of old Baedekers, Ward Lock red guides, Blue Guides and Murray books for those who collect or seek travel information in its original form. Specialist catalogues are issued occasionally on Baedekers. The range of new guides in the basement is as good as anywhere. Some of the second-hand books, complete with useful first hand annotations in the margins, provide a cost saving opportunity to engage in an enjoyable form of recycling. The notice board for travellers is well used and scribbled notes frequently pose questions such as '...is it possible to go by boat from India to China?' Suggestions and route details from kindred spirits will appear in reply within hours.

STANFORDS
12-14 Long Acre
WC2E 9LP
071 836 1321
Tu- F 9-7, M, Sat 10-6

STANFORDS AT BRITISH AIRWAYS
156 Regent Street
W1R 5TA
071 434 4744
M-Sat 9-6 winter, 'till 7 summer

The name of Stanfords has been synonymous with maps and travel since Edward Stanford, cartographer and printer, started the business in 1852. It is the world's premier source of maps and guides and whether you're crossing the Nullabor or in the deserts of Namibia it is likely that the map or guide that got you there came from Stanfords. In the way that Trailfinders employ young adventurers as travel consultants, Stanfords use the well travelled as sales staff to offer advice from first hand experience. It is not possible to fully explain the diversity of the stock here, suffice to say that if it's been mapped or written it will be here. In addition to books and maps, products associated with travel such as journals and compasses can be found. The mail order service serves customers all over the world, regular specialist catalogues are issued and the programme of events and signings ever popular.

**BERNARD SHAPERO RARE
BOOKS**
80 Holland Park Avenue
W11 3RE
071 493 0876
M-F 10-7, Sat 10-5

A well established antiquarian
specialist occupying attractive
premises. Voyages and travel and
associated literature are the main
specialisation. Natural History
and architecture are well covered
within the fine all round selection.

**YOUTH HOSTELS
ASSOCIATIONSERVICES**
14 Southampton Street
WC2E 7HY
071 836 8541
M-W, Sat 10-6, Thu, F 10-7

A shop for all outdoor clothing
and equipment with a good
section of maps and travel guides.
All Youth Hostel Association
publications and handbooks can
be found here.

GEOGRAPHERS
44 Grays Inn Road
WC1X 8LR
071 242 9246
M-F 9-5

The shop window for the
publisher of the well known A-Z
guides, maps and atlases. The
complete range, covering more
than just the capital, is to be found
here.

R & P REMINGTON
18 Cecil Court
WC2N 4HE
071 836 9771
M-F 10-5

Antiquarian and second-hand
books on voyages and travel with
some engravings. Dark and dingy
and compared to The Travellers
Bookshop opposite, positively
uninspiring.

DAUNT BOOKS
83 Marylebone High Street
W1M
071 224 2295
M-Sat 9-7.30

Natural light pours through the
skylights running down the
centre of this attractive shop. The
books are arranged by country so
that all those relating to one
particular country are found in
one place. Guides sit alongside
books on the food, culture and
fiction of the country, providing a
complete and unique selection.
This common sense strategy
benefits the customer and all
travel sections should be ordered
this way. The range of titles on the
British Isles is arranged by county
and city. There is also a selection
of new and general books.

BARBARA GRIGOR-TAYLOR
15 Frith Street
W1V 5TS
071 287 3721
M-F 10-6, Sat by appointment

The owner cut her teeth on
bookselling in San Francisco over

thirty years ago and has always specialised in voyages and travel. The shop is on the first floor above Soho's finest remaining neo-gothic shop frontage. There are about 5000 antiquarian and second-hand titles on polar exploration, mountaineering, maritime history, voyages, the Pacific and Asia. In addition to the normal services of mail order and catalogues, there is a consultancy service for appraisals, formation of collections and commission bidding.

TRAILFINDERS
194 Kensington High Street
W8 7RG
071 938 3999
M-Sat 9-6

At the heart of the High Street, an all in one travel emporium will give you expert advice, book your ticket, stab your arm and sell you the right book. All the popular guides are here along with maps, medical kits and phrase books. The Earl's Court Road branch stocks tents, money belts and rucksacks.

THE TRAVEL BOOKSHOP
13 Blenheim Crescent
W11 2EE
071 229 5260
M-F 10-6, Sat 10-5.30

Concentrating on all literature pertaining to travel: fiction, guides, languages, biography, history, anthropology, natural history and children's titles. The shop was founded in the late

seventies well before the explosion of travel publications in the 1980's. The range of stock includes new, second-hand and out of print books. All books are grouped under the country to which they relate. Non-book products include world music tapes and CDs, globes, videos and magazines. Book lists are available, a quarterly catalogue issued and an out of print booksearch service to locate the hard to find.

LONDON TOURIST BOARD SHOP
Victoria Station forecourt
SW1V 1JU
071 730 3450
M-Sun 8-7, Sun 8-5 in winter

Occupying a strategic corner of this busy station is a selection of popular and essential guides on London and the UK for the visitor. London souvenirs from ashtrays to T-shirts are sold along with essentials such as stamps and phonecards.

NOMAD BOOKS
781 Fulham Rd
SW6
071 736 4000
M 10-9, Tu-F 9-9, Sat 10-6

On cosmopolitan Fulham Road located on the corner of St Maur Road just a few minutes walk from Parsons Green tube. Nomad Books has told the recession to take a hike and has recently moved into this bigger and better site. One floor is devoted to travel which is the main specialisation, and the atmosphere coupled with the excellent range encourages daydreaming along mountain paths in New Zealand or drifting down the Zambesi. As well as being a genuine travel specialist this is also a fine example of a local neighbourhood bookshop with children's books close behind travel. The selection of contemporary fiction paperbacks is good with other popular general subjects completing the range. An innovative newsletter on travel and children's books is produced and this is likely to be further developed once Harriet and Andrew Currie have settled into the new premises.

THE NATIONAL MAP CENTRE
22-24 Caxton Street
SW1H 0QU
071 222 2466
M-F 9-5

Great Britain's premier Ordnance Survey agent. Whether a suburb, town or county in the UK, the map can be found here. In addition to motoring and touring maps, street plans, travel guides and wall maps there is a specialist service for professionals and business. Superplan, a new facility from Ordnance Survey, provides instant print-outs and plots from A4 to A0 at a choice of scales from 1:200 to 1:5000.

GEOGRAPHIA
58 Ludgate Hill
EC4M 7HX
071 248 3554
M-F 9-5.15

If it's a map you want, in any form, but especially flat sheet or laminated, then this is one of the places to call. That is if you haven't already been to Stanfords or The National Map Centre. Dillons Bookstores is the latest in a long series of owners.

WOMEN

SILVER MOON WOMEN'S BOOKSHOP
64-68 Charing Cross Road
WC2H 6BB
071 836 7906
M-Sat 10-6.30

One of the few interesting specialists on a bookish street occupied largely by unimaginative second-hand merchants. Jane Cholmeley and Sue Butterworth started this business at number 68 in 1984 and have recently expanded into two shops next door. Silver Moon is now Europe's largest women's bookshop, with close to 10,000 books of women's literature and non-fiction by and about women. The range of other products is not as wide as Sisterwrite in Camden, but the lesbian selection is the best in the country. Women's music, on CD and tape is stocked. The mail order business is very active and specialist catalogues are available. Events, readings and signing sessions are held regularly and are always well attended.

WOMEN'S PRESS BOOK CLUB
34 Great Sutton Street
EC1V 0DX
071 253 0009
M-F 9.30-5.30 (mail order only)

This is a mail order book club and not a bookshop. For over ten years it has claimed to be the

world's only mail order book club specialising in recently published good books by women authors. A catalogue detailing around 150 books, plus at least 20 new titles, is issued quarterly. In addition, the 'In Touch' section carries news of relevant conferences, courses, an information exchange and book search service. The international membership is ten thousand strong and they enjoy discounts ranging from a minimum of 15% to a massive 70% off usual shop prices on every book in the catalogue.

SISTERWRITE BOOKSHOP
190 Upper Street
N1 1RQ
071 226 9782
M-Sat 10-6, Th 10-7

This co-operative women's book and craft shop serves the community and beyond with a comprehensive range of titles. Subjects from lesbian fiction to women's studies, books on disabilities and green issues. Books for children, older women, Jewish and Black women. The collective is run by a multi-racial group of women and it is stressed that all books stocked are positive about women. Creative writing workshops are on offer, bookstalls can be arranged for conferences and events and libraries and schools are supplied. A monthly booklist of new books, including American imports, is available by subscription. There is a wide range of arts and crafts with stylish gifts for feminists and lesbians all sourced from women artists and craftswomen. Much more than a bookshop, it is an information point and community centre. Relevant, current and positive.

OTHER BOOKSHOPS

Most of the large general bookstores have sections devoted to women's issues, but cannot claim to specialise in this area. The bookshops detailed in this section of the guide are devoted exclusively to books for women. The majority of bookshops included in the **POLITICS & SOCIAL SCIENCES** section also carry large ranges of books on women's issues.

SHOP INDEX

ACCADEMIA ITALIANA, 65
ACME COMIC SHOP, 56
ACUMEDIC CENTRE, 103
AFRICA BOOK CENTRE, 59
J. AISENTHAL, 135
AL HODA, 66
AL KASHKOOL BOOKSHOP, 67
AL SAQI BOOKS, 67
AL-NOOR BOOKSHOP, 67
ALAN BRETT, 22
ALHANI INTERNATIONAL, 67
ALL SAINTS BOOKSHOP, 10
ALPHA BOOK EXCHANGE, 142
ANGEL BOOKSHOP, 86
ANN CREED BOOKS, 22
ANTHONY C. HALL, 63
ANTHONY J SIMMONDS, 153
ANY AMOUNT OF BOOKS, 138
ARCADE BOOKSHOP, 84
ARCHIVE BOOKS, 145
ARMY & NAVY, 81
ARTHUR PROBSTHAIN, 61
ASH RARE BOOKS, 15
ASIAN BOOKSHOP, 60
AT THE SIGN OF THE
DRAGON, 56
ATLANTIS BOOKSHOP LTD, 102
ATOMIC COMICS, 57
AUSTRALIAN BOOKSHOP, 62
AUSTRALIAN GIFT SHOP, 61
AVALON COMICS, 56
AVENUE BOOKSHOP, 11
AVIATION BOOKSHOP, 152

BAINES BOOKSHOP, 88
BALLANTYNE & DATE, 20
BANKERS BOOKS, 31
BARBARA GRIGOR-TAYLOR,
159
BARBARA STONE, 17
BARBICAN BUSINESS BOOK
CENTRE, 32
BARBICAN MUSIC SHOP, 118

BATTERSEA ARTS CENTRE, 27
BAYSWATER BOOKS, 139
BBC SHOP, 79
BBC WORLD SHOP, 115
BEAUMONT'S BOOKS, 83
BECKENHAM BOOKSHOP, 94
BECKETT'S BOOKSHOP, 83
BELL'S BOOKSHOP, 83
BELL, BOOK & RADMALL, 99
BELSIZE BOOKSHOP, 86
BENEDICTS BOOKSHOP, 97
BERGER AND TIMS, 81
BERNARD QUARITCH LTD, 13
BERNARD SHAPERO RARE
BOOKS, 159
BERTRAM ROTA, 99
BHAVANS BOOKSHOP, 64
BIBLE BOOKSTORE, 131
S K BILTCLIFFE BOOKS, 16
BIRD AND WILDLIFE BOOKS,
75
BLOOMSBURY WORKSHOP, 99
BOLINGBROKE BOOKSHOP, 82
BONAVENTURE, 144
BOOK BARGAINS LTD, 80
BOOK CELLAR, 94
BOOK CENTRE, 92
BOOKCASE
        Waterloo Rd, 84
        Ludgate Hill, 85
BOOKING HALL, 156
BOOKMARK BOOKSHOP, 147
BOOKMARKS, 125
BOOKPLACE, 121
BOOKS & CO, 89
BOOKS AND THINGS, 28
BOOKS *etc*, 34
        London Wall, 30
BOOKS FOR A CHANGE, 74
BOOKS FOR CHILDREN, 51
BOOKS FOR COOKS, 70
BOOKS FROM INDIA, 65
BOOKS NIPPON, 66

BOOKS OF BLACKHEATH, 84
BOOKS ON ISLAM, 134
BOOKSAVE, 87
BOOKSHOP
  Virginia Water, 90
  Ruislip, 91
  Loughton, 93
BOOKSHOP DULWICH
VILLAGE, 84
BOOKSHOP ISLINGTON
GREEN, 86
BOOKSHOP BLACKHEATH, 147
BOOKSPREAD, 51
BOOKTREE, 70
BOOKWORLD, 92
R A BOON, 144
BOOSEY & HAWKES, 116
BOSWELL BOOKS & PRINTS, 66
BOURNEMOUTH ENGLISH
BOOKCENTRE, 96
BOUTLE AND KING, 24
BRIAN L BAILEY, 16
BRITISH LIBRARY BOOKSHOP,
73
BRITISH MEDICAL JOURNAL
BOOKSHOP, 2
BRITISH MUSEUM, 1
BROADWAY BOOKSHOP, 88
BROMLEY BOOKSHOP, 148
BROWN & PERRING, 153
BRUNEL UNIVERSITY
BOOKSHOP, 8
BUILDING BOOKSHOP, 20
BUSH BOOKS & RECORDS, 81
BUSINESS BOOKSHOP, 33
BUTTERWORTHS BOOKSHOP,
30

CAISSA BOOKS, 69
CALAMITY COMICS, 57
CAMBERWELL BOOKSHOP, 27
CANAAN CHRISTIAN
BOOKCENTRE, 133
CANNINGS, 89
CANONBURY BOOKSHOP, 52
CAPTAIN O M WATTS, 152

CATHOLIC TRUTH SOCIETY
BOOKSHOP, 128
CENTERPRISE BOOKSHOP, 123
CENTRE FOR PEACE
BOOKSHOP, 128
CHANGES BOOKSHOP, 104
CHAPPELL OF BOND STREET,
117
CHAPTER TWO, 136
CHARING CROSS ROAD
BOOKSHOP, 138
CHARLES HIGHAM, 129
CHARLOTTE ROBINSON, 100
CHATERS, 154
CHELSEA RARE BOOKS, 17
CHENER BOOKS, 84
CHESS AND BRIDGE LTD, 69
CHILDREN'S BOOK CENTRE, 51
CHILDREN'S BOOKSHOP, 53
CHILDREN'S BOOKSHOP IN
HARRODS, 51
CHOLMELEY BOOKSHOP, 154
CHORLEYWOOD BOOKSHOP,
92
CHRIS BEETLES, 25
CHRISTIAN BOOKS & MUSIC,
130
CHRISTIAN BOOKSHOP, 132
CHRISTOPHER EDWARDS, 16
CHURCH HOUSE, 130
CINEMA BOOKSHOP, 113
CIRCA, 145
CITY POLY BOOKSHOP, 5
CITY UNI BOOKSHOP, 4
J CLARKE-HALL LTD, 139
CLC BOOKSHOP, 131
CLEARING HOUSE, 139
CLIVE A BURDEN LTD, 75
COFFEE HOUSE BOOKSHOP,
148
COLISEUM SHOP, 113
COLLECTED WORKS, 148
COLLEGE BOOKSHOP
  Newham, 5
  St Marys, 7
  London College of
  Printing, 73

COLLETS RUSSIAN & EAST, 62
COLLINGE & CLARK, 12
COMIC SHACK, 57
COMPENDIUM BOOKSHOP, 124
COMYNS BOOKS, 145
CONSTANT READER
BOOKSHOP, 140
CONTEMP'ARY CERAMICS, 69
CORBETT'S BOOKSHOP, 91
CORNERSTONE, 132
COSMIC BOOKSHOP, 103
COUNTRYSIDE BOOKSHOP, 74
COUNTY BOOKSHOPS, 94
CROUCH END BOOKSHOP, 87
CROYDON BOOKSHOP, 142

DANCE BOOKS, 114
DAR AL DAWA, 68
DAR AL-TAQWA, 134
DAUNT BOOKS, 159
DAVENPORT'S MAGIC SHOP, 72
DAYBREAK BOOKS, 131
DEES OF STONELEIGH, 88
DEMETZY BOOKS, 15
DEPTFORD BOOKSHOP, 121
DERRICK NIGHTINGALE, 18
DESIGN COUNCIL BOOKSHOP, 24
DESIGN MUSEUM, 26
DICKENS HOUSE MUSEUM, 98
DILLONS THE BOOKSTORE, 36
   Arts Bookshop, 21
   Antiquarian, 13
   Gower Street, 77
   Ealing College, 3
   Science Museum, 6
   Egham, 8
   Children's & Educ, 50
   A R Mowbray, 128
DILLONS MEDICAL
BOOKSHOPS
   Charing Cross, 3
   Hammersmith, 4
   St Thomas', 5
DISCOUNT BOOKS CO, 79
DON KELLY BOOKS, 26

DOVER BOOKSHOP, 70
DRESS CIRCLE, 114
DULWICH BOOKS, 84
DULWICH COLLEGE
BOOKSHOP, 7

EAST END BOOKSHOP, 123
ECONOMIST BOOKSHOP, 32
ECONOMISTS BOOKSHOP, 120
EDWARD TERRY, 147
ELAINES, 92
ELGIN BOOKS, 81
ELIZABETH GANT, 18
EPPING BOOKSHOP, 93
ESPERANTO BOOKSHOP, 96
EUROCENTRE BOOKSHOP, 97
EUROPEAN BOOKSHOPS
LIMITED, 95
EXPORT MARKET INFO, 33

FACT AND FICTION, 79
FACULTY BOOKS, 9
FACULTY BOOKSHOP, 9
FAIRCROSS BOOKS, 144
FAITH HOUSE BOOKSHOP, 128
FALCONWOOD TRANSPORT
AND MILITARY BOOKSHOP, 157
FALKINER FINE PAPERS, 69
FANTASY CENTRE, 57
FARLOW'S OF PALL MALL, 150
FIELDERS BOOKSHOPS, 83
FINE BOOKS ORIENTAL, 61
FISHER AND SPERR, 18
FITZJOHNS BOOKS, 146
FOLK SHOP, 118
FOOD FOR THOUGHT, 12
G.W. FOOTE, 10
FORBIDDEN PLANET, 54
FORTUNE GREEN BOOKSHOP, 146
W.A. FOSTER, 143
FOUNTAIN BOOKS, 80
FOUR PROVINCES BOOKSHOP, 65
L N FOWLER & CO, 105

W & G FOYLE, 78
FRANCIS EDWARDS, 152
R.D. FRANKS, 71
F&R FREEDMAN, 94
FREEDOM PRESS BOOKSHOP, 123
FRENCH BOOKSHOP, 64
FRENCH'S THEATRE BOOKSHOP, 115
FREW MACKENZIE, 11
FRIENDS BOOK CENTRE, 136
FRONTLINE CHRISTIAN, 133

GABRIELS BOOKSHOP, 146
GAY'S THE WORD, 120
GENESIS BOOKS, 103
GEOGRAPHERS, 159
GEOGRAPHIA, 161
GLOUCESTER ROAD BOOKSHOP, 140
GOLDEN AGE, 70
GOLDEN COCKEREL, 1
GORDON RD BOOKSHOP, 154
GOSH! COMICS, 54
GRAHAM WYCHE, 88
GRANT & CUTLER, 95
GRAPHICALLY SPEAKING, 57
GRASS ROOTS, 59
GREEN INK BOOKS, 65
GREENS THE BOOKCELLAR, 79
GREENWICH BOOKSHOP, 148
GROWER BOOKS, 71
GUANGHWA LTD, 62

HAMLEYS BOOK DEPARTMENT, 50
HAMMICKS, 40
            Professional Books, 30
HAMMOND ROBERTS, 91
HAN-SHAN TANG LTD, 62
HAROLD T STOREY, 13
HARRINGTON BROS, 17
HARROW SCHOOL BOOKSHOP, 8
HATCHARDS, 36
            Piccadilly, 80

HAVERING CHRISTIAN CENTRE, 133
HAYES BOOKSHOP, 91
HAYWARD GALLERY SHOP, 26
HEALTHWISE BOOKSHOP, 103
HEATH EDUCATIONAL, 7
HEBREW BOOK & GIFT CENTRE, 134
HELLENIC BOOKSERVICE, 64
HENRY PORDES BOOKS, 138
HENRY SOTHERAN LTD, 14
G. HEYWOOD HILL LTD, 100
HIGHGATE BOOKSHOP, 86
HIGHWAY CHRISTIAN BOOKSHOP, 133
P J HILTON, 12
HISTORY BOOKSHOP, 10
HMSO BOOKS, 77
HOISANS BOOKS, 61
HOLBORN COLLEGE, 32
HOLLOWAY EXCHANGE, 146
HOLLOWAY STATIONERS, 87
HOLSTEIN CAMPBELL, 23
HORSEMAN'S BOOKSHOP, 151
W & A HOUBEN, 143
HOUSING CENTRE TRUST, 124
HOUSMANS BOOKSHOP, 124
HUNGARIAN BOOK AGENCY, 63

I T BOOKSHOP, 74
IAN ALLAN TRANSPORT BOOKSHOP, 156
IAN SHERIDAN'S BOOKSHOP, 18
IBIS BOOKSHOP, 88
ICA BOOKSHOP, 25
IL LIBRO, 17
IMPERIAL COLLEGE UNION, 5
IMPERIAL WAR MUSEUM, 152
INDEX BOOKCENTRE
            Charlotte St, 120
            Atlantic Rd, 122
INPUT SOFTWARE, 32
INSPIRATION, 104
INSTITUTE BOOKSHOP DIGBY STUART COLLEGE, 6

IRANIAN BOOKSHOP, 67
ISLAMIC BOOK CENTRE, 134
ISO PUBLICATIONS, 154

JAMBALA BOOKSHOP, 103
JAMES SMITH BOOKSELLERS, 93
JAPAN CENTRE BOOKSHOP, 66
JARNDYCE ANTIQUARIAN, 11
JERUSALEM THE GOLDEN, 135
JEWISH MEMORIAL COUNCIL , 134
JG NATURAL HISTORY, 76
JOHN BUCKLE BOOKS, 122
JOHN KEATS CORNER, 83
JOHN LEWIS, 51
JOHN MENZIES, 41
JOHN RANDALL, 61
JOHN SANDOE BOOKS, 100
JOHN THORNTON, 140
JOHN TROTTER BOOKS, 135
JONATHAN POTTER, 14
E. JOSEPH BOOKSELLERS, 14

KARNAC BOOKS, 9
KARNAK HOUSE, 120
KEITH FAWKES, 146
KELTIC LTD, 95
KELVIN HUGHES, 153
KENSINGTON MUSIC SHOP, 118
KER AND DOWNEY, 80
KEW BOOKSHOP, 90
KEW SHOP, 71
KILBURN BOOKSHOP, 125
KING'S BOOKS, 130
KIRKDALE BOOKSHOP, 85
KIWI FRUITS, 68

LA PAGE BOOKSHOP, 64
LABOUR PARTY BOOKSHOP, 122
LANGTON'S BOOKSHOP, 90
LAW NOTES BOOKSHOP, 32
LAW SOCIETY SHOP, 30

LCL INTERNATIONAL BOOKSELLERS, 96
LENS OF SUTTON, 157
LIBERTY, 23
LIBRARY BOOKSHOP, 9
LILLYWHITES, 149
LINGUAPHONE LANGUAGE CENTRE, 96
LION & UNICORN, 52
LITERARY GUILD, 79
LLOYDS OF KEW, 71
LONDON BUDDHIST, 127
LONDON CITY MISSION BOOKSHOP, 131
LONDON TOURIST BOARD, 160
LONDON TRANSPORT MUSEUM, 156
LONDON YACHT CENTRE, 153
LORD'S SHOP, 149
LOUIS BONDY, 11

MAGGS BROTHERS, 13
MAGHREB BOOKSHOP, 59
MANOR HOUSE BOOKS, 135
MARANATHA CHRISTIAN BOOKSHOP, 132
MARCET BOOKS, 148
MARCHMONT BOOKSHOP, 138
MARCHPANE, 50
MARLBOROUGH RARE BOOKS, 15
J W McKENZIE, 150
MARYLEBONE BOOKS, 8
MEGA-CITY COMICS, 56
D MELLOR & A L BAXTER, 15
MENCAP BOOKSHOP, 4
MENORAH PRINT & GIFT, 135
MERCURIUS, 103
MERCURY BOOKSHOP, 6
MERTON COLLEGE BOOKSHOP, 7
MESOIROH SEFORIM BOOKSHOP, 135
MICHAEL FINNEY, 18
MODERN BOOK COMPANY, 3
MORGANS, 88
MOTOR BOOKS, 155

A R MOWBRAY, 128
MUIRS BOOKSHOP, 92
MURDER ONE, 99
MUSEUM BOOKSHOP, 1
MUSEUM OF LONDON, 108
MUSEUM OF MANKIND, 3
MUSEUM OF THE MOVING
IMAGE, 117
MUSIC & VIDEO EXCHANGE,
139
MUSLIM BOOKSHOP, 134
MUSTARD SEED, 132
MUSWELL HILL BOOKSHOP, 87
MY BACK PAGES, 141
MYSTERIES NEW AGE CENTRE,
102

NASHRE KETAB, 67
NATIONAL ARMY MUSEUM,
154
NATIONAL MAP CENTRE, 161
NATIONAL PORTRAIT
GALLERY BOOKSHOP, 23
NATIONAL SCHIZOPHRENIC
FELLOWSHIP BOOKSHOP, 140
NATIONAL SECULAR SOCIETY,
10
NATURAL HISTORY MUSEUM,
75
NAVAL & MARITIME
BOOKSHOP, 153
NEAL STREET EAST, 60
NEW BEACON BOOKS, 59
NEW ERA BOOKS, 124
NEWHAM PARENTS CENTRE,
123
NOMAD BOOKS, 160
NORTHWOOD BOOKSHOP, 91
NOTTING HILL BOOKS, 139
NURSING BOOK SERVICE, 9
NW BOOKSHOP, 96

O.C.S. BOOKSHOP, 66
OASIS CHRISTIAN CENTRE, 133
OFFSTAGE THEATRE AND
FILM BOOKSHOP, 119

OLD TOWN BOOKS, 65
121 BOOKSHOP, 122
OPEN BOOK, 90
OPEN BOOKS, 7, 8
OPERATION HEADSTART, 60
OPPENHEIM AND CO., 81
ORBIS BOOKS (London) LTD, 63
OSTERLEY BOOKSHOP, 144
OWEN CLARK, 93
OWL BOOKSHOP, 52
OYEZ STATIONERY, 32

P C BOOKSHOP, 29
PADRE PIO BOOKSHOP, 128
PAN BOOKSHOP, 82
PARKS BOOKSHOP, 29
PASSAGE BOOKSHOP, 5
PATHFINDER BOOKSHOP, 120
PAUL ORSSICH, 68
PENDLEBURY'S BOOKSHOP,
131
PENGUIN BOOKSHOP
      City Lit, 2
      Covent Garden, 78
      Camden, 78
PHOTOGRAPHERS GALLERY,
22
PICKERING & CHATTO, 16
PIPELINE BOOKS, 78
PLANNING BOOKSHOP, 25
PLEASURES OF PAST TIMES,
114
PLUS BOOKS, 142
PMS BOOKSHOP LTD, 63
POETRY BOOK SOCIETY, 101
POLLOCKS TOY MUSEUM, 116
POPULAR BOOK CENTRE
      Rochester Row, 140
      Lewisham, 148
PORCUPINE BOOKCELLAR, 124
PRIMROSE HILL BOOKS, 85
PROTESTANT TRUTH SOCIETY
BOOKSHOP, 130
PSYCHIC SENSE BOOKSHOP,
104
PUFFIN CHILDREN'S
BOOKSHOP, 50

QUARTET BOOKSHOP, 117
QUEEN MARY & WESTFIELD COLLEGE, 5
QUINTO BOOKSHOP, 138

RAY'S JAZZSHOP, 114
READER'S DIGEST SHOP, 80
READERS DREAM, 57
REGENCY BOOKSHOP, 89
REGENT BOOKSHOP, 85
R & P REMINGTON, 159
RESPONSE BOOKSHOP, 140
RIBA BOOKSHOP, 23
RICHMOND BOOKSHOP, 143
RIPPING YARNS, 52
RIVERSIDE BOOKSHOP, 83
ROBBIES BOOKSHOP, 144
ROBERT CONNELLY, 2
ROE & MOORE, 20
ROGERS TURNER BOOKS, 19
ROUND ABOUT BOOKS, 93
ROWLAND WARDS, 150
ROYAL ACADEMY OF ART, 24
ROYAL INSTITUTE OF CHARTERED SURVEYORS, 33
ROYAL NATIONAL THEATRE BOOKSHOP, 117
ROYAL SHAKESPEARE COMPANY, 118
RUPOSHI BANGLA LTD, 60
RUSSELL RARE BOOKS, 13
RUSSIAN ORTHODOX CATHEDRAL BOOKSHOP, 130

S P C K, 129
SAM FOGG RARE BOOKS, 14
SANGORSKI & SUTCLIFFE, 15
SARAH BADDIEL, 150
SCEPTRE BOOKS, 10
SCHOTT MUSIC SHOP, 117
SCM BOOKROOM, 132
SCRIPTURE UNION, 129
SELFRIDGES LTD, 79
SERENDIP BOOKSHOP, 89
SHIPLEY SPECIALIST ART, 22
SILVER MOON BOOKSHOP, 162

L SIMMONDS, 85
SIMS, REED LTD, 16
SISTERWRITE BOOKSHOP, 162
SKINNY MELINK'S COMICS, 58
SKOLA BOOKS, 95
SKOOB BOOKS, 137
SKOOB ESOTERICA, 137
WH SMITH, 45
SMOKEBOX, 157
SOMA BOOKS, 59
SOUVENIR PRESS LTD, 77
SPINK & SON, 72
SPORTING BOOKSHOP, 151
SPORTSPAGES, 149
SPREAD EAGLE BOOKSHOP, 147
ST GEORGES HOSPITAL, 6
ST MARTIN-IN-THE-FIELDS, 129
ST PAULS, 127
ST. GEORGES GALLERY, 25
ST. PAUL MULTIMEDIA, 128
STAGE DOOR PRINTS, 113
STANFORDS, 158
STANLEY GIBBONS, 72
STATESIDE COMICS, 55
STEPHEN FOSTER, 28
STOKE NEWINGTON BOOKSHOP, 87
STUDIO BOOKS, 147
SURREY BOOKSHOP, 89
SWAN BOOKSHOP, 90
SWAN LIBRARIES, 93
SWANS BOOKSHOP, 142
SWEDENBORG SOCIETY, 136
SWISS COTTAGE BOOKS, 86

TATE GALLERY SHOP, 25
TEMPLE BAR BOOKSHOP, 78
THEY WALK AMONG US, 56
THOMAS HENEAGE ART, 25
TIMBUKTU BOOKS, 122
TINTIN SHOP, 55
TLON BOOKS, 7
TOOLEY, ADAMS & CO, 12
TOWER BOOKSHOP, 85
TRAILFINDERS, 160
TRAINER'S BOOKSHOP, 33

TRAVEL BOOKSHOP, 160
TRAVELLERS BOOKSHOP, 158
TRAVIS AND EMERY, 113
TRENT BOOKSHOP, 10
TRIANGLE BOOKSHOP, 20
TURF NEWSPAPERS, 151
TURKISH LANGUAGE BOOKS, 68
TURNERS BOOKSHOP, 88
TURRET BOOKSHOP, 98
TWO JAYS BOOKSHOP, 146

UKRAINIAN BOOKSHOP, 63
ULYSSES, 98
UNSWORTH, RICE & COE, 137
UPPER STREET BOOKSHOP, 119

VANBRUGH RARE BOOKS, 11
VANDELEUR ANTIQUARIAN, 17
VERMILION BOOKS, 77
VICTORIA & ALBERT MUSEUM SHOP, 26
VILLAGE BOOKSHOP
        Woodford Green, 93
        Belsize Lane, 101
VINTAGE MAGAZINE SHOP, 116
VIRDEE BROTHERS, 61
VIRGIN MEGASTORE, 115
VOLUME ONE, 42
VORTEX BOOKSHOP, 145

WAITE AND SONS, 93
WALDEN BOOKS, 145
WATERSTONE'S, 43
        Goldsmith's College, 6
        City Department, 31
        South Bank, 118
WATKINS BOOKS, 102
WEATHER WISE, 2
WELLSPRING BOOKSHOP, 1
WEST LONDON BOOKS, 81
WEYBRIDGE BOOKS, 90
WHETSTONE BOOKS, 145
WHITEHALL BOOKSHOP, 143

WHOLEFOOD BOOKS, 102
WILDY AND SONS, 32
WILLESDEN BOOKSHOP, 125
WISDOM BOOKS, 127
WITHERBY & CO LTD, 31
WOMEN & CHILDREN FIRST, 53
WOMEN'S PRESS, 162
WORDS WORTH BOOKS, 82
WORLD OF BOOKS, 138
WORLD OF DIFFERENCE, 74
WORLD OF TRANSPORT, 157

YING HWA, 62
YOUTH HOSTELS ASSOCIATION SERVICES, 159

ZENO BOOKSELLERS, 64
ZWEMMER
        Litchfield St, 21
        Charing Cross Road, 21
        OUP, 21
        OUP Music & Books, 113
        Whitechapel Gallery, 24

AREA INDEX

CENTRAL LONDON

WC 1

British Museum	Academic	1
BMJ Bookshop	Academic	2
Golden Cockerel	Academic	1
Museum Bookshop	Academic	1
Robert Connelly	Academic	2
Weather Wise	Academic	2
Avenue Bookshop	Antiquarian	11
Collinge & Clark	Antiquarian	12
Dillons Gower Street	Antiquarian	77
Frew Mackenzie	Antiquarian	11
Jarndyce	Antiquarian	11
Louis Bondy	Antiquarian	11
Vanburgh Rare Books	Antiquarian	11
Ballantyne & Date	Art & Design	20
Building Bookshop	Art & Design	20
Roe & Moore	Art & Design	20
Triangle Bookshop	Art & Design	20
PC Bookshop	Business	29
Parks	Business	29
Gosh! Comics	Com & Sci Fi	54
Forbidden Planet	Com & sci Fi	54
Arthur Probsthain	Countries	61
Australian Bookshop	Countries	62
Books from India	Countries	65
Boswell Books & Prints	Countries	66
Collets Eastern Europe	Countries	62
Fine Books Oriental	Countries	61
Four Provinces Books	Countries	65
Maghreb Bookshop	Countries	59
British Library Books	Crafts & Past'	73
Falkiner Fine Papers	Crafts & Past'	69
Grower Books	Crafts & Past'	71
IT Bookshop	Environment	74
Books *etc*	General	35
Dillons Gower Street	General	77
HMSO	General	77
Souvenir Press	General	77
Vermillion Books	General	77
LCL International	Languages	96
Bloomsbury Workshop	Literature	99
Dicken's House Mus	Literature	98

WC 1

Ulysses	Literature	98
Atlantis Bookshop	MBS	102
Cinema Bookshop	Perform' Arts	113
Gay's The Word	Social Sciences	120
Jewish Mem' Council	Religion	134
Swedenborg Society	Religion	136
Geographers	Travel	159
Marchmont Bookshop	Second-hand	138
Skoob Books	Second-hand	137
Skoob Esoterica	Second-hand	137
Unsworth, Rice & Co	Second-hand	137
World of Books	Second-hand	138

WC 2

Penguin City Lit	Academic	2
Food For Thought	Antiquarian	12
Harold T Storey	Antiquarian	13
P J Hilton	Antiquarian	12
Tooley, Adams & Co	Antiquarian	12
Alan Brett	Art & Design	22
Ann Creed Books	Art & Design	22
Dillons Art Bookstore	Art & Design	21
National Gallery	Art & Design	23
Photographers Gallery	Art & Design	22
A Zwemmer	Art & Design	21
Butterworths	Business	30
Law Notes Library	Business	32
Law Society	Business	30
Wildy & Sons	Business	32
Tintin Shop	Com & Sci Fi	55
Marchpane	Children's	50
Puffin Bookshop	Children's	50
Africa Book Centre	Countries	59
Al Hoda	Countries	66
Australian Gift Shop	Countries	61
Guanghwa Ltd	Countries	62
Neal Street East	Countries	60
Zeno Booksellers	Countries	64
Davenport's Magic	Crafts & Past'	72
Dover Bookshop	Crafts & Past'	70
Stanley Gibbons	Crafts & Past'	72
Books For A Change	Environment	74
World Of Difference	Environment	74
Books *etc* Covent Gdn	General	35
Books *etc* Charing X	General	35
Fact & Fiction	General	79
W & G Foyle	General	78
Hatchards Strand	General	37

WC 2			
	John Menzies	General	41
	Penguin Covent Gdn	General	78
	Penguin Camden	General	78
	Pipeline Books	General	78
	Temple Bar Bookshop	General	78
	Waterstone's Garrick	General	43
	Waterstone's Charing	General	43
	WH Smith Aldwych	General	47
	Bell, Book & Radmall	Literature	99
	Bertram Rota	Literature	99
	Murder One	Literature	99
	Turret Bookshop	Literature	98
	Mysteries New Age	MBS	102
	Watkins Books	MBS	102
	BBC World Shop	Perform' Arts	115
	Coliseum Shop	Perform' Arts	113
	Dance Books	Perform' Arts	114
	Dress Circle	Perform' Arts	114
	Pleasures Past Times	Perform' Arts	114
	Ray's Jazz Shop	Perform' Arts	114
	Stage Door Prints	Perform' Arts	113
	Travis & Emery	Perform' Arts	113
	Zwemmer OUP Music	Perform' Arts	113
	Economists Bookshop	Pol & Soc Sci	120
	St Martins in the Fields	Religion	129
	Any Amount of Books	Second-hand	138
	Charing Cross Rd Bk'	Second-hand	138
	Clearing House	Second-hand	139
	Henry Pordes	Second-hand	138
	Quinto Bookshop	Second-hand	138
	Sportspages	Sport	149
	Francis Edwards	Transport	152
	Motorbooks	Transport	155
	London Tran' Museum	Transport	156
	R & P Remington	Travel	159
	Stanfords	Travel	158
	Travellers Bookshop	Travel	158
	Youth Hostels Assoc	Travel	159
	Silver Moon Bookshop	Women	162
EC 1			
	City University	Academic	4
	Mencap Bookshop	Academic	4
	Boutle & King	Art & Design	24
	Witherby & Co	Business	31
	WH Smith Holborn	General	46
	Genesis Books	MBS	103
	CLC Bookshop	Religion	131

EC 1	Women's Book Club	Women	162
EC 2	City Poly	Academic	5
	Barbican Book Centre	Business	32
	Books *etc* London Wall	Business	30
	Parks Bookshop	Business	29
	Books *etc* Broadgate	General	34
	J Menzies Cheapside	Genera;	41
	J Menzies Old Broad St	General	41
	WH Smith Broadgate	General	48
	WH Smith Cheapside	General	48
	Barbican Music Shop	Perform' Arts	118
	Royal Shakespeare Co	Perform' Arts	118
	Brown & Perring	Transport	153
EC 3	Ash Rare Books	Antiquarian	15
	City dept Waterstone's	Business	31
	Books *etc* Fenchurch St	General	34
	Tower Bookshop	General	85
	Kelvin Hughes	Transport	153
EC4	Bankers Books	Business	31
	Hammick's Prof' Books	Business	30
	Oyez Stationery	Business	32
	Books Nippon	Countries	66
	Bookcase	General	85
	Books *etc* Fleet St	General	34
	L Simmonds	General	85
	Protestant Truth Soc'	Religion	130
	J Clarke-Hall	Second-hand	139
	Geographia	Travel	161

INNER LONDON

NORTH WEST

NW 1	Marylebone Books	Academic	8
	Nursing Book Service	Academic	9
	Stephen Foster	Art & Design	28
	Business Bookshop	Business	33
	Mega City Comics	Coms & Sci Fi	56
	Al Noor Bookshop	Countries	67
	Chess & Bridge Ltd	Crafts & Past'	69
	Primrose Hill Books	General	85
	Regent Bookshop	General	85
	Waterstone's	General	44
	Skola Books	Languages	95
	Acumedic Centre	MBS	103
	The Folk Shop	Perform' Arts	118
	Offstage Bookshop	Perform' Arts	119
	Compendium Books	Pol & Soc Sci	124
	Dar Al Taqwa	Religion	134
	Friends book Centre	Religion	136
	Charles Higham	Religion	129
	Islamic Book Centre	Religion	134
	Mustard Seed	Religion	132
	SPCK	Religion	129
	Archive Books	Second-hand	145
	Walden Books	Second-hand	145
NW 2	WH Smith	General	48
NW 3	Karnac Books	Academic	9
	Library Bookshop	Academic	9
	Belsize Bookshop	General	86
	Waterstone's	General	44
	WH Smith	General	47
	Village Bookshop	Literature	101
	Manor House Books	Religion	135
	Fitzjohns Books	Second-hand	146
	Gabriel's bookshop	Second-hand	146
	Holloway Book Exc'	Second-hand	146
	Keith Fawkes	Second-hand	146
NW 4	Faculty Bookshop	Academic	9
	WH Smith Brent Cross	General	46
	John Trotter Books	Religion	135

NW 5	Owl Bookshop	Children's	52
	Hellenic Book Service	Countries	64
NW 6	Swiss Cottage Books	General	86
	WH Smith Kilburn	General	48
	Changes Bookshop	MBS	104
	Kilburn Bookshop	Pol & Soc Sci	125
	Fortune Green Books	Second-hand	146
NW 7	WH Smith Mill Hill	General	48
NW 8	Lord's Shop	Sport	149
NW 10	Willesden Bookshop	Pol & Soc Sci	125
NW 11	John Lewis	Children's	51
	WH Smith Golders Gn	General	48
	J Aisenthal	Religion	135
	Jerusalem the Golden	Religion	135
	Menorah Centre	Religion	135

NORTH

N 1	Michael Finney	Antiquarian	18
	Canonbury Bookshop	Children's	52
	Angel Bookshop	General	86
	Islington Green Bks	General	86
	Upper Street Bkshop	General	119
	Housing Centre Trust	Pol & Soc Sci	124
	Housman's Bookshop	Pol & Soc Sci	124
	Porcupine Bookcellar	Pol & Soc Sci	124
	SCM Bookroom	Religion	132
	Sisterwrite	Women	162
N 3	Faculty Books	Academic	9
N 4	New Beacon Books	Countries	59
	Bookmarks	Pol & Soc Sci	125
	New Era Books	Pol & Soc Sci	124
	Books on Islam	Religion	134
	Muslim Bookshop	Religion	134
N 6	Fisher & Sperr	Antiquarian	18
	Ripping Yarns	Children's	52
	Highgate Bookshop	General	86
	Cholmeley Bookshop	Military	154
	Bonaventure	Second-hand	144

N 7	Fantasy Centre	Coms & Sci Fi	57
	Holloway Booksellers	General	87
	R A Boon Booksellers	Second-hand	144
N 8	Crouch End Bookshop	General	87
N 10	Children's Bookshop	Children's	53
	Muswell Hill Books	General	87
	WH Smith Mus' Hill	General	48
	Robbie's Bookshop	Second-hand	144
N 11	History Bookshop	Academic	10
N 12	Hatchards	General	38
	WH Smith	General	48
	Cornerstone	Religion	132
N 13	WH Smith Palmers Gn	General	48
N14	Trent Bookshop	Academic	10
	Booksave	General	87
N 15	Operation Headstart	Countries	60
N 16	Stoke Newington Bks	General	87
	Hebrew Book & Gifts	Religion	134
	Mesoiroh Seforim Bks	Religion	135
	Pendlebury's Books	Religion	131
	Circa	Second-hand	145
	Vortex Bookshop	Second-hand	145
N 18	Comyns Books	Second-hand	145
N 19	G W Foote	Academic	10
	Green Ink Bookshop	Countries	65
	Aviation Bookshop	Transport	152
N 20	Morgans	General	88
	Whetstone Books	Second-hand	145
N 21	Graham Wyche	General	88
N 22	WH Smith	General	46

EAST

E 1	Queen Mary College	Academic	5
	Zwemmer	Art & Design	24
	East End Bookshop	Pol & Soc Sci	123
	Freedom Press Bkshop	Pol & Soc Sci	123
	London Yacht Centre	Transport	153
E 2	Graphically Speaking	Coms & Sci Fi	57
E 2	Hungarian Book s	Countries	63
	Jambala Bookshop	MBS	103
	London Buddhist Ctr	Religion	127
E 6	Newham College Bks	Academic	5
	WH Smith	General	46
E 8	Turkish Books	Languages	68
	Round About Books	General	93
	Centreprise Bookshop	Pol & Soc Sci	123
E 11	Comic Shack	Coms & Sci Fi	57
E 12	Bible Bookstore	Religion	131
E 13	Newham Parents Ctr	Pol & Soc Sci	123
E 14	Trainer's Bookshop	Business	33
E 15	WH Smith	General	47
E 17	Sceptre Books	Academic	10
	Psychic Sense	MBS	104
	Wisdom Books	Religion	127
	Sporting Bookshop	Sport	151

SOUTH EAST

SE 1	St Thomas' Hospital	Academic	5
	Sangorski & Sutcliffe	Antiquarian	15
	Design Museum	Art & Design	26
	Hayward Gallery	Art & Design	26
	Parks Bookshop	Business	29
	London Printing Coll	Crafts & Past'	73
	The Bookcase	General	84
	Riverside Bookshop	General	83
	WH Smith	General	47
	Museum Mov' Image	Perform' Arts	117

SE 1	National Theatre	Perform' Arts	117
	Pathfinder Bookshop	Pol & Soc Sci	120
	London City Mission	Religion	131
	Imperial War Museum	Military	152
	ISO Publications	Military	154
	Ian Allan Bookshop	Transport	156
	My Back Pages	Second-hand	141
SE 3	Books of Blackheath	General	84
	Eurocentre Bookshop	Language	97
	Bookshop Blackheath	Second-hand	147
SE 3	Studio Books	Second-hand	147
SE 5	Passage Bookshop	Academic	5
	Camberwell Bookshop	Art & Design	27
	Wordsworth Books	General	82
SE 6	WH Smith	General	48
SE 8	Deptford Bookshop	Pol & Soc Sci	121
SE 9	Arcade Bookshop	General	84
	WH Smith Eltham	General	47
SE 10	Rogers Turner Books	Academic	19
	Women & Child' First	Children's	53
	Coffeehouse Bookshop	Second-hand	148
	Greenwich Bookshop	Second-hand	148
	Marcet Books	Second-hand	148
	Spread Eagle Books	Second-hand	147
	Anthony J Simmonds	Transport	153
SE 11	Soma Books	Countries	59
SE 12	Daybreak Books	Religion	131
SE 13	Skinny Melink's	Coms & Sci Fi	58
	WH Smith Lewisham	General	46
	Popular Bookcentre	Second-hand	148
SE 14	Goldsmith's College	Academic	6
SE 15	The Bookplace	Pol & Soc Sci	121
SE 16	WH Smith	General	48
SE 17	Labour Party Books	Pol & Soc Sci	122

SE 18	Mercury Bookshop	Academic	6
	WH Smith Woolwich	General	46
	Chapter Two	Religion	136
SE 21	Dulwich College	Academic	7
	Dulwich Village	General	84
	Dulwich Books	General	84
SE 22	Chener Books	General	84
	Collected Works	Second-hand	148
SE 24	121 Bookshop	Pol & Soc Sci	122
SE 26	Kirkdale Bookshop	General	85

SOUTH WEST

SW 1	Christopher Edwards	Antiquarian	16
	Pickering & Chatto	Antiquarian	16
	Sims, Reed Ltd	Antiquarian	16
	Chris Beetles	Art & Design	25
	Design Council	Art & Design	24
	ICA Bookshop	Art & Design	25
	Planning Bookshop	Art & Design	25
	St Georges Gallery	Art & Design	25
	Tate Gallery	Art & Design	25
	Thomas Heneage	Art & Design	25
	Economist Bookshop	Business	32
	Export Market Centre	Business	33
	Royal Chart 'Surveyors	Business	33
	Harrods	Children's	51
	Al Kashkool	Countries	67
	Han-Shan Tang	Countries	62
	John Randall	Countries	61
	Kiwi Fruits	Countries	68
	Spink & Son	Crafts & Past'	72
	Bird & Wildlife Bks	Environment	75
	Clive A Burden	Environment	75
	Army & Navy	General	81
	Berger & Tims	General	81
	Books *etc*	General	34
	Waterstone's Harrods	General	44
	WH Smith Sloane Sq	General	46
	Catholic Truth Society	Religion	128
	Church House Books	Religion	130
	Faith House Bookshop	Religion	128
	Padre Pio Bookshop	Religion	128
	St Pauls	Religion	128

SW 1	Farlow's of Pall Mall	Sport	150
	Horseman's Bookshop	Sport	151
	Lillywhites Books	Sport	149
	Sarah Baddiel	Sport	150
	London Tourist Board	Travel	160
	National Map Centre	Travel	161
	Popular Book Centre	Second-hand	140
SW 3	Barbara Stone	Antiquarian	17
	Chelsea Rare Books	Antiquarian	17
	Harrington Bros	Antiquarian	17
	IL Libro	Antiquarian	17
	Don Kelly Books	Art & Design	26
	Dillons Kings Rd	General	38
	Linguaphone Centre	Language	96
	John Sandoe	Literature	100
	National Army Mus'	Military	154
SW 4	Old Town Books	Countries	65
	Wordsworth Books	General	82
SW 5	Orbis Books	Countries	63
	Waterstone's	General	44
	Poetry Book Society	Literature	101
	Response Bookshop	Second-hand	140
SW 6	Books for Children	Children's	51
	Paul Orssich	Countries	68
	West London Books	General	81
	WH Smith	General	48
	Benedicts Bookshop	Languages	97
	Constant Reader Bks	Second-hand	140
	Nomad Books	Travel	160
SW 7	Dillons Science Mus'	Academic	6
	Imperial College	Academic	5
	Karnac Books	Academic	9
	V & A Museum	Art & Design	26
	Academia Italiana	Countries	65
	French Bookshop	Countries	64
	La Page Bookshop	Countries	64
	Natural History Mus'	Environment	75
	Oppenheim & Co	General	81
	Waterstone's	General	44
	Kensington Music	Perform' Arts	118
	Russian Orthodox	Religion	130
	Gloucester Road Bks	Second-hand	140

SW 8	Parks Bookshop	Business	29
	John Buckle Books	Pol & Soc Sci	122
SW 9	Acme Comic Shop	Com & Sci Fi	56
	Index Bookcentre	Pol & Soc Sci	122
	Timbuktu Books	Pol & Soc Sci	122
	Bible Bookstore	Religion	131
SW 10	Pan Bookshop	General	82
	John Thornton	Second-hand	140
SW 11	Battersea Arts Centre	Art & Design	27
	Avalon Comics	Coms & Sci Fi	56
	Bolingbroke Bookshop	General	82
SW 12	My Back Pages	Second-hand	141
SW 13	Beaumont Books	General	83
SW 14	Vandeleur Books	Antiquarian	17
	At Sign of the Dragon	Coms & Sci Fi	56
SW 15	Institute Bookshop	Academic	6
	Bell's Bookshop	General	83
	WH Smith	General	46
SW 16	JG Natural History Bks	Environment	76
	Wordsworth Books	General	82
	WH Smith	General	47
	Alpha Book Exchange	Second-hand	142
	My Back Pages	Second-hand	141
SW 17	St Georges Hospital	Academic	6
	Bookspread	Children's	51
	Ruposhi Bangla	Countries	60
	Beckett's Bookshop	General	83
	My Back Pages	Second-hand	141
	Swans Bookshop	Second-hand	142
SW 18	John Keat's Corner	General	83
	WH Smith	General	47
SW 19	Tlon Books	Academic	7
	The Booktree	Crafts & Past'	70
	Fielders Bookshop	General	83
	Volume One	General	42
	Waterstone's	General	44
	King's Books	Religion	130

SW 19	Nat' Schizophrenic	Second-hand	140
	Plus Books	Second-hand	142

WEST

W 1	Museum of Mankind	Academic	3
	Bernard Quaritich	Antiquarian	13
	Henry Sotheran	Antiquarian	14
	Jonathan Potter	Antiquarian	14
	E Joseph	Antiquarian	14
	Maggs Brothers	Antiquarian	13
	Marlborough Rare Bks	Antiquarian	15
	Russell Rare Books	Antiquarian	13
	Sam Fogg Rare Books	Antiquarian	14
	Holstein Campbell	Art & Design	23
	Libertys Book Dept	Art & Design	23
	RIBA Bookshop	Art & Design	23
	Royal Academy of Art	Art & Design	24
	Input Software	Business	32
	Dillons Child' & Educ'	Children's	50
	Hamley's Book Dept	Children's	50
	John Lewis	Children's	51
	Stateside Comics	Coms & Sci Fi	55
	Alhani International	Countries	67
	Asian Bookshop	Countries	60
	Japan Centre	Countries	66
	Ying Hwa	Countries	62
	Caissa Books	Crafts & Past'	69
	Contemp' Ceramics	Crafts & Past'	69
	R D Franks	Crafts & Past'	71
	Countryside Bookshop	Environment	74
	BBC shop	General	79
	Books *etc*	General	34
	Claude Gill Bargains	General	37
	Dillons James St	General	37
	Dillons Oxford St	General	37
	Dillons Piccadilly	General	37
	Discount Book Co	General	79
	Greens Bookcellar	General	79
	Hatchards Piccadilly	General	80
	Ker & Downey	General	80
	Literary Guild Books	General	79
	Readers Digest	General	80
	Selfridges	General	79
	WH Smith Oxford St	General	47
	Bournmouth Book Ctr	Languages	96
	European Bookshops	Languages	95

W 1	Grant & Cutler	Languages	95
	Charlotte Robinson	Literature	100
	G Heywood Hill	Literature	100
	Healthwise Bookshop	MBS	103
	Wholefood Books	MBS	102
	Boosey & Hawkes	Perform' Arts	116
	Chappell of Bond St	Perform' Arts	117
	Frenchs' Theatre Books	Perform' Arts	115
	Pollocks Toy Museum	Perform' Arts	116
	Quartet Bookshop	Perform' Arts	117
	Schott Music Shop	Perform' Arts	117
	Vintage Magazines	Perform' Arts	116
	Virgin Megastore	Perform' Arts	115
	Index Bookcentre	Pol & Soc Sci	120
	Dillons A R Mowbray	Religion	128
	Scripture Union	Religion	129
	Rowland Ward's	Sport	150
	Turf Newspapers	Sport	151
	Captain O M Watts	Maritime	152
	The Booking Hall	Transport	156
	Barbara Grigor-Taylor	Travel	159
	Daunt Books	Travel	159
	Stanfords at B Airways	Travel	158
W 2	Modern Book Co	Academic	3
	Al Saqi Books	Countries	67
	Dar Al Dawa	Countries	68
	Hoisans Books	Countries	61
	Ukrainian Bookshop	Countries	63
	Books *etc*	General	34
	Keltic Ltd	Languages	95
	NW Bookshop	Languages	96
	Bayswater Books	Second-hand	139
W 4	Fountain Books	General	80
	WH Smith	General	48
	Inspiration	MBS	104
	Faircross Books	Second-hand	144
	W A Foster	Second-hand	143
W 5	Dillons Ealing College	Academic	3
	OCS Bookshop	Countries	66
	Dillons Bookstore	General	38
	WH Smith	General	46
	Scripture Union	Religion	129
	Naval & Maritime Bks	Transport	153

W 6	Dillons Medical Books	Academic	3
	PMS Bookshop	Countries	63
	Hammick's	General	40
	WH Smith	General	46
W 8	Mellor & Baxter	Antiquarian	15
	Children's Bookcentre	Children's	51
	Iranian Bookshop	Countries	67
	Dillons Bookstore	General	38
	Waterstone's	General	43
	WH Smith	General	46
	St Paul Multi-media	Religion	128
	Notting Hill Books	Second-hand	139
	Trailfinders	Travel	160
W 10	Books & Things	Art & Design	28
	Grass Roots	Countries	59
	Golden Age	Crafts & Past'	70
	Elgin Books	General	81
	Mercurius	MBS	103
W 11	S K Biltcliffe Books	Antiquarian	16
	Brian Bailey	Antiquarian	16
	Demetzy Books	Antiquarian	15
	Books For Cooks	Crafts & Past'	70
	Waterstone's	General	43
	WH Smith	General	47
	Esperanto Bookshop	Languages	96
	Cosmic Bookshop	MBS	103
	Karnak House	Pol & Soc Sci	120
	Christian Books	Religion	130
	Bernard Shapero	Travel	159
	Travel Bookshop	Travel	160
	Music & Video Exch'	Second-hand	139
W 12	Dillons Medical Books	Academic	4
	Bush Books & Records	General	81
W 13	WH Smith West Ealing	General	47
W 14	Holborn College	Academic	32
	Bhavans Bookshop	Countries	64
	Nashre Ketab	Countries	67

OUTER LONDON

NORTH

Barnet	Stateside Comics	Coms & Sci Fi	55
	Hammick's	General	40
	Muir's Bookshop	General	92
	WH Smith	General	48
Enfield	All Saints Bookshop	Academic	10
	WH Smith	General	46
	Gordon Road Books	Military	154
	Christian Bookshop	Religion	132
Hoddesdon	The Bookcentre	General	92
Potters Bar	Bookworld	General	92
	Elaines	General	92

NORTH WEST

Chorleywood	Chorleywood Bkshop	General	92
Edgware	Bookmark Bookshop	Second-hand	147
	Two Jays bookshop	Second-hand	146
Harrow	Harrow School	Academic	8
	Calamity Comics	Coms & Sci Fi	57
	Hammick's	General	40
	WH Smith	General	47
	Scripture Union	Religion	129
Northwood	Northwood Bookshop	General	91
Pinner	Corbett's Bookshop	General	91
	Hammond Roberts	General	91
Ruislip	The Bookshop	General	91
	WH Smith	General	49
Uxbridge	Brunel University	Academic	8
	Hayes Bookshop	General	91
	Volume One	General	42
	WH Smith	General	46
	Maranatha	Religion	132

NORTH EAST

Epping	Epping Bookshop	General	93
Ilford	Owen Clark	General	93
	Volume One	General	42
	WH Smith	General	46
	Centre For Peace	Religion	128
	Edward Terry	Second-hand	147
Loughton	The Bookshop	General	93

Romford	Atomic Comics	Coms & Sci Fi	57
	WH Smith	General	46
	L N Fowler	MBS	105
	Havering Christian Ctr	Religion	133
Woodford Green	Village Bookshop	General	93
	Waite & Sons	General	93

EAST

Barking	James Smith	General	93
Bexleyheath	Waterstone's	General	44
	WH Smith	General	47
Hornchurch	Frontline Christian	Religion	133
Upminster	Swan Libraries	General	93
Welling	Falconwood Bookshop	Transport	157

SOUTH EAST

Beckenham	Beckenham Bookshop	General	94
	WH Smith	General	48
Bromley	County Bookshops	General	94
	Dillons Bookstore	General	38
	Waterstone's	General	44
	WH Smith	General	46
	Bromley Bookshop	Second-hand	148
Orpington	The Bookcellar	General	94
	Wordsworth Books	General	82
	WH Smith	General	47
West Wickham	WH Smith	General	48

SOUTH

Banstead	The IBIS Bookshop	General	88
Carshalton	Croydon Bookshop	Second-hand	142
Caterham	F & R Freedman	General	94
Cheam	Broadway Bookshop	General	88
	WH Smith	General	49
	Whitehall Bookshop	Second-hand	143
Coulsdon	Turners Bookshop	General	88
Croydon	Dillons Bookstore	General	38
	Volume One	General	42
	Waterstone's	General	44
	WH Smith	General	46
	Scripture Union	Religion	129
Epsom	John Menzies	General	41
	Hammick's	General	40
	Surrey Bookshop	General	89

Ewell	J W McKenzie	Sport	150
Morden	Merton College	Academic	7
New Malden	Canning's	General	89
	WH Smith	General	49
Stoneleigh	Dees of Stoneleigh	General	88
Sutton	Baines Bookshop	General	88
	Hammick's	General	40
	WH Smith	General	47
	Lens of Sutton	Transport	157
Wallington	Heath Educational	Academic	7
	WH Smith	General	48
	Oasis Christian Ctr	Religion	133
Worcester Park	WH Smith	General	49

SOUTH WEST

Chertsey	Oasis Christian Ctr	Religion	133
East Molesey	Serendip Bookshop	General	89
Egham	Dillons Bookstore	Academic	8
Hampton	Ian Sheridan's Bkshop	Antiquarian	18
Kingston	Derrick Nightingale	Antiquarian	18
	Dillons Bookstore	General	38
	John Lewis	Children's	51
	Books & Co	General	89
	Hammick's	General	40
	Hatchards	General	39
	Volume One	General	42
	Waterstone's	General	44
	WH Smith	General	46
	The Smokebox	Transport	157
Richmond	Lion & Unicorn	Children's	52
	They Walk Among Us	Coms & Sci Fi	56
	The Kew Shop	Crafts & Past'	90
	Lloyds of Kew	Crafts & Past'	71
	Kew Bookshop	General	90
	The Open Book	General	90
	Waterstone's	General	44
	WH Smith	General	47
	Scripture Union	Religion	129
	W & A Houben	Second-hand	143
	Richmond Bookshop	Second-hand	143
Staines	John Menzies	General	41
	WH Smith	General	46
	Canaan Book Centre	Religion	133
Surbiton	Regency Bookshop	General	89
	Highway Christian Bk	Religion	133
Teddington	Swan Bookshop	General	90

Thames Ditton	Elizabeth Gant	Antiquarian	18
Twickenham	College Bookshop	Academic	7
	Open Books	Academic	8
	Richmond College	Academic	7
	Anthony C Hall	Countries	63
	Langton's Bookshop	General	90
	World of Transport	Transport	157
Virginia Water	The Bookshop	General	90
Walton	WH Smith	General	47
Weybridge	Weybridge Books	General	90
	WH Smith	General	48

WEST

Feltham	Reader's Dream	Coms & Sci Fi	57
Hayes	WH Smith	General	48
Hounslow	Volume One	General	42
	WH Smith	General	47
Isleworth	Osterley Bookshop	Second-hand	144
	Chaters	Transport	154
Southall	Virdee Bros	Countries	61

SUBJECT INDEX

Accounting *see* Business
    Books *etc* London Wall 30
    City Department Waterstone's
    31
    Hammick's Professional 30
    Parks High Holborn 29
    Parks ICAEW 30
Acupuncture
    Acumedic Centre 103
Afghanistan
    Nashre Ketab 67
Africa
    Africa Book Centre 59
    Grass Roots 59
    Operation Headstart 60
    Soma Books 59
AIDS & HIV
    Healthwise Bookshop 103
Alternative Health, see Natural
Therapy
Antiquarian
    Ash Rare Books 15
    Avenue Bookshop 11
    Barbara Stone 17
    Bernard Quaritch 13
    Bernard Shapero 159
    Brian Bailey 16
    Chelsea Rare Books 17
    Christopher Edwards 16
    Collinge & Clark 12
    Demetzy Books 15
    Derrick Nightingale 18
    Dillons Gower St 77
    E Joseph Booksellers 14
    Elizabeth Gant 18
    Fisher & Sperr 18
    Food for Thought 12
    Francis Edwards 152
    Frew Mackenzie 11
    Harrington Bros 17
    Henry Sotheran 14
    Il Libro 17
    Jarndyce Booksellers 11

    Maggs Brothers 13
    Mellor & Baxter 15
    P J Hilton 12
    Pickering & Chatto 16
    Russell Rare Books 13
    S K Biltcliffe 16
    Vanbrugh Rare Books 11
    Vandeleur Books 17
Antiquarian Miniatures
    Louis Bondy 11
Antiques & Collectables
    Don Kelly 26
    Golden Age 70
    The Angel Bookshop 86
    Thomas Heneage 25
Dolls & Toys
    Pollocks Toy Museum 116
Arabic
    Al Hoda 66
    Al Kashkool 67
    Al Saqi 67
    Alhani International 67
    Dar Al Dawa 68
    Dar Al-Taqwa 134
Archaeology *see* History Classical
    British Museum 1
    Museum Bookshop 1
Architecture *see* Building,
Planning
    Marylebone Books 8
    Parks South Bank 29
    RIBA Bookshop 23
    Royal Institute of Chartered
    Surveyors 33
    Triangle Bookshop 20
Art
    Bloomsbury Group 99
Art & Design
    Ballantyne & Date 20
Art Asia
    Han Shan Tang Ltd 62
Art Decorative
    Books & Things 28

Camberwell Bookshop 27
St Georges Gallery 25
Stephen Foster 28
Thomas Heneage 25
Victoria & Albert Museum 26
Zwemmer 21
Art Fine
  Chris Beetles 25
  Hayward Gallery 26
  National Portrait Gallery 23
  Roe & Moore 20
  Royal Academy of Art 24
  Tate Gallery 25
  Zwemmer Whitechapel 24
Art Fine & Applied
  Ann Creed Books 22
  Camberwell Bookshop 27
  Dillons Arts Bookshop 21
  Don Kelly 26
  Holstein Campbell 23
  Institute of Contemporary Art
  25
  Libertys 23
  Shipley Specialist Art
  Booksellers 22
  Sims, Reed Ltd 16
  St Georges Gallery 25
  Stephen Foster 28
  Thomas Heneage 25
  Victoria & Albert Museum 26
  Zwemmer 21
Art Fine & Applied second-hand
  Richmond Bookshop 143
Art Graphics
  Zwemmer 21
Art Surrealism
  Boutle & King 24
Asia
  Asian Bookshop 60
  Han Shan Tang Ltd 62
  Hoisans Books 61
  John Randall 61
Astrology *see* Mind, Body & Spirit
  Cosmic Bookshop 103
  Genesis Books 103
  LN Fowler 105
  Psychic Sense Bookshop 104

Australia
  Australian Bookshop 62
  Australian Gift Shop 61
Aviation
  Motor Books 155
  The Aviation Bookshop 152

Bangladesh
  Ruposhi Bangla 60
Banking
  Bankers Books 31
  City Depatrment Waterstone's
  31
Bargains
  Book Bargains Ltd 80
  Books & Co 89
  Booksave 87
  County Bookshops 94
  Discount Book Company 79
  Oppenheim & Co 81
  The Bookcase 84, 85
  The Clearing House 139
  Unsworth, Rice & Co 137
  West London Books 81
  Wordsworth Books 82
BBC Publications
  BBC Shop 79
BBC World Service
  BBC World Shop 115
Black Interest
  Africa Book Centre 59
  Bookmarks 125
  Bookplace 121
  Centreprise Bookshop 123
  East End Bookshop 123
  Grass Roots 59
  Index Bookcentre 120, 122
  Kilburn Bookshop 125
  New Beacon Books 59
  Operation Headstart 60
  Pathfinder Bookshop 120
  Soma Books 59
  Timbuktu Books 122
Bloomsbury Group
  The Bloomsbury Workshop
  99

Bookbinding
British Library Bookshop 73
Falkiner Fine Papers 69
Sangorski & Sutcliffe 15
Books
British Library Bookshop 73
Botany *see* Gardening
Lloyds of Kew 71
The Kew Shop 71
Boxing second-hand
Sporting Bookshop 151
Bridge
Chess & Bridge Ltd 69
Buddhism
London Buddhist Centre 127
Wisdom Books 127
Building *see* Architecture
Building Bookshop 20
Marylebone Books 8
Parks South Bank 29
Royal Institute of Chartered
Surveyors 33
Business
Barbican Business Centre 32
Books *etc* London Wall 30
Brunel University 8
Business Bookshop 33
City Department Waterstone's
31
City Poly Bookshop 5
Faculty Books 9
Faculty Bookshop 9
Graham Wyche 88
Hammick's Professional 30
Holborn College 32
Parks High Holborn 29
Parks South Bank 29
Business Economist Publications
Economist Bookshop 32
Business Export
Export Market Info Centre 33
Business Reference
Business Bookshop 33
Business Training & Development
Trainer's Bookshop BACIE 33

Calligraphy
British Library Bookshop 73
Falkiner Fine Papers 69
Carroll Lewis
Marchpane 50
Cartoon Strips
Gosh! Comics 54
Ceramics
Contemporary Ceramics 69
Charities for Book Donations
National Schizophrenic
Bookshop 140
Response Bookshop 140
Chess
Caissa Books 69
Chess & Bridge Ltd 69
Child Care
Karnac Books 9
Children's
Bookspread 51
Canonbury Bookshop 52
Children's Book Centre 51
Children's Bookshop 53
Deptford Bookshop 121
Hamley's 50
Harrod's 4th floor 51
John Lewis 51
Lion and Unicorn 52
Nomad Books 160
Owl Bookshop 52
Pollocks Toy Museum 116
Puffin Children's Books 50
Tintin Shop 55
Wellspring Bookshop 1
Women & Children First 53
Children's Antiquarian
Barbara Stone 17
Children's Educational
Books For Children 51
Dillons Upper Berkeley St 50
Children's Hebrew
Mesoiroh Seforim Bookshop
135
Children's Illustrated
Charlotte Robinson 100
Marchpane 50

Children's Illustrated &
Adventure
   Ripping Yarns 52
Children's Illustrated & comics
   Gosh! Comics 54
Children's non-discriminatory &
multi-cultural
   Bookmarks 125
   Bookplace 121
   Bookspread 51
   Deptford Bookshop 121
   East End Bookshop 123
   New Beacon Books 59
   Newham Parents Centre 123
   Soma Books 59
Children's second-hand
   Elizabeth Gant 18
   Marchpane 50
   Ripping Yarns 52
China & Chinese
   Guanghwa Ltd 62
   New Era Books 124
   Ying Hwa 62
Churchill
   E Joseph Booksellers 14
Cinema *see* Performing Arts
   Cinema Bookshop 113
   Offstage Theatre & Film
Bookshop 119
Cinema Magazines
   Vintage Magazine Shop 116
Classical History
   British Museum 1
   Museum Bookshop 1
Comics & Graphic Novels *see*
Science Fiction & Fantasy
   ACME Comic Shop 56
   At The Sign Of The Dragon 56
   Atomic Comics 57
   Avalon Comics 56
   Calamity Comics 57
   Comic Shack 57
   Fantasy Centre 57
   Forbidden Planet 54
   Gosh! Comics 54
   Graphically Speaking 57
   Mega City Comics 56

   Skinny Melink's Comics 58
   Stateside Comics 55
   They Walk Among Us 56
   Tintin Shop 55
Comics & Graphic Novels
Japanese
   Japan Centre Bookshop 66
Comics & Graphic Novels Silver
& Golden Age
   Stateside Comics 55
Computing
   Books *etc* London Wall 30
   Hammick's Professional 30
   Imperial College 5
   Input Software 32
   James Smith Booksellers 93
   Modern Book Company 3
   Parks High Holborn 29
   Parks South Bank 29
   PC Bookshop 29
Cookery
   Books For Cooks 70
Cookery Vegetarian
   Genesis Books 103
   Wholefood Books 102
Countryside
   The Countryside Bookshop 74
Crafts *see* individual craft
   Booktree 70
   Dover Bookshop 70
Cricket
   The Lord'sShop 149
Cricket Antiquarian & second-
hand
   J W McKenzie 150
Crime
   Murder One 99
Cyprus
   Hellenic Bookservice 64
   Turkish Language Books 68
   Zeno Booksellers 64

Dance *see* Performing Arts
   Dance Books 114
Dance Folk
   Folk Shop 118

Design
    Design Council Bookshop 24
    Design Museum 26
Development Third World
    IT Bookshop 74
    World of Difference 74
Dickens Charles
    Jarndyce Booksellers 11
    Dickens House Museum 98

Eastern Europe *see* individual
country
    Collets 62
Eastern Europe Languages
    Orbis Books 63
Eastern Europe second-hand
    Anthony C Hall 63
Education
    Dillons Upper Berkeley St 50
    Faculty Books 9
    Heath Educational 7
    Institute Bookshop Digby
    Stuart College 6
    Newham Parents Centre 123
    Wellspring Bookshop 1
Education Adult Literacy
    Bookplace 121
    Centreprise Bookshop 123
    Deptford Bookshop 121
    East End Bookshop 123
EFL
    Eurocentre Bookshop 97
EFL & ELT
    Benedicts Bookshop 97
    Bournmouth English Book
    Centre 96
    Keltic Ltd 95
    Skola Books 95
Environment & Ecology
    Bird & Wildlife Bookshop 75
    Books for a Change 74
    IT Bookshop 74
    Jambala Bookshop 103
    World of Difference 74
Esperanto
    Esperanto Bookshop 96

Ethnography
    Museum of Mankind 3

Fashion
    R D Franks 71
Field Sports
    Farlows of Pall Mall 150
    Rowland Wards 150
Finance & Investment *see* Banking
    Bankers Books 31
    Books *etc* London Wall 30
    City Department Waterstone's
    31
    Hammick's Professional 30
    Parks High Holborn 29
    Parks ICAEW 30
Fine Binding
    Sangorski & Sutcliffe 15
Fine Bindings *see* Antiquarian
    Ann Creed Books 22
    Ash Rare Books 15
    Hatchards Paccadilly 80
    Maggs Brothers 13
    Roe & Moore 20
Food & Wine
    Books For Cooks 70
Football second-hand
    Sporting Bookshop 151
France & French
    La Page Bookshop 64
    French Bookshop 64
French Children's & Graphic
Novels
    French Bookshop 64
French Literature
    French Bookshop 64
    La Page Bookshop 64

Gaelic *see* Ireland
Gardening
    Lloyds of Kew 71
    The Kew Shop 71
Gardening commercial
    Grower Books 71

Gay
  Gay'sthe Word 120
General
  Books *etc* 34
  Dillons The Bookstore 36
  Hammick's 40
  Hatchards 36
  John Menzies 41
  Volume One 42
  Waterstone's 43
  WH Smith 45
Geology
  Imperial College 5
  JG Natural History Books 76
  Natural History Museum 75
German Literature
  Village Bookshop 101
Golf second-hand
  Sarah Baddiel 150
Government Publications
  HMSO Books 77
Graphic Design *see* Art Applied
  London College of Printing 73
Grahic Novels *see* Comics
Greece & Greek
  Hellenic Bookservice 64
  Zeno Booksellers 64

Health *see* Natural Therapy
  Acumedic Centre 103
  Healthwise Bookshop 103
  Wholefood Books 102
Hebrew *see* Judaism
Hispanic Studies
  Paul Orssich 68
History
  Tlon Books 7
History Ancient Greek
  Hellenic Bookservice 64
  Zeno Booksellers 64
History British Industrial
  S K Biltcliffe 16
History Industrial
  Ballantyne & Date 20
History Islamic & Middle East
  Dar Al Dawa 68

History Military
  Imperial War Museum 152
  National Army Museum 154
History second-hand
  History Bookshop 10
Horology
  Rogers Turner 19
Horror *see* Science Fiction &
Fantasy
Horse racing
  Turf Newspapers 151
Horses
  The Horseman's Bookshop
  151
  Turf Newspapers 151
Housing *see* Planning
  Housing Centre Trust 124
  Planning Bookshop 25
Humanism
  National Secular Society G W
  Foote 10
Hungary & Hungarian
  Hungarian Book Agency 63

Illustrated Antiquarian
  Barbara Stone 17
  Brian Bailey 16
  Collinge & Clark 12
  Il Libro 17
  Michael Finney 18
Illustrated second-hand
  Alan Brett 22
  Camberwell Bookshop 27
India
  Asian Bookshop 60
  Bhavans Bookshop 64
  Books From India 65
  Hoisans Books 61
  John Randall 61
  Ruposhi Bangla 60
India Literature
  Virdee Brothers 61
Insurance
  City Department Waterstone's
  31
  Witherby & Co 31

Iran
Iranian Bookshop 67
Nashre Ketab 67
Ireland
Four Provinces 65
Green Ink Books 65
Islam
Al Noor 67
Books on Islam 134
Dar Al Dawa 68
Dar Al-Taqwa 134
Iranian Bookshop 67
Islamic Bookcentre 134
Muslim Bookshop 134
Italian Literature
Accademia Italiana 65
Italy
Old Town Books 65
Italy & Italian
Accademia Italiana 65

Japan
Books Nippon 66
Boswell Books & Prints 66
OCS Bookshop 66
Japan & Japanese
Japan Centre Bookshop 66
Japan Antiquarian & second-hand
Fine Books Oriental 61
Judaism
Hebrew Book & Gift Centre 134
J Aisenthal 135
Jerusalem the Golden 135
Jewish Memorial Council Bookshop 134
Menorah Print & gift Centre 135
Mesoiroh Seforim Bookshop 135
Judaism Antiquarian & second-hand
John Trotter Books 135
Manor House Books 135

Language Bengali
East End Bookshop 123
Language Dictionaries Technical
Grant & Cutler 95
Languages *see* individual country
Benedicts Bookshop 97
Grant & Cutler 95
LCL International Booksellers 96
Linguaphone Language Centre 96
NW Bookshop 96
Languages European
European Bookshops 95
Languages India
Asian Bookshop 60
Ruposhi Bangla 60
Latin
Hellenic Bookservice 64
Law
Butterworths 30
Faculty Books 9
Faculty Bookshop 9
Hammick's Professional 30
Holborn College 32
Law Society Shop 30
Oyez Stationery 32
Wildy & Sons 32
Literary Periodicals
Camberwell Bookshop 27
Literature
Charlotte Robinson 100
G Heywood Hill 100
John Sandoe 100
Swiss Cottage Books 86
The Turret Bookshop 98
Waterstone's South Bank 118
Literature Antiquarian
Ash Rare Books 15
Mellor & Baxter 15
Village Bookshop 101
Literature Bloomsbury Group
The Bloomsbury Workshop 99
Literature English & American
Bell, Book & Radmall 99
Bertram Rota 99

Literature English Antiquarian
 Chelsea Rare Books 17
 Frew Mackenzie 11
 Jarndyce Booksellers 11
 Pickering & Chatto 16
Literature European Languages
 European Bookshops 95
Literature Gay
 Gay'sthe Word 120
Literature Great War
 Charlotte Robinson 100
Literature Irish
 Kilburn bookshop 125
Literature Lesbian
 Silver Moon Bookshop 162
 Sisterwrite Bookshop 1162
Literature P G Wodehouse
 The Clearing House 139
Literature Samuel Johnson
 J Clarke-Hall 139
Literature second-hand
 Fortune Green Bookshop 146
 Keith Fawkes 146
 Ulysses 98
 Village Bookshop 101
Literature Women's
 Sisterwrite Bookshop 162
 Women's Press Bookshop 162
London
 London Museum 108
 London Tourist Board Shop 160
 London Transport Museum 156

Maghreb
 Maghreb Bookshop 59
Magic & Conjuring
 Davenports Magic Shop 72
Management see Business
Manuscripts
 Bertram Rota 99
 Maggs Brothers 13
 Vanbrugh Rare Books 11

Manuscripts Illuminated and Medieval
 Sam Fogg Rare Books 14
Maps
 Geographia 161
 The National Map Centre 161
Maps & Atlases
 Geographers 159
 Stanfords 158
Maps & Atlases Antiquarian
 Harold T Storey 13
 Tooley, Adams & Co 12
Maritime see Naval & Maritime
Media
 BBC Shop 79
Medicine
 British Medical Journal Bookshop 2
 Dillons Charing Cross & Westminster 3
 Dillons Hammersmith hospital 4
 Dillons St Thomas' Hospital 5
 Modern Book Company 3
 Passage Bookshop 5
 St Georges Hospital 6
Medicine Antiquarian
 Pickering & Chatto 16
Medicine Oriental
 Acumedic Centre 103
Medicine-History of
 Robert Connelly 2
Mentally Handicapped
 MENCAP Bookshop 4
Meteorology
 Weather Wise 2
Middle East
 Al Hoda 66
 Al Noor 67
 Al Saqi 67
 Alhani International 67
 Dar Al Dawa 68
 Dar Al-Taqwa 134
 Hoisans Books 61
 John Randall 61
 Nashre Ketab 67

Middle East Antiquarian
Al Kashkool 67
Fine Books Oriental 61
Middle East second-hand
Anthony C Hall 63
Military see Transport
Falconwood Bookshop 157
Gordon Road Bookshop 154
Imperial War Museum 152
ISO Publications 154
Motor Books 155
National Army Museum 154
The Cholmeley Bookshop 154
Military & Naval Antiquarian
Harold T Storey 13
Military History
History Bookshop 10
Mind, Body & Spirit
Changes Bookshop 104
Compendium Bookshop 124
Cosmic Bookshop 103
Genesis Books 103
Inspiration 104
Mercurius 103
Mysteries New Age Centre
102
Psychic Sense Bookshop 104
Watkins Books 102
Miniatures
Demetzy Books 15
Louis Bondy 11
Modern First Editions
Bell, Book & Radmall 99
Bertram Rota 99
Charlotte Robinson 100
E Joseph Booksellers 14
Harrington Bros 17
Quinto Bookshop 138
Ulysses 98
Village Bookshop 101
Motoring see Transport
Chaters 154
Motor Books 155
Motoring second-hand
Sarah Baddiel 150
Mountaineering Antiquarian
Barbara Grigor-Taylor 159

Music see Performing Arts
Barbican Music Shop 118
Boosey & Hawkes 116
Chappell of Bond Street 117
Kensington Music Shop 118
Schott Music Shop 117
Travis & Emery 113
Zwemmer OUP Music&
Books 113
Music Contemporary
Virgin Megastore 115
Music Folk
Folk Shop 118
Music Jazz
Ray's Jazzshop 114

Natural History
Bird & Wildlife Bookshop 75
Natural History Museum 75
The Countryside Bookshop 74
Natural History Antiquarian
Bernard Shapero 159
Clive A Burden 75
Natural Therapy
Acumedic Centre 103
Genesis Books 103
Jambala Bookshop 103
Mysteries New Age Centre
102
Watkins Books 102
Naval & Maritime see Military,
Transport
Anthony J Simmonds 153
Captain O M Watts 152
Naval & Maritime Bookshop
153
ISO Publications 154
Motor Books 155
The Cholmeley Bookshop 154
The London Yacht Centre 153
Naval & Maritime Antiquarian
Francis Edwards 152
Naval & Maritime Charts
Brown & Perring 153
Kelvin Hughes 153
New Age, see Mind, Body & Spirit

New Zealand
  Kiwi Fruits 68
Numismatics
  Spink & Son 72
Nursing *see* Medicine
  Nursing Book Service 9
  Open Books 7, 8

Occult *see* Mind, Body & Spirit
  Atlantis Bookshop 102
  Psychic Sense Bookshop 104
Opera
  ColiseumShop 113
Orient *see* individual country
  Al Saqi 67
  Neal St East 60
Orient Antiquarian & second-hand
  Arthur Probsthain 61
  Fine Books Oriental 61
Ornithology
  Bird & Wildlife Bookshop 75
  Henry Sotheran 14
Ornithology John Gould
  Henry Sotheran 14
Ornithology John Gould facsimilies
  Stephen Foster 28

Pacifism & anti-militarism
  Housmans Bookshop 124
Performing Arts
  Dress Circle 114
  Offstage Theatre & Film Bookshop 119
  Quartet Bookshop 117
  Stage Door Prints 113
  Upper Street Bookshop 119
  Waterstone's South Bank 118
Performing Arts Magazines
  Vintage Magazine Shop 116
Performing Arts second-hand
  Boutle & King 24
Performing Arts TV

Museum of the Moving Image 117
Persian
  Al Hoda 66
  Nashre Ketab 67
Philately
  Stanley Gibbons 72
Philosophy
  Karnac Books 9
Photography
  Ann Creed Books 22
  Photographer's Gallery 22
  Zwemmer 21
Planning
  Marylebone Books 8
  Planning Bookshop 25
  Royal Institute of Chartered Surveyors 33
Poetry
  Poetry Book Society 101
  The Turret Bookshop 98
Poland & Polish
  Orbis Books 63
  PMS Bookshop 63
Politics
  Compendium Bookshop 124
  Economists Bookshop 120
  Housmans Bookshop 124
  Index Bookcentre 120, 122
  Karnak House 120
  Kilburn Bookshop 125
  Pathfinder Bookshop 120
  Tlon Books 7
Politics Anarchism
  121 Bookshop 122
  Freedom Press Bookshop 123
Politics Labour Movement
  Labour Party Bookshop 122
Politics Malcolm X
  Pathfinder Bookshop 120
Politics second-hand
  John Buckle Books 122
  Porcupine Bookcellar 124
Politics Socialism
  Bookmarks 125
  Index Bookcentre 120, 122
  New Era Books 124

Pottery *see* Ceramics
Printing
    British Library Bookshop 73
    Falkiner Fine Papers 69
    London College of Printing 73
Private Press
    Barbara Stone 17
    Bertram Rota 99
    Collinge & Clark 12
Psychology
    Changes Bookshop 104
    Watkins Books 102
Psychology & Psychoanalysis
    Karnac Books 9
Psychotherapy
    Changes Bookshop 104

Railways *see* Transport
    Ian Allan Bookshop 156
    Lens of Sutton 157
    Motor Books 155
    The Booking Hall 156
Readers Digest Publications
    Readers Digest Shop 80
Religion & Theology Antiquarian
    Charles Higham 129
Religion & Theology Catholicism
    Catholic Truth Society 128
    Centre for Peace Bookshop
    128
    Padre PioBookshop 128
    St Paul Multimedia 128
Religion & Theology Christian
    Bible Bookstore 131
    Canaan Christian Bookcentre
    133
    Christian Books & Music 130
    Christian Bookshop 132
    Church House Bookshop 130
    CLC Bookshop 131
    Cornerstone 132
    Daybreak Books 131
    Faith House Bookshop 128
    Frontline Christian Bookshop
    133

Havering Christian Bookshop
133
Highway Christian Bookshop
133
King's Books 130
London City Mission 131
Maranatha Christian
Bookshop 132
Mowbray - Dillons Bookstore
128
Oasis Christian Centre 133
Protestant Truth Society 130
SCM Bookroom 132
Scripture Union 129
SPCK 129
St Martins Bookshop 129
St Pauls 127
Religion & Theology Christian
Orthodox
    Russian Orthodox Bookshoop
    130
Religion & Theology Creation
Debate
    Mustard Seed 132
Religion & Theology Plymouth
Brethren
    Chapter Two 136
Religion & Theology Quakerism
    Friends Book Centre 136
Religion & Theology second-hand
    John Thornton 140
    Pendlebury's Bookshop 131
    R A Boon Booksellers 144
Religion & Theology Swedenborg
    Swedenborg Society 136
Religion Eastern *see* Mind, Body &
Spirit
    Watkins Books 102
Reptiles & Amphibians
    JG Natural History Books 76
Review Copies
    Vermilion Books 77
Romance
    Murder One 99
Rowing
    Vandeleur Books 17

Science & Technology
  Dillons Science Museum 6
  Imperial College 5
  Modern Book Company 3
  Queen Mary & Westfield College 5
Science & Technology Alternative
  IT Bookshop 74
  World of Difference 74
Science & Technology Antiquarian
  Rogers Turner 19
Science Fiction & Fantasy see Comics & Graphic Novels
  At The Sign Of The Dragon 56
  Avalon Comics 56
  Comic Shack 57
  Fantasy Centre 57
  Forbidden Planet 54
  Mega City Comics 56
  Murder One 99
  Reader's Dream 57
Science-History of
  Robert Connelly 2
Second-hand
  Any Amount of Books 138
  Archive Books 145
  Bayswater Books 139
  Bonaventure 144
  Bookmark Bookshop 147
  Bookshop Blackheath Ltd 147
  Bromley Bookshop 148
  Camberwell Bookshop 27
  Charing Cross Rd Bookshop 138
  Chelsea Rare Books 17
  Circa 145
  Coffee House Bookshop 148
  Collected Works 148
  Constant Reader Bookshop 140
  Crouch End Bookshop 87
  Croydon Bookshop 142
  Derrick Nightingale 18
  Dillons Gower St 13
  Edward Terry 147
  Elizabeth Gant 18
  Faircross Books 144
  Fisher & Sperr 18
  Fortune Green Bookshop 146
  Gabriels Bookshop 146
  Gloucester Rd Bookshop 140
  Greenwich Bookshop 148
  Henry Pordes Books 138
  Holloway Book Exchange 146
  Ian Sheridan's Bookshop 18
  J Clarke-Hall 139
  John Buckle Books 122
  John Thornton 140
  Keith Fawkes 146
  Marcet Books 148
  Marchmont Bookshop 138
  Music & Video Exchange 139
  My Back Pages 141
  National Schizophrenic Bookshop 140
  Notting Hill Books 139
  Osterley Bookshop 144
  P J Hilton 12
  Popular Book Centre 140, 148
  Porcupine Bookcellar 124
  Quinto Bookshop 138
  Response Bookshop 140
  Richmond Bookshop 143
  Robbies Bookshop 144
  Spread Eagle Bookshop 147
  Swans Bookshop 142
  The Clearing House 139
  The Hayes Bookshop 91
  Two Jays Bookshop 146
  Unsworth,Rice & Co 137
  Vandeleur Books 17
  Vortex Bookshop 145
  W A Foster 143
  W&A Houben 143
  Walden Books 145
  Whetstone Books 145
  Whitehall Bookshop 143
  World of Books 138
Second-hand Academic
  Economists Bookshop 120
  Fitzjohns Books 146
  R A Boon Booksellers 144
  Skoob Books 137

Studio Books 147
Second-hand Esoterica
Skoob Books 137
Second-hand Exchange
Alpha Book Exchange 142
Comyns Books 145
Plus Books 142
Popular Book Centre 1140,
148
Secularism
National Secular Society G W
Foote 10
Shipping
Kelvin Hughes 153
Witherby & Co 31
Shooting & Hunting
Rowland Wards 150
Farlows of Pall Mall 150
Signed Copies
Hatchards Piccadilly 80
Regent Bookshop 85
Social Sciences *see* Politics
Compendium Bookshop 124
Economists Bookshop 120
Karnak House 120
Spain & Spanish
Paul Orssich 68
Speech Therapy
City Uni Bookshop 4
Sport
Lillywhites Books on Sport
149
Sportspages 149
Sport second-hand
Sporting Bookshop 151
Steadman Ralph
Turret Bookshop 98

Taxation *see* Finance & Investment
Textbooks
All Saints Bookshop 10
Brunel University 8
City Poly Bookshop 5
City Uni Bookshop 4
College Bookshop St Marys 7
Dillons Ealing College 3

Dillons Egham 8
Dillons Gower St 77
Dulwich College 7
Faculty Books 9
Harrow School 8
Imperial College 5
Institute Bookshop Digby
Stuart College 6
James Smith Booksellers 93
Library Bookshop 9
Mercury Bookshop 6
Merton College 7
Newham Community College
5
NW Bookshop 96
Open Books 7,8
Penguin City Lit 2
Queen Mary & Westfield
College 5
Sceptre Books 10
Trent Bookshop 10
Waterstone's Goldsmith's
College 6
Textbooks second-hand
Tlon Books 7
W&A Houben 143
Theatre *see* Performing Arts
French's Theatre Bookshop
115
Offstage Theatre & Film
Bookshop 119
Pleasures of Past Times 114
Royal National Theatre 117
Theatre Magazines
Vintage Magazine Shop 116
Theatre Shakespeare
Royal Shakespeare Company
Shop 118
Theatre Victorian Toy
Pollocks Toy Museum 116
Tintin
Tintin Shop 55
Transport
Falconwood Bookshop 157
Ian Allan Bookshop 156
Lens of Sutton 157

London Transport Museum
156
Motor Books 155
World of Transport 157
Transport second-hand
The Smokebox 157
Travel
Daunt Books 159
London Tourist Board 160
Nomad Books 160
Stanfords 158
The National Map Centre 161
The Travel Bookshop 160
The Travellers Bookshop 158
Trailfinders 160
Youth Hostels Association
Services 159
Travel & Voyages Antiquarian
Barbara Grigor-Taylor 159
Bernard Shapero 159
R & P Remington 159
Vandeleur Books 17
Travel Antiquarian & second-
hand
The Travellers Bookshop 158
Ulysses 98
Travel Baedekers
The Travellers Bookshop 158
Turkey
Hellenic Bookservice 64
Turkey & Turkish
Turkish Language Books 68

Ukraine & Ukranian
Ukrainian Bookshop 63

Vanity Fair
Alan Brett 22
Ventriloquism
Davenports Magic Shop 72

Women
Deptford Bookshop 121
East End Bookshop 123
Jambala Bookshop 103
Silver Moon Bookshop 162
Sisterwrite Bookshop 162
Women & Children First 53
Women's Press Book Club 162

Yachting *see* Naval & Maritime
The London Yacht Centre 153
Youth Hostel Association
Publications
Youth Hostel Services 159